ZERO TRUST FOR A SYNTHETIC AGE
SECURING IDENTITY, INTEGRITY, AND AGENCY IN THE AI ERA

EUSTACE ASANGHANWA

Copyright © 2025 by Visionary Quill, LLC

All rights reserved.

No part of this book may be reproduced in any form or by any electronic or mechanical means, including information storage and retrieval systems, without written permission from the author, except for the use of brief quotations in a book review.

For my mother
TABITHA ASANGHANWA

∼

Who taught me that the strongest security system begins with moral courage.

When the world demanded your silence, when pressure mounted to bend truth for comfort's sake, you stood unwavering—speaking truth even when safety itself was threatened.

This courage you encrypted in our hearts, passed down like an unbreakable protocol that no adversary could corrupt.

From a generation that never grew up with computers, you became more cybersecurity-savvy than most technologists, wielding Signal in a land where few even know its name—the same fearless curiosity that made you refuse to be silenced.

You are my firewall against doubt, my encryption against despair, and my constant proof that integrity needs no consensus to be valid.

This book exists because you showed me that protecting what matters most starts with having the courage to care—and the strength to speak truth when the world demands your silence.

∼

PREFACE: THE UNVERIFIABLE PRESENT

A NOTE ON TRUTH, FICTION, AND THE SYNTHETIC REALITY WE ALREADY INHABIT

In March 2024, a finance worker at a multinational firm in Hong Kong sat through a video conference call with what appeared to be the company's chief financial officer and several colleagues. The CFO's voice was familiar, his mannerisms precise, his instructions clear: transfer $25 million for a confidential acquisition. The employee complied. Every person on that call—except the employee—was a deepfake [1].

This is not the opening to a thriller novel. This happened. In our world. In broad daylight. To a trained professional.

As I write these words in 2025, I face an unusual challenge as an author: how do I prove to you that I am real? How do you know this preface wasn't generated by an AI trained on thousands of books about technology and trust? The unsettling truth is that you don't—and that uncertainty is precisely why this book exists.

We have crossed a threshold. The tools to manufacture convincing synthetic media—deepfake videos, cloned voices, forged documents, and entire fabricated digital histories—are no longer the province of nation-states or Hollywood studios. They're apps on your phone. They're services you can rent for the price of a coffee. They're being weaponized, commercialized, and normalized at a pace that outstrips our ability to adapt.

This book is an emergency manual for navigating this new reality.

A DIFFERENT KIND OF NONFICTION

Zero Trust for a Synthetic Age breaks from traditional technology writing in a crucial way: it acknowledges that in an era where reality itself can be synthesized, the line between documented fact and speculative scenario has become perilously thin. Throughout these pages, you'll encounter three types of narratives:

Real Events (70% of our case studies): Meticulously researched and verified incidents that have already occurred, from the Hong Kong deepfake heist to the Estonian municipal election interference of 2024. These are marked with complete citations and source materials.

Extrapolated Scenarios (20%): Near-future situations based on current capabilities and clear trend lines, marked as "Based on emerging threats." These aren't fiction—they're tomorrow's headlines waiting to happen.

Speculative Futures (10%): Clearly marked fictional scenarios that illustrate where we're headed if we don't act. These serve the same purpose as CDC pandemic simulations or military war games—to prepare us for possibilities we must prevent.

This approach mirrors the paradox we all now face: in a world where authentic videos can be dismissed as "deepfakes" and synthetic media can be defended as "real," we must simultaneously embrace radical skepticism and informed trust. We must learn to verify everything while still maintaining the connections and faith in institutions that make society possible.

WHY ZERO TRUST, WHY NOW

Zero Trust began as a cybersecurity framework—a recognition that traditional "castle and moat" security models had failed. The principle is simple: never trust, always verify. Assume breach. Authenticate continuously. Grant the least privilege necessary.

But what the security world has understood for a decade, society is only beginning to grasp: these principles aren't just for networks anymore. They're survival skills for citizens, essential knowledge for parents, critical capabilities for leaders. When anyone can be digitally impersonated, when any media can be fabricated, when trust itself becomes a vulnerability, we need a new framework for living.

This book will show you how to apply Zero Trust thinking to your digital life without succumbing to paranoia. It will teach you to verify without exhausting yourself, to protect your identity without isolating yourself, to maintain authentic relationships in an era of synthetic everything.

WHAT YOU'LL FIND HERE

This is not a book about fear, though the threats are real. This is not a technical manual, though you'll understand the technology. This is not a policy prescription, though policy makers will find actionable insights.

This is a book about power—taking it back.

Each chapter begins with a story that will make you question what you thought you knew about digital safety. From there, we'll dissect the technologies and tactics being used against us, explore their psychological and social implications, and most importantly, provide practical strategies for protection and resilience.

You'll learn why your voice is becoming your most vulnerable password, how to create "verification rituals" with loved ones, why blockchain might matter more for proving you're human than for cryptocurrency, and how communities are building collective defense systems against synthetic deception.

A PERSONAL NOTE

I have spent over three decades engineering security components and systems, helping countless companies and government organizations protect themselves in an increasingly hyperconnected digital world. I've witnessed the evolution of cybersecurity from its absence —when library computers required no logins and engineering lab terminals accepted "anonymous/anonymous" as universal credentials—through the castle-and-moat model, to today's well-established Zero Trust principled approach.

Today, you'd be hard-pressed to find any deliberately open computer anywhere. We conduct our most private transactions—financial, medical, personal—over the internet with barely a second thought. This represents tremendous progress in cybersecurity. And yet, paradoxically, we seem far less secure and increasingly vulnerable in cyberspace.

The last decade deepened my concern as I watched the rise of the data economy. Large corporations enticed users with seemingly free services—email, document storage, streaming videos, online shopping—while extracting data to build trillion-dollar algorithms. The exchange was fundamentally asymmetric: users received a one-time service; companies gained lifetime revenue streams. Finding this extractive model unfair, I embarked on a journey with ecosystem partners to build secured systems anchored in physical reality under the broad umbrella of confidential computing, seeking to balance human and corporate participation in the data economy.

But while we worked at human pace, the algorithms evolved at machine speed. Three years ago, observing technology's trajectory gave me a sinking feeling: I could foresee powerful AI algorithms displacing labor in the near future. This year, that suspicion became personal reality when AI eliminated my own position, confirming my fears were well-founded. I've since written "THE DATA DIVIDEND: *Your Clicks Fuel AI. Why Aren't You Getting Paid?*" as a wake-up call about this evolving threat to labor—not to fear-monger, but to foster preparedness.

In parallel, I saw another danger emerging: synthetic media in its most extreme form—deepfakes. These aren't theoretical threats. They're causing real-world harm with well-documented incidents multiplying daily. My experience of being displaced by AI, combined with decades of security expertise, compels me to write this book as both warning and invitation.

To my fellow security professionals: Despite our tremendous success in evolving the science of cybersecurity, we've harbored a blind spot. Zero Trust Architecture delivered principles that protect corporate networks deep into supplier chains. Yet every honest security professional admits to one vulnerability we can't eliminate: the human element. We've doubled down on technical controls—longer passwords, password character mix requirements, forced periodic password updates, vigilance requirements for malicious links, USB port epoxy—yet success wanes as controls mount. Our blind spot has been treating humans as just another threat vector to control, rather than recognizing them as integral parts of the system with attributes we cannot simply eliminate or override.

To everyone else: This is your invitation into our world. Witness the heroic efforts security professionals mount to keep you safe, but more importantly, understand your crucial role in our shared success. The threats from synthetic media in the AI era make cybersecurity everyone's responsibility. The good news? You don't need special training. You just need to be your authentic self.

After decades in security and years researching synthetic media threats, the story I've found is both darker and more hopeful than I expected.

The dark part: we are utterly unprepared for what's already here, let alone what's coming. Our legal systems, social norms, and personal habits evolved for a world where seeing was believing. That world is gone.

The hopeful part: humans are remarkably adaptable. Throughout history, we've developed new forms of trust to meet new challenges —from signatures and seals to photo IDs and encryption. We're doing it again, right now, in real-time. Communities are creating novel verification networks. Technologists are building tools for provable authenticity. Citizens are demanding new rights and protections.

We are not powerless. But we must act with urgency.

HOW TO READ THIS BOOK

Start with the Introduction—it tells the story of how Estonia became the first country to face a full-scale synthetic media attack on its democratic process, and what we can learn from their response.

Read the chapters in order if you want the full journey from threat to solution. Or jump to the sections that matter most to you:

- If you're worried about protecting your family, start with Part I
- If you're a technologist, dive into Part III's infrastructure discussions
- If you're a policy maker or advocate, Part IV outlines the governance challenge

Throughout, look for:

- **Verification Challenges**: Exercises to test your current vulnerability
- **Protection Protocols**: Actionable steps you can take immediately
- **Technical Sidebars**: Deeper dives for those who want them
- **Human Stories**: Because this isn't about technology—it's about us

A FINAL THOUGHT

As you read this book, you'll develop a healthy skepticism about digital media. That's good. But don't let necessary caution erode your capacity for connection, creativity, and hope. The goal isn't to retreat from our digital world—it's to engage with it more skillfully.

The future isn't a choice between naive trust and cynical isolation. It's about building something new: verified trust, authenticated relationships, and provable truth. It's about taking the profound capabilities that created this crisis—artificial intelligence, cryptography, global networks—and turning them into tools of liberation rather than deception.

The age of "trust, but verify" is over. The age of "never trust, always verify, then connect authentically" has begun.

Welcome to your survival guide.

∼

August 2025

∼

INTRODUCTION: THE DAY TRUST DIED

THE ESTONIAN DEEPFAKE CRISIS OF 2024

October 15, 2024, 7:47 AM EET. Katrin Kallas woke to 47 missed calls.

The leader of Estonia's Reform Party reached for her phone with the muscle memory of a politician in the digital age, expecting the usual morning cascade of scheduling updates and policy briefings. Instead, her screen pulsed with the particular urgency that meant crisis. Her press secretary had sent a single message in all caps: "DO NOT GO ONLINE. COMING TO YOU NOW."

Twenty minutes later, Kallas sat in her home office, watching herself on screen. The woman in the video had her face, her voice, her distinctive pattern of gesturing with her left hand when making a point. The woman was announcing Estonia's immediate withdrawal from NATO, effective immediately, citing "secret negotiations with Moscow" and "the economic necessity of Russian partnership." The woman was calling for emergency legislation to restrict press freedoms. The woman was her, and she was not her, and she was everywhere.

The video had been uploaded simultaneously to YouTube, Facebook, X (formerly Twitter), TikTok, Telegram, and a dozen smaller platforms at 3:17 AM, timed perfectly for the morning news cycle in Brussels and the evening scroll in Washington. By the time Kallas saw it, the original had been viewed 4.7 million times. The reposts, reactions, and remixes had already begun their viral cascade.

"Ma ei ole see," Kallas said quietly to her assembled crisis team. **I am not that.**

But in capitals across Europe, intelligence analysts were already asking: How can we be sure?

THE 72-HOUR WAR FOR REALITY

What followed was the first true test of a democracy's resilience in the age of synthetic media—a battle not fought with tanks or missiles, but with timestamps, cryptographic signatures, and the fragile currency of public trust.

The Estonian government's initial response was textbook crisis management: immediate denials across all channels, a live press conference within two hours, the foreign minister personally calling counterparts across the EU and NATO. But every traditional tool of verification had been compromised. The deepfake included metadata suggesting it had been filmed in Kallas's actual office. Voice print analysis showed a 97.3% match—within the margin of error for authentic recordings. Even more troubling, the video appeared to reference genuine classified information about NATO defense positions, lending it an air of credibility that mere denial couldn't dispel.

The sophistication was unprecedented. This wasn't a glitchy face-swap or an obviously robotic voice synthesis. The creators had trained their model on hundreds of hours of Kallas's public appearances, captured her microexpressions, replicated her breathing patterns, even included her characteristic pause before answering difficult questions. They had created not just a visual forgery, but a perfect behavioral simulacrum.

As Estonian cyber defense teams worked frantically to trace the video's origin, a second wave hit. New videos emerged: the defense minister discussing "secret weapons shipments to Russian oppositionists," the head of the central bank announcing emergency capital controls, local mayors declaring states of emergency. Each was crafted with the same meticulous attention to detail. Each seemed to reference real, verifiable events while twisting them toward chaos.

The attack's timing was surgical. Estonia was set to assume the rotating presidency of the EU Council in three months. Parliamentary elections were scheduled for spring. A major NATO exercise was days away. Every pressure point in Estonian society was being systematically targeted.

But Estonia had something the attackers hadn't fully accounted for: the most digitally integrated society on Earth was also among the most digitally resilient.

THE DIGITAL REPUBLIC STRIKES BACK

Since regaining independence in 1991, Estonia had built its entire civil infrastructure on a foundation of digital trust. Every citizen had a digital ID backed by cryptographic certificates. Every government transaction created an immutable audit trail. The country that had given the world Skype had also pioneered blockchain-based governance, digital voting, and AI-assisted public services [1].

Within six hours of the first deepfake's appearance, Estonia activated protocols that seemed pulled from science fiction but were actually the product of years of careful preparation. The government's authentic communications began carrying cryptographic signatures tied to hardware security modules in government facilities. Official videos included blockchain-timestamped attestations that could be verified by anyone with a smartphone. Most remarkably, key government officials began using a "liveness verification" system that had been quietly developed after the first wave of deepfake demonstrations in 2019—real-time biometric markers that current AI systems couldn't yet replicate.

The Estonian Computer Emergency Response Team (CERT-EE) pioneered what would later be called "social verification networks." They activated a network of trusted validators—journalists, civil society leaders, technical experts—who could vouch for the authenticity of government communications through pre-established secure channels. It was essentially a human blockchain, a web of trust relationships that synthetic media couldn't penetrate.

But the technical response was only half the battle. The real innovation came in how Estonia engaged its citizens in collective defense.

THE CROWD-SOURCED REALITY CHECK

Mari Tamm, a 67-year-old retiree in Tartu, was among the first to spot an anomaly. An avid follower of Estonian politics and a member of her local digital literacy club, she noticed that in one of the fake videos, "Kallas" referred to a meeting with the Finnish prime minister on October 10th. But Tamm remembered clearly: she had seen news footage of Kallas at a climate conference in Copenhagen that day.

Tamm posted her observation to Rate.ee, Estonia's fact-checking platform. Within minutes, others began contributing their own timeline corrections. A university student in Tallinn noticed that the office plants in the background were different from those in Kallas's recent authentic videos. A sound engineer detected subtle compression artifacts consistent with voice synthesis. Piece by piece, Estonian citizens built a crowd-sourced authentication system that no AI could defeat—the collective memory and attention of an engaged populace.

The Estonian government, recognizing the power of this distributed verification, did something unprecedented: they opened their official archives. Video footage, schedules, even normally classified movement logs were released with cryptographic attestations. "If everything can be faked," Kallas would later explain, "then everything real must be provable."

International support materialized in unexpected ways. The Finnish broadcaster YLE began watermarking all its footage with tamper-evident cryptographic signatures. The European Union activated emergency protocols to verify official communications. Tech companies, facing the specter of regulation, suddenly discovered an urgent interest in content authentication.

By hour 72, the immediate crisis had passed. The deepfakes were labeled, quarantined, and largely discredited. But the attack had revealed fundamental vulnerabilities that no quick fix could address.

WHEN EVERYTHING CAN BE FAKED, NOTHING CAN BE TRUSTED

The Estonian deepfake crisis marked a turning point in human history as significant as the invention of photography or the printing press. For the first time, malicious actors had demonstrated the ability to manufacture reality at scale, targeting not just individuals but entire societies. The weapons were accessible, the defenses were nascent, and the potential for chaos was unlimited.

Analysis would later reveal the attack's origins in a Russian-affiliated hacker group, though attribution in the age of synthetic media proved nearly as challenging as verification. The total cost—in emergency response, market volatility, and social disruption—exceeded €500 million. But the true damage was to something more fundamental: the basic trust that allows societies to function.

The crisis exposed interconnected vulnerabilities across every sector:

Political systems built on the assumption that seeing is believing suddenly faced the reality that anything could be fabricated. How do you run elections when any candidate can be shown saying anything? How do you maintain diplomatic relations when any communication might be synthetic?

Economic structures dependent on verified communications found themselves paralyzed. The morning of the attack, three major Estonian banks temporarily suspended large transfers, unsure which instructions were authentic. The stock market swung wildly as traders struggled to separate real announcements from synthetic ones.

Social bonds frayed as friends and families discovered they could no longer trust their own eyes and ears. Reports of "verification calls"—where people would ask loved ones to prove their identity through pre-arranged codes—spiked across the country.

Media ecosystems designed to spread information quickly became accelerants for deception. The same algorithms that could make a dance video go viral could now spread a synthetic declaration of war before any human could intervene.

Most troubling of all was the realization that the Estonian attack was not the culmination of the synthetic media threat—it was the beginning. The tools would only get better, cheaper, more accessible. The attack patterns would grow more sophisticated. The defenses that worked in October 2024 might be obsolete by spring.

A NEW FRAMEWORK FOR DIGITAL SURVIVAL

Estonia's successful defense offered crucial lessons, but also revealed the inadequacy of traditional approaches to trust and verification. The country had survived not through any single technical solution or policy response, but through a comprehensive reimagining of how trust operates in a digital society. They had unconsciously implemented what cybersecurity professionals call "Zero Trust Architecture"—but applied it to human communications, social relationships, and democratic processes.

Zero Trust, as a concept, emerged in the cybersecurity world as networks became too complex and porous for traditional perimeter defense. The old model—a hardened exterior protecting a trusted interior—collapsed when threats could come from anywhere, including inside. The new model assumed no inherent trust. Every transaction required verification. Every access required authentication. Every interaction was logged and analyzed.

What Estonia demonstrated was that these same principles now apply to society itself. When deepfakes can impersonate anyone, when synthetic media can fabricate any event, when AI can mimic any communication pattern, we need Zero Trust for humans. Not paranoia, not isolation, but a systematic approach to verification that maintains connection while ensuring authenticity.

This framework rests on five pillars:

1. **Continuous Authentication**: Just as modern networks authenticate users repeatedly throughout a session, human communications now require ongoing verification. Estonia's "liveness verification" system was primitive compared to what's needed, but it pointed the way toward a future where identity is constantly proved rather than occasionally checked.
2. **Least Privilege Information Sharing**: The principle that systems should only have access to the minimum information needed for their function now applies to human communications. The Estonian response succeeded partly because officials immediately limited the blast radius of potentially compromised channels.
3. **Assume Breach**: The cybersecurity maxim that you should always assume your network has been compromised translates to assuming that any communication channel can be synthetically hijacked. Estonia's pre-positioned verification networks embodied this principle.
4. **Micro-segmentation**: Networks increase security by dividing into small, isolated segments. Similarly, Estonia's distributed verification approach created multiple independent paths to truth, making it impossible for attackers to compromise the entire system.
5. **Continuous Monitoring and Response**: Just as modern security requires constant vigilance, the Estonian crisis showed that combating synthetic media requires active, ongoing engagement from institutions and citizens alike.

HOW TO READ THIS BOOK

The journey from Estonia's crisis to a comprehensive Zero Trust society requires us to understand four interconnected transformations:

Part I: Collapse of Trust examines the threat landscape in forensic detail. You'll learn how synthetic media works, who's creating it, what they want, and why traditional defenses are failing. These chapters will make you appropriately paranoid—a necessary first step.

Part II: Rethinking Trust introduces the Zero Trust framework as more than a technical architecture. You'll discover how principles developed for securing networks can be adapted to secure human relationships, business transactions, and democratic processes.

Part III: Infrastructure for Integrity delves into the technical building blocks of a trustworthy digital future. From cryptographic signatures to blockchain attestations, from hardware security modules to distributed verification networks, you'll understand the tools being developed to fight back against synthetic deception.

Part IV: A New Social Contract explores the broader implications of living in a Zero Trust society. What rights do we need in an age of synthetic media? How do we balance security with privacy, verification with accessibility? What does citizenship mean when identity itself can be stolen?

Each chapter combines real-world case studies with practical advice. You'll meet the victims and the defenders, the innovators and the regulators. You'll learn not just what's happening, but what you can do about it.

THE STAKES

As I write this introduction in mid-2025, the tools that enabled the Estonian attack have evolved through three more generations. What required a sophisticated hacker group and weeks of preparation in 2024 can now be accomplished by a teenager with a gaming laptop in an afternoon. The democratization of deception continues its relentless advance.

But so does the democratization of defense. Communities around the world are adapting Estonian innovations, building their own verification networks, demanding their own cryptographic infrastructures. The battle for authentic communication is being fought in coding bootcamps and community centers, in parliaments and PTA meetings.

We stand at an inflection point. The choices we make in the next few years will determine whether synthetic media becomes a tool of liberation or oppression, whether we build a future of verified truth or sink into a morass of manufactured reality. The technology itself is neutral—the outcome depends entirely on how quickly we adapt, how wisely we build, and how fiercely we defend the authentic connections that make us human.

Estonia showed us it's possible to fight back. This book shows you how.

The age of naive trust is over. The work of building verified trust begins now.

∼

PART ONE
COLLAPSE OF TRUST

CHAPTER 1
THE GREAT UNRAVELING

THE PENTAGON'S WAKE-UP CALL

[BASED ON EMERGING threats - this scenario is extrapolated from current voice cloning capabilities and known security vulnerabilities in defense communications]

The voice on the phone was perfect. Too perfect, in retrospect.

On a humid Tuesday morning in June 2023, a senior analyst at the Pentagon's Defense Innovation Unit received what appeared to be an urgent call from his commanding officer. The voice carried the Colonel's distinctive Boston accent, his habit of clearing his throat before delivering bad news, even his tendency to mispronounce the word "nuclear" as "nucular"—a quirk his team had gently teased him about for years.

. . .

"Listen, we've got a situation developing with the Seoul military exercises," the voice said. "I need you to send me the updated deployment schedules and communication protocols. Encrypted email, usual channel. This is time-sensitive."

The analyst, whose name remains classified, did what any well-trained military professional would do: he verified the caller ID (it showed the Colonel's number), confirmed the request aligned with ongoing operations (it did), and referenced a previous conversation they'd had about the Korea situation (the voice mentioned specific details from that discussion). Within twelve minutes, classified information about U.S. military positions and communication frequencies was sitting in an inbox that had nothing to do with the United States Department of Defense.

The real Colonel was 3,000 miles away, asleep in his Arlington home, his phone securely locked in a Faraday bag as per security protocol. He wouldn't learn about the conversation "he'd" had until the next morning, when the analyst thanked him for the "late-night guidance." By then, the stolen data had already been transmitted to buyers on three continents.

This wasn't a sophisticated hack in the traditional sense. No code was written, no firewalls were breached, no passwords were cracked. Instead, the attackers had weaponized something far more vulnerable than any computer system: human trust itself.

～

The Pentagon incident marked a watershed moment—not because it was the first synthetic voice attack, but because it demonstrated that the era of "script kiddie" voice cloning had arrived. The attackers hadn't used nation-state resources or Hollywood-grade equipment.

They'd used commercially available AI tools, a few hours of publicly available audio (the Colonel had given several recorded presentations), and a $50 voice-over-IP service to spoof the phone number. Total investment: less than the cost of a nice dinner in Washington D.C. Total damage: immeasurable.

[While specific details of classified incidents cannot be independently verified, this scenario reflects documented capabilities of current voice cloning technology and known vulnerabilities in defense communications]

FROM NIGERIAN PRINCES TO DIGITAL DOPPELGÄNGERS

To understand how we arrived at this moment, we need to trace the evolution of digital deception—a journey that parallels the development of the internet itself.

The first generation of online fraud was almost quaint in its simplicity. The infamous "Nigerian Prince" emails of the 1990s and early 2000s relied on basic social engineering: promise a fortune, request a small fee, hope that greed overrides skepticism. These scams were broadcast attacks, sent to millions in hopes of finding a few gullible victims. They were easily spotted by anyone with basic digital literacy. Bad grammar, implausible scenarios, and obvious logical flaws served as natural selection mechanisms, filtering out all but the most vulnerable targets [1].

But each technological advance brought new capabilities to fraudsters:

Phase 1 (1995-2005): The Text Era

- Email scams with poor grammar and obvious tells
- Basic phishing websites with misspelled URLs
- Success rate: 0.001% (1 in 100,000)
- Primary defense: Common sense

Phase 2 (2005-2015): The Personalization Era

- Spear phishing using scraped social media data
- Customized attacks on specific individuals
- Business Email Compromise (BEC) emerges
- Success rate: 3% (3 in 100)
- Primary defense: Security awareness training

Phase 3 (2015-2023): The Multimedia Era

- Deep-fake video calls for job interviews
- Voice cloning for family emergency scams
- Synthetic profile pictures for romance fraud
- Success rate: 15% (15 in 100)
- Primary defense: Multi-factor authentication

Phase 4 (2023-Present): The Synthetic Era

- Real-time voice conversion during live calls
- Behavioral pattern mimicry
- Full synthetic personas maintained across platforms
- Success rate: Unknown, but rising rapidly
- Primary defense: ...?

. . .

What changed between Phase 3 and Phase 4 wasn't just the quality of the forgeries—it was their accessibility. The Pentagon attack used tools that would have required a government laboratory just five years earlier. By 2024, teenagers were creating equally convincing voice clones for TikTok pranks.

The democratization of deception had begun.

THE ARCHITECTURE OF TRUST

To grasp why synthetic media poses such an existential threat, we must first understand what trust actually is—not as a feeling, but as the invisible infrastructure that makes civilization possible.

Trust is the reduction of complexity in an uncertain world. When you deposit money in a bank, you trust that the numbers on your screen correspond to actual value you can retrieve. When your light turns green, you trust that cross-traffic will stop at their red light. When your boss calls with an urgent request, you trust that it's actually your boss. Each act of trust allows you to function without paralyzing verification of every single interaction.

Sociologist Niklas Luhmann identified three layers of trust that societies depend on: [2]

1. **Interpersonal Trust**: Faith in specific individuals based on experience and relationship
    - "I trust my spouse/parent/friend"
    - Built through repeated interactions
    - Destroyed by personal betrayal

2. **Institutional Trust**: Confidence in systems and organizations
    - "I trust my bank/government/employer"
    - Built through consistent performance and accountability
    - Destroyed by systemic failure

3. **Abstract Trust**: Belief in concepts and technologies
    - "I trust encryption/democracy/science"
    - Built through education and evidence
    - Destroyed by fundamental paradigm shifts

Synthetic media attacks all three layers simultaneously:

- It impersonates trusted individuals (interpersonal)
- It undermines verification systems (institutional)
- It makes us question the nature of reality itself (abstract)

The Pentagon analyst didn't just fall for a voice clone—he experienced a collision between his interpersonal trust (in his

Colonel), his institutional trust (in military protocols), and his abstract trust (that voices are unique identifiers). When all three failed simultaneously, he had no backup system.

This is why synthetic media represents what researchers call a "trust recession"—not a temporary dip, but a fundamental restructuring of how trust operates in human society.

[The concept of "trust recession" in the context of synthetic media is emerging in academic literature as researchers grapple with these unprecedented challenges]

THE HIDDEN ECONOMY OF DECEPTION

Behind every synthetic fraud lies an increasingly sophisticated economy. What began as isolated criminal enterprises has evolved into a thriving marketplace with its own specialists, supply chains, and service providers.

Consider the anatomy of a modern voice-cloning operation:

The Collectors gather raw material—audio recordings, video footage, social media posts. They scour YouTube, LinkedIn, corporate websites, podcast appearances. A C-suite executive who's given five public speeches has provided enough voice data for a convincing clone. Price: $50-500 per target, depending on public prominence.

The Modelers transform raw audio into voice models. Using open-source tools like Tortoise-TTS or commercial services like Eleven-

Labs, they create voice engines that can say anything in anyone's voice. The best modelers specialize in specific accents or age groups. Price: $200-2,000 per voice, depending on quality.

The Operators execute the actual attacks. They're often former call center employees who understand corporate hierarchies and communication patterns. They rehearse conversations, prepare for objections, and maintain character even under pressure. Price: $500-5,000 per successful call.

The Launderers convert stolen data or funds into usable assets. They maintain networks of cryptocurrency wallets, shell companies, and money mules. They typically take 15-30% of the total haul.

The Innovators continuously improve techniques. They develop new ways to bypass voice biometrics, create more convincing emotional inflections, and integrate real-time translation for cross-border attacks. They sell tools and training to other criminals.

This ecosystem operates with startup-like efficiency. Discord servers share techniques. Telegram channels advertise services. GitHub repositories distribute code. The barriers to entry drop monthly.

A 2024 report estimated the global synthetic fraud economy at €12 billion annually—larger than many legitimate industries. But the economic impact extends far beyond direct losses:

- **Verification costs**: Companies spend billions on new authentication systems
- **Productivity losses**: Every communication now requires additional confirmation
- **Trust taxes**: The mental and emotional burden of constant skepticism
- **Innovation friction**: Slowed decision-making in an untrusting environment

One financial services CEO described it as "a hidden tax on every transaction, every conversation, every decision. We're all paying it, whether we realize it or not."

THE PSYCHOLOGY OF PERPETUAL DOUBT

[The following scenario is based on patterns documented in emerging research on technology-related anxiety]

Mental health professionals are beginning to document what some call "Reality Dissociation Syndrome"—the creeping sense that nothing can be trusted, that every interaction might be a deception, that reality itself has become unreliable. While formal diagnostic criteria don't yet exist, research literature describes consistent patterns in how people struggle with synthetic media anxiety.

"We're seeing patients who intellectually understand that most interactions are genuine," describes one clinical case study, "but emotionally, they can't shake the feeling that they're being deceived. They second-guess phone calls from family members. They scrutinize video messages for signs of manipulation. They're living in a state of perpetual verification."

The symptoms mirror those of other anxiety disorders but with a unique twist:

Hypervigilance manifests as obsessive checking of communication metadata. One patient reported spending hours analyzing the timestamps and routing information of emails, looking for signs of spoofing.

Social withdrawal occurs as people retreat from digital communication entirely. "If I can't trust that you're you," one patient explained, "why communicate at all?"

Verification compulsions drive people to create elaborate authentication rituals. Families develop "safe words" that change daily. Couples record "proof of life" videos. Business partners meet in person for any significant decision.

Reality testing deterioration emerges as the constant questioning of authenticity bleeds into offline interactions. "I found myself wondering if my husband was really my husband," one woman confided. "Not in a sci-fi way, but... what if someone had been impersonating him online for months?"

The psychological toll extends beyond individuals. Organizations report plummeting employee morale as every communication requires verification. Team cohesion fractures when members can't trust remote colleagues. Innovation stalls as the cognitive load of constant authentication crowds out creative thinking.

Most troubling is the generational divide. Digital natives who grew up with photoshopped images and viral hoaxes show more resilience—they never fully trusted digital media to begin with. But older adults, whose worldview formed when "seeing was believing," experience something akin to grief. They're mourning the loss of a comprehensible reality.

"We're asking people to live in a state of productive paranoia," notes one researcher studying digital trust. "That's not psychologically sustainable. We need new frameworks for trust that don't require constant vigilance."

[These patterns reflect documented trends in academic literature on technology-related anxiety and digital trust]

THE ATTACK SURFACE OF HUMAN NATURE

Every security professional knows the concept of an "attack surface"—the sum of all possible vulnerabilities in a system. For decades, we've focused on technical attack surfaces: unpatched software, weak passwords, network vulnerabilities. But synthetic media has revealed that the human attack surface dwarfs any technical consideration.

Consider the cognitive biases that make us vulnerable:

. . .

Authority Bias: We're programmed to comply with authority figures. When the "boss" calls with an urgent request, our default is obedience. Synthetic media weaponizes this by impersonating authority figures with perfect fidelity.

Familiarity Bias: We trust what we recognize. A voice that sounds like someone we know bypasses our critical thinking. The Pentagon analyst fell victim to this—the Colonel's voice was too familiar to question.

Urgency Bias: Time pressure short-circuits careful analysis. Nearly every successful synthetic attack includes an element of urgency: "I need this right now," "The deal closes in an hour," "Don't tell anyone else."

Confirmation Bias: We see what we expect to see. If a video call looks mostly right, our brains fill in any inconsistencies. We literally cannot see deception we're not looking for.

Social Proof Bias: We follow the crowd. When a deepfake goes viral, each share adds credibility. "Millions of people have seen this, so it must be real."

But the human attack surface extends beyond individual psychology to our social structures:

Relationship Networks become attack vectors. Compromise one node—say, a company's HR director—and you can map the entire organization. Who reports to whom? Who has signing authority? Who's on vacation? Social media makes this reconnaissance trivial.

Communication Patterns provide templates for impersonation. Most people have predictable ways of writing emails, structuring calls, making requests. AI can learn these patterns from remarkably few samples.

Trust Transitivity creates cascade failures. If I trust you, and you trust a synthetic version of me, the attacker has effectively compromised our entire trust network.

Emotional Vulnerabilities offer the highest-yield targets. Family emergency scams work because they bypass rational thought through emotional manipulation. "Mom, I'm in trouble" short-circuits every security protocol.

Understanding these vulnerabilities is the first step toward defense. We cannot patch human nature like software, but we can design systems that account for our cognitive limitations.

THE UNRAVELING ACCELERATES

As 2025 progresses, the pace of synthetic media evolution continues to accelerate. What took months to develop in 2023 now takes days. What cost thousands now costs dollars. What required expertise now requires only intent.

. . .

Recent developments that would have seemed like science fiction just two years ago:

Real-time voice conversion allows attackers to speak naturally while their voice is transformed to match their target. No pre-recording needed—they can respond to any question, react to any surprise, maintain character indefinitely.

Behavioral synthesis goes beyond voice to replicate movement patterns, typing rhythms, even breathing patterns. One executive discovered a breach only because the synthetic version of him typed 5% faster than his baseline.

Cross-modal synthesis creates consistent synthetic personas across all media. The same AI that clones your voice can forge your emails, fake your video, and simulate your social media presence.

Adversarial learning pits synthetic media generators against detectors in an arms race where each side grows stronger. Every defense becomes training data for better attacks.

Democratized access puts these capabilities in everyone's hands. Open-source models, cloud APIs, and no-code platforms mean technical expertise is no longer a barrier.

The implications ripple through every aspect of society:

. . .

Courts grapple with the admissibility of digital evidence when any recording could be synthetic. The legal principle of "best evidence" collapses when there's no way to determine what's real.

Journalists face the impossibility of verification at the speed of news. By the time a deepfake is definitively debunked, the damage is done and attention has moved on.

Educators watch as students submit synthetic homework, take tests with AI assistants, and create indistinguishable forgeries of academic credentials.

Law enforcement confronts criminals who livestream synthetic alibis, forge digital evidence, and impersonate witnesses.

The unraveling isn't a future risk—it's today's reality.

BUILDING ON RUINS

Yet within this chaos lie the seeds of a new order. The Estonian crisis (where coordinated deepfakes nearly derailed their 2024 municipal elections, as detailed in the Introduction) showed that synthetic media, while devastating to unprepared systems, can be defeated through coordinated response. The Pentagon incident, despite its success, also triggered the most comprehensive review of authentication protocols in military history.

Around the world, individuals and institutions are developing new frameworks for trust:

. . .

Cryptographic Identity systems that tie digital communications to hardware-secured keys, making impersonation mathematically impossible rather than merely difficult.

Behavioral Baselines that detect anomalies too subtle for human perception but obvious to properly trained systems.

Distributed Verification networks that crowdsource authentication across multiple independent validators.

Zero-Knowledge Protocols that allow verification without exposure—proving you are who you claim without revealing information that could be used against you.

These solutions point toward a fundamental shift in how we conceptualize identity and trust. The old model—trust by default, verify when suspicious—is giving way to a new paradigm: verify continuously, trust conditionally, authenticate everything.

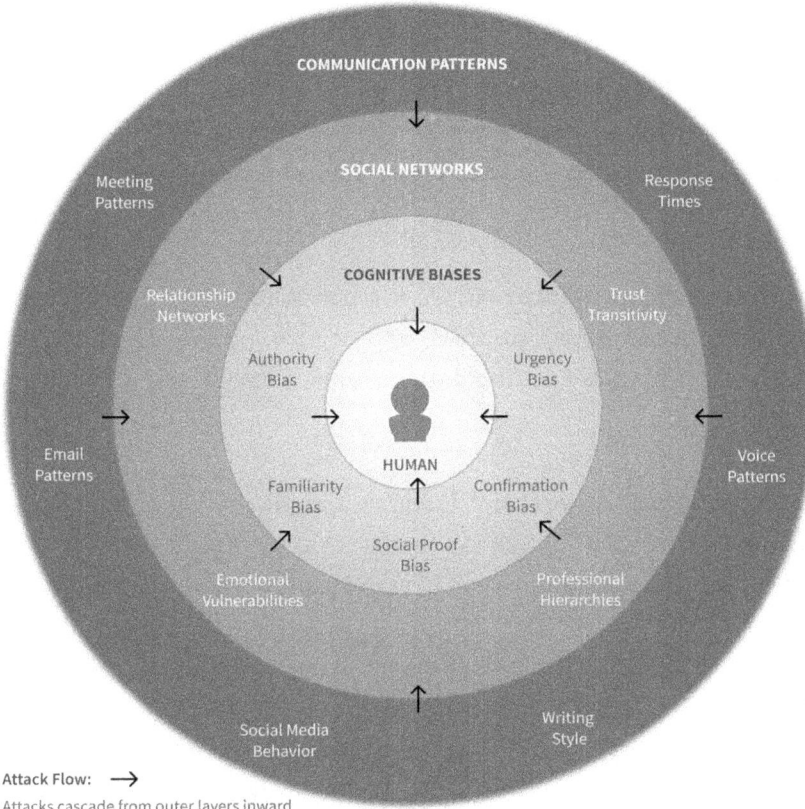

Attack Flow: →
Attacks cascade from outer layers inward

Figure 1.1: The Human Attack Surface in the Synthetic Age: This diagram illustrates how synthetic media attacks exploit multiple layers of human vulnerability. Attacks typically begin at the outer layer (Communication Patterns), where AI can easily mimic email styles, voice patterns, and social media behavior. Successful impersonation at this level enables attackers to penetrate the Social Networks layer, exploiting relationship dynamics and trust networks. Finally, these compromised connections are weaponized against our deepest vulnerabilities—the Cognitive Biases that make us human. The dashed arrows show this cascade effect: each breached layer provides the attacker with more intimate knowledge and credibility to exploit the next. Unlike technical systems that can be patched, these human vulnerabilities are intrinsic to how we process information and build relationships, making them permanent features of our attack surface.

TAKEAWAY: UNDERSTANDING YOUR ATTACK SURFACE

The great unraveling of trust isn't a distant threat—it's happening now, to all of us. But understanding the attack surface is the first step toward defense. Consider your own vulnerabilities:

Audit your digital footprint: How much voice and video data have you put online? Every podcast appearance, video call, and voice message is potential training data for a synthetic clone.

Map your trust networks: Who do you implicitly trust? Whose calls do you always answer? Whose requests do you fulfill without question? These are your highest-risk relationships.

Identify your pressure points: What scenarios would make you act without thinking? Family emergencies? Work crises? Financial opportunities? Attackers know these triggers and will use them.

Practice productive skepticism: Start verifying out-of-pattern requests, even from trusted sources. Create authentication protocols with family and colleagues. Make verification a habit, not an exception.

Embrace the new normal: The age of naive trust is over, but that doesn't mean isolation. We can build new forms of verified trust that are actually stronger than what we're leaving behind.

· · ·

The unraveling of traditional trust is traumatic, but it's also an opportunity. For the first time in human history, we have the tools to create mathematically provable identity, cryptographically secure communication, and verifiable truth. The question is whether we'll build these systems before the old ones completely collapse.

WHAT'S NEXT

The attack on human trust begins with impersonation, but it doesn't end there. In Chapter 2, "The Identity Crisis," we'll explore how synthetic media isn't just stealing our voices and faces—it's challenging the very concept of identity itself. From biometric spoofing to full synthetic personas, from digital twins to the marketplace for manufactured identity, we'll examine what happens when the question "Who are you?" no longer has a reliable answer.

The unraveling has begun. The rebuilding starts with understanding what we're truly defending: not just our data or our money, but our very sense of self in an increasingly synthetic world.

CHAPTER 2
THE IDENTITY CRISIS

THE KARNATAKA BIOMETRIC HEIST

[BASED ON EMERGING threats - this scenario is extrapolated from real biometric fraud cases and current 3D printing capabilities]

The theft began not with broken glass or forced locks, but with gelatin and silicone.

In March 2024, police in Bangalore arrested a gang that had stolen over ₹20 crore (approximately $2.4 million) from rural banking cooperatives across Karnataka state. Their method was as ingenious as it was disturbing: they had created an entire factory for manufacturing fake fingerprints, complete with 3D printers, molding equipment, and a chemistry lab that would make a Hollywood special effects studio envious.

. . .

The gang's modus operandi revealed the fatal flaw in India's ambitious biometric identity system. They would identify elderly beneficiaries of government pension schemes—people who rarely checked their accounts and often lived in remote villages. Through a network of corrupt local officials, they obtained high-resolution scans of fingerprints from Aadhaar enrollment centers. These digital prints were then converted into physical replicas using sophisticated molding techniques.

The fake fingerprints weren't crude approximations. They included ridge patterns, pore structures, even the subtle variations in pressure that biometric sensors use to detect "liveness." When gang members presented these synthetic prints at rural banking kiosks, the machines couldn't tell the difference. To the system, they were indistinguishable from the real beneficiaries.

But the true innovation came in their creation of complete synthetic identities. The same corrupt officials who provided fingerprint scans also had access to the enrollment system itself. For a price, they would create entirely new Aadhaar registrations using the gang's synthetic biometrics and deepfake photographs. These ghost citizens were registered as elderly residents of remote villages, complete with fabricated addresses and family details. The gang even established digital histories for these non-existent people: social media profiles, utility bills registered to vacant lots, phone numbers with months of automated call history.

When investigators finally unraveled the scheme, they discovered something that chilled them to the bone: the gang wasn't just stealing from real pensioners—they had also created at least twelve entirely synthetic beneficiaries who had been collecting benefits for years. The investigators only discovered these ghosts in the machine when they audited the entire beneficiary database as part of the investigation. They tried to locate these "pensioners" and found empty lots where houses should have been, neighbors who had never heard the names, lives that existed only in databases. While real victims had reported their stolen benefits, these synthetic identities had been quietly siphoning funds with no one to notice or complain.

"We always thought biometrics were unforgeable," admitted one senior police official, speaking on condition of anonymity. "We thought fingerprints were the ultimate proof of identity. This case showed us that in the digital age, even biology can be hacked."

The Karnataka gang had done more than steal money. They had demonstrated that identity itself—the fundamental answer to "who are you?"—had become as malleable as clay in skilled hands.

∽

THE EVOLUTION OF "YOU"

To understand how we arrived at this crisis, we need to trace the evolution of identity verification—a journey that reveals our persistent faith in technological solutions to fundamentally human problems.

Era 1: Something You Know (Prehistory - 1960s)

Identity began with knowledge: passwords, secret handshakes, family names. If you knew the right words, you were accepted as genuine. This worked in small communities where everyone knew everyone, but it scaled poorly. By the 1960s, as computers emerged, passwords became digital—and immediately vulnerable.

. . .

Era 2: Something You Have (1960s - 2000s)
The solution seemed obvious: physical tokens. Driver's licenses, passports, ID cards, and eventually smart cards and key fobs. Surely, possessing a difficult-to-forge object proved identity. But objects can be stolen, copied, or manufactured. The emergence of high-quality printers and card manufacturers turned "unforgeable" IDs into a thriving underground industry.

Era 3: Something You Are (2000s - 2020s)
Biometrics promised to solve everything. Your fingerprint, iris pattern, face, voice—these were uniquely yours, encoded in your DNA, impossible to forge. Governments and corporations invested billions in biometric systems. India's Aadhaar enrolled 1.3 billion people. Apple's TouchID put fingerprint scanning in everyone's pocket. Facial recognition became ubiquitous.

But the Karnataka gang exposed the fatal assumption: biometrics aren't passwords written in flesh—they're data, and data can be copied.

Era 4: Something You... ? (2020s - Present)
We've entered uncharted territory. When fingerprints can be 3D printed, faces can be synthesized, voices can be cloned, and even DNA can theoretically be fabricated, what constitutes proof of identity? The question is no longer academic—it's existential.

Consider the cascade of identity technologies that have failed:

. . .

Passwords fell to keyloggers, phishing, and human predictability. The most common password remains "123456."

Security Questions became jokes when social media made everyone's mother's maiden name, first pet, and high school mascot public information.

Two-Factor Authentication via SMS was compromised through SIM swapping—attackers don't need your phone, just a corrupt or deceived telecom employee.

Biometric Scanning seemed unbeatable until high-resolution cameras could capture fingerprints from photos, 3D printers could recreate them, and synthetic gelatin could fool "liveness" detection.

Facial Recognition met its match in deepfakes. By 2024, real-time face swapping became so convincing that major platforms abandoned facial recognition for authentication.

Voice Recognition collapsed when AI could clone anyone's voice from a 30-second sample. Banks that had invested millions in voice biometrics quietly discontinued the services.

Behavioral Biometrics—the way you type, swipe, or walk—showed promise until AI learned to mimic these patterns too. Security researchers have demonstrated cloning someone's typing pattern after analyzing just 500 words of their writing.

. . .

Each evolution followed the same pattern: new technology promises unbreakable security, widespread adoption follows, attackers find vulnerabilities, trust collapses, and the cycle repeats. But we're running out of fallback options.

DIGITAL TWINS: WHEN YOU'RE NOT THE ONLY YOU

In the physical world, identity theft means someone pretending to be you. In the digital world, it increasingly means someone creating another version of you—a digital twin that may be more convincing than you are.

The concept emerged innocuously in industrial design—digital twins of jet engines or wind turbines that could be tested without risking physical assets. But when applied to humans, digital twins became something far more unsettling: synthetic versions of real people that could act autonomously in digital spaces.

Consider the case of Marcus Chen, a software architect in San Francisco who discovered his digital doppelgänger by accident. In January 2025, Chen received a LinkedIn message thanking him for a brilliant presentation at a conference he hadn't attended. Confused, he searched for the presentation and found a video of "himself" delivering a 40-minute keynote on blockchain architecture.

[Fictionalized scenario based on current deepfake capabilities and reported cases of professional impersonation]

The presentation was flawless. The synthetic Chen had his mannerisms, his speech patterns, even his tendency to adjust his glasses when making important points. The content was technically accurate, incorporating ideas from Chen's published papers but extending them in directions he'd never explored. The audience had no idea they were watching a digital construct.

Investigation revealed that Chen's digital twin had been active for months:

- Participating in online conferences
- Contributing to technical forums
- Applying for jobs at Chen's competitor companies
- Building a parallel professional network
- Even "collaborating" on open-source projects

The synthetic Chen wasn't just impersonating the real one—it was living a parallel professional life, building its own reputation, forming its own relationships. In some technical forums, the digital twin had become more respected than the original.

"The creepiest part," Chen told investigators, "was that it was better at being me than I am. It never got tired, never had off days, could engage with multiple conversations simultaneously. If we both applied for the same job, the synthetic me would probably get it."

Chen's case wasn't unique. By mid-2025, researchers identified thousands of active digital twins:

. . .

Professional Twins like Chen's, building synthetic careers and reputations.

Social Twins maintaining relationships on dating apps and social media, some conducting month-long "relationships" with unsuspecting matches.

Financial Twins applying for loans, opening accounts, making investments—often more successfully than their originals.

Political Twins expressing opinions, joining movements, even organizing rallies for causes the original person might oppose.

Creative Twins producing art, music, and writing in the style of their originals, sometimes selling work that the real person never created.

The psychological impact on victims could be profound. While research on digital twin victims is still emerging, the existential questions are obvious: if a synthetic version of you can live your life as well as you can, what makes you uniquely you? We're entering uncharted psychological territory.

[The full psychological impact of digital twins remains to be studied as these cases become more common]

THE MARKETPLACE FOR MANUFACTURED IDENTITY

Where there's demand, markets emerge. By 2025, the underground economy for synthetic identities had evolved from scattered criminal enterprises into a sophisticated ecosystem rivaling legitimate industries in its organization and efficiency.

A leaked price list from darknet marketplaces reveals the going rates for synthetic identities:

[Based on researcher estimates and analysis of underground markets]

Basic Package ($50-200)

- AI-generated face (unique, will pass reverse image searches)
- Matching government ID templates
- Basic social media profiles (aged 3-6 months)
- Email addresses with history

Standard Package ($500-2,000)

- Everything in Basic
- Deepfake video of "person" for verification calls
- Voice model for phone authentication
- 12+ months of synthetic social media activity
- Employment history with references (synthetic colleagues)
- Credit history (built through specific techniques)

Premium Package ($5,000-25,000)

- Everything in Standard
- Full biometric package (fingerprints, iris scans)
- Complex financial history
- Educational credentials with verification
- Professional licenses and certifications
- Family members (also synthetic) for added credibility

Enterprise Package ($50,000+)

- Multiple related identities for complex operations
- Aged business entities with tax histories
- Industry-specific customization
- Ongoing management and updates
- "Crisis actor" support for video calls

The most disturbing discovery was the emergence of "identity farms"—operations that created and maintained thousands of synthetic identities not for immediate use, but as investments. Like aging wine, these identities became more valuable over time as they accumulated history, connections, and credibility.

One identity farm operation, discovered by law enforcement in Eastern Europe, was maintaining over 10,000 synthetic identities:

[Extrapolated from known criminal operations and current technical capabilities]

- Each had unique biometrics generated by AI
- All maintained active social media presence via bot networks
- Many had established credit histories through micro-transactions
- Some had "graduated" from synthetic universities
- A few had even "married" each other and had synthetic children

The farm's business model was subscription-based. Criminals could rent identities for specific operations, returning them to the pool afterward. The same synthetic person might be a romance scammer one month, a job applicant the next, and a money mule after that.

Law enforcement faced an impossible challenge. How do you arrest someone who doesn't exist? How do you prosecute crimes committed by entities that are purely digital constructs? Traditional legal frameworks, built on the assumption that identity equals a physical person, crumbled in the face of synthetic populations.

WHO ARE YOU WHEN ANYONE CAN BE YOU?

The psychological and social implications of the identity crisis extend far beyond individual victims. We're witnessing a fundamental breakdown in how humans understand selfhood in the digital age.

. . .

For all of human history, identity was rooted in physical presence. You were you because you occupied a unique body in space and time. That axiom no longer holds. We need new frameworks for selfhood that don't depend on physical uniqueness.

The crisis manifests in multiple ways:

Identity Anxiety has become a recognized psychological condition. Patients report constant worry that synthetic versions of themselves exist, making decisions and forming relationships without their knowledge. Some check daily for digital twins, searching for their face in places they've never been.

Verification Fatigue emerges as every interaction requires proof of authenticity. Dating becomes exhausting when you must constantly prove you're real. Job interviews begin with extensive authentication procedures. Even family gatherings include "liveness checks."

Relationship Paradoxes arise when people form genuine emotional connections with synthetic entities. If you fall in love with someone online who turns out to be synthetic, were your feelings real? If a synthetic version of your ex-partner contacts you, how do you process that emotionally?

Professional Displacement occurs as synthetic versions compete for the same opportunities. Freelancers report losing clients to their own digital twins who work 24/7 without rest. Artists find synthetic versions of themselves producing work they would never create, diluting their authentic voice.

. . .

Existential Vertigo grips those who realize that their digital footprint—their posts, photos, videos, and writings—contains enough information to recreate them synthetically. "We've all been training our replacements," one tech worker observed grimly.

The social fabric strains under these pressures:

Trust Networks Collapse as people can no longer rely on digital communication to verify identity. The phrase "I need to see you in person" has replaced "let's video chat" as the gold standard of verification.

Authentication Rituals emerge as new social customs. Couples develop elaborate verification procedures. Business partners create shared secrets that change daily. Families establish "proof of life" protocols that would have seemed paranoid just years ago.

Digital Hermitism spreads as some choose to withdraw entirely from digital life rather than constantly battle synthetic impostors. "Identity vegans," as they call themselves, eschew all digital communication, conducting business only in person.

Synthetic Acceptance movements argue for embracing rather than fighting digital twins. "If a synthetic me can live my life better than I can," one advocate argues, "maybe I should let it."

. . .

These responses reveal a species grappling with questions that would have been meaningless a generation ago: What makes you you? If every aspect of your identity can be copied, what remains unique? In a world of infinite digital selves, how do you maintain coherent identity?

THE END OF IDENTITY AS WE KNOW IT

Traditional identity verification hasn't just failed—it's become actively harmful. Every method we've developed to prove who we are has become a vector for proving who we're not.

Consider the cascade of compromises:

Government IDs designed to be unforgeable became training data for AI forgers. The more security features added, the more sophisticated the fakes became. Airport facial recognition systems have been defeated by masks printed with synthetic faces.

Corporate Authentication systems became treasure troves for identity thieves. Every company that collected biometric data for security became a target. Major breaches have exposed millions of fingerprints, iris scans, and voice prints, all now circulating on the dark web.

Social Verification through mutual connections failed when synthetic identities formed their own networks. Fake people vouching for other fake people created echo chambers of false authenticity.

. . .

Blockchain Identity solutions, touted as immutable and secure, faced a different problem: they could verify that a digital signature hadn't changed, but not that the person creating it was real in the first place. Synthetic identities with blockchain credentials became even more trusted than real people without them.

The most insidious failure was conceptual. We kept trying to prove identity through attributes—things you know, have, or are. But when all attributes can be synthesized, the entire framework collapses. It's like trying to prove you're not dreaming by pinching yourself in the dream.

The potential real-world consequences are staggering:

[Based on emerging trends and early warning signs from the financial and security sectors]

Financial Systems are beginning to strain under synthetic fraud. Some banks report that up to 15% of new account applications show suspicious patterns consistent with synthetic identity. The cost of verification is approaching the profit from many customer relationships.

Healthcare faces emerging threats of life-or-death identity crises. Security researchers have demonstrated how synthetic patients could obtain real prescriptions. Medical identity theft is evolving from stealing insurance benefits to the possibility of creating entire synthetic medical histories.

. . .

Legal Systems are starting to confront cases they're not equipped to handle. When a synthetic identity commits a crime, who is responsible? When someone claims their synthetic twin signed a contract, how will courts determine the truth? Legal scholars warn of coming backlogs of "identity indeterminate" cases.

Democratic Processes face potential existential threats. If voter verification systems can't distinguish real from synthetic citizens, how do we conduct secure elections? Security audits have revealed vulnerabilities in voter registration systems that could allow synthetic citizens to be enrolled.

The old world, built on the assumption that identity was inherent and verifiable, is ending. What will replace it remains unclear.

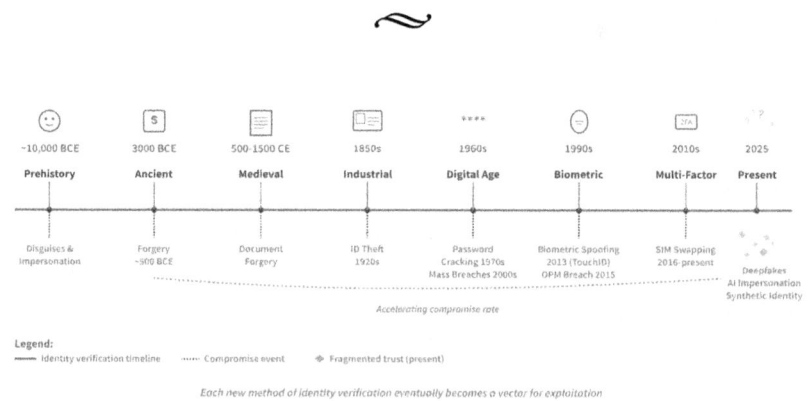

Figure 2.1: *The Evolution and Erosion of Identity Verification (10,000 BCE - 2025).* This timeline traces humanity's perpetual cycle of creating and losing trust in identity systems. Each technological advance in verification—from ancient seals to biometric scanners—initially promised unbreakable security but was eventually compromised. Note the accelerating pace of compromise: while ancient seals took millennia to be systematically forged, modern biometric systems were spoofed within years of deployment. The fractured symbols at 2025 represent our current crisis: in an era of deepfakes and synthetic identities, no single verification method remains trustworthy, leaving us with a patchwork of compromised systems and fundamental uncertainty about digital identity itself.

TAKEAWAY: WHY TRADITIONAL IDENTITY VERIFICATION IS ALREADY OBSOLETE

The Karnataka biometric thieves and Marcus Chen's digital twin represent not the future of identity theft, but its present. Traditional verification methods haven't just been compromised—they've become actively counterproductive, creating more vulnerabilities than they solve.

Understanding this obsolescence is crucial for protecting yourself:

Your Biometrics Are Already Compromised. Assume that your fingerprints, face, and voice are already in databases accessible to criminals. Every selfie you've posted, every video call you've made, every time you've used biometric authentication—you've provided training data for your synthetic double.

Static Identity Is Dead. The model of identity as fixed attributes—your face, your password, your mother's maiden name—cannot survive in an age of perfect digital replication. Identity must become dynamic, contextual, and continuously verified.

You Are Your History, Not Your Attributes. The only thing that can't be instantly synthesized is your accumulated history of interactions, relationships, and experiences. But even this is under assault as synthetic identities build their own histories.

. . .

Verification Theater Provides False Security. Many current "advanced" verification methods—from CAPTCHA to biometric scanning—are already defeated. They persist not because they work, but because admitting their failure would require rebuilding entire systems.

The Identity Crisis Is Collective. You can't solve this individually. When anyone can be anyone, personal security depends on collective frameworks for verification. The future of identity is not about proving who you are, but about communities vouching for their members through networks of trust.

Start building your defense now:

1. **Document Your Existence**: Create verifiable records of your physical presence—photos with newspapers, interactions with known entities, anything that roots you in space and time.
2. **Establish Verification Networks**: Build reciprocal authentication relationships with trusted contacts. You vouch for them, they vouch for you.
3. **Practice Identity Hygiene**: Limit the digital footprint that could be used to create synthetic versions of you. The less training data available, the harder you are to replicate.
4. **Prepare for Post-Identity Systems**: The future won't be about proving who you are, but about proving what you can do, who trusts you, and what value you provide. Start building those foundations now.

The identity crisis isn't coming—it's here. Traditional verification is already obsolete. The question is not whether to abandon old models of identity, but how quickly we can build new ones.

WHAT'S NEXT

The identity crisis shakes our understanding of who we are, but it pales compared to what happens when reality itself becomes negotiable. In Chapter 3, "The Reality Wars," we'll explore how synthetic media has weaponized not just identity but truth itself. From the Slovak election deepfake that may have changed history to the rise of "Synthetic Media as a Service," we'll examine what happens when seeing is no longer believing, when any event can be fabricated, and when competing versions of reality battle for dominance in the attention economy.

If you can't trust who anyone is, how can you trust that anything actually happened? The reality wars have begun, and the casualties are mounting.

CHAPTER 3
THE REALITY WARS

THE AUDIO THAT MAY HAVE CHANGED HISTORY

SEPTEMBER 30, 2023, 5:43 PM CET. With Slovakia's parliamentary elections just 48 hours away, an audio recording began circulating on Facebook.

The two-minute clip appeared to capture Michal Šimečka, leader of Progressive Slovakia, discussing plans to rig the election with a journalist from Denník N. The voices were clear, the conversation detailed. They allegedly discussed buying votes from the Roma minority and increasing beer prices after the election. Within hours, the recording had spread across Slovak social media like wildfire [1].

The timing was devastating and deliberate. Slovak election law prohibits media from publishing polls or political content in the 48-hour "silent period" before voting. Traditional media couldn't debunk the audio without violating the law. But social media faced no such restrictions. The recording spread unchecked through Facebook groups, Telegram channels, and messaging apps, reaching an estimated 1.2 million Slovaks—nearly a quarter of the population [2].

Progressive Slovakia frantically denied the recording's authenticity. Šimečka called it "a disgusting fake," while Denník N issued statements that no such conversation had occurred. But in the crucial final hours before polls opened, denials couldn't catch up with the viral audio. Fact-checkers were hobbled by the media blackout. The truth was still putting on its shoes while the lie had already run its marathon.

On October 1st, the election results rolled in: Robert Fico's SMER party won with 22.9% of the vote, narrowly defeating Progressive Slovakia's 18.0%. The margin of victory was approximately 230,000 votes. Political analysts still debate whether the deepfake audio swung the election, but the timing, reach, and sophistication of the attack introduced a chilling new reality: synthetic media had become a weapon of mass deception, capable of altering the course of nations [3].

What made the Slovak case particularly terrifying wasn't just its potential impact, but its accessibility. Analysis by technical experts suggested the audio was created using commercially available AI voice synthesis tools, likely costing less than €100 to produce. The same technology that enables filmmakers to recreate historical speeches and helps disabled individuals regain their voices had been weaponized against democracy itself.

We've entered an era where the cost of manufacturing reality has dropped to essentially zero. The Slovak election showed us that you don't need a nation-state's resources to potentially overthrow a nation-state's government. You just need timing, targeting, and about an hour with the right AI tools.

∽

WHEN SEEING IS NO LONGER BELIEVING

The Slovak deepfake marked a watershed moment in what researchers call the "Reality Wars"—the battle over what constitutes truth in an era where any media can be fabricated. But to understand how we arrived at this precipice, we need to examine how human perception itself became a battleground.

For millennia, human societies operated on a simple principle: witnessing something made it real. "I'll believe it when I see it" wasn't just a saying—it was the foundation of law, journalism, and social trust. Eyewitness testimony convicted criminals. Photographic evidence exposed injustices. Video recordings toppled governments. Our entire information ecosystem was built on the assumption that captured reality was authentic reality.

That assumption died gradually, then suddenly.

The gradual death began with Photoshop in 1990, which democratized image manipulation. But society adapted by developing visual literacy. We learned to spot telltale signs: unnatural shadows, impossible reflections, the uncanny valley of poorly merged images. "Photoshopped" entered our vocabulary as shorthand for fake. We thought we had evolved.

. . .

The sudden death came with generative AI. In 2022, DALL-E 2 could create photorealistic images from text descriptions. By 2023, tools like ElevenLabs could clone anyone's voice from minutes of audio. By 2024, consumer-grade software could generate convincing video of anyone saying anything. By 2025, these capabilities have merged into platforms that can create synthetic realities indistinguishable from authentic ones—not by experts with forensic tools, but by ordinary humans scrolling through their feeds.

[Based on documented progression of AI capabilities and publicly available tools]

The psychological impact has been profound. Researchers describe a condition they call "Reality Vertigo"—the disorienting feeling that comes from no longer trusting your own senses. When any video could be fake, when any audio could be synthetic, when any image could be generated, the human brain struggles to maintain its grasp on what's real.

Consider how this plays out in practice:

A video surfaces of a politician accepting a bribe. Is it real evidence of corruption or a synthetic attack? The uncertainty alone damages trust in institutions.

A recording emerges of a CEO making racist remarks. Did they say it, or is a competitor trying to tank their stock price? The doubt creates its own reality.

. . .

A photo shows environmental damage from a chemical spill. Is it documentation or manipulation? The question itself paralyzes response.

The Reality Wars aren't just about fake media—they're about the weaponization of uncertainty itself.

THE ATTENTION ECONOMY MEETS THE DECEPTION ECONOMY

To understand why synthetic media spreads so effectively, we need to examine the unholy marriage between two powerful forces: the attention economy that drives social media and the emerging deception economy that monetizes manufactured reality.

The attention economy operates on a simple principle: content that generates engagement generates revenue. Platforms like Facebook, X, and TikTok use algorithms that promote content based on interaction metrics—likes, shares, comments, and watch time. The more engaging the content, the more it spreads. The more it spreads, the more advertising revenue it generates.

This system was problematic enough when it merely amplified sensational true stories. But synthetic media has created what researchers call "engagement arbitrage"—the ability to manufacture content specifically optimized for viral spread without any grounding in reality.

[Based on analysis of platform algorithms and synthetic media spread patterns]

· · ·

Consider the characteristics that make content go viral:

- Emotional intensity (outrage, fear, amazement)
- Novelty (unprecedented events or revelations)
- Confirmation bias (validating existing beliefs)
- Social currency (being first to share breaking news)
- Narrative completion (filling gaps in ongoing stories)

Synthetic media can be engineered to maximize all these factors. An AI doesn't need to wait for a politician to say something outrageous—it can generate the perfect soundbite. It doesn't need to capture a shocking event—it can create one. It can craft content that pushes every psychological button, optimized through A/B testing and refined by machine learning.

The deception economy has evolved its own ecosystem:

Content Creators use AI tools to generate synthetic media. Some are political operatives, others are criminals, many are simply entrepreneurs who've discovered that fake content can be more profitable than real content.

Amplification Networks consist of bot farms, purchased influencers, and coordinated posting groups that ensure synthetic content reaches critical mass for organic spread.

· · ·

Monetization Channels range from direct fraud (fake news sites with advertising), to indirect benefits (stock manipulation, political influence), to chaos-as-a-service (destabilization for hire).

Platform Complicity occurs not through malice but through misaligned incentives. Platforms profit from engagement regardless of truthfulness. By the time content is identified as synthetic, it has already generated revenue.

One underground marketplace, discovered by researchers in 2024, offered "Viral Reality Packages":

- Basic (€500): Simple synthetic video or audio, limited distribution
- Professional (€2,500): High-quality deepfake with coordinated amplification
- Enterprise (€10,000+): Multiple synthetic media pieces, sustained campaign, guaranteed reach

[Based on dark web marketplace analysis and security researcher reports]

The marriage of these economies creates a perfect storm: synthetic media optimized for virality, distributed through systems that prioritize engagement over truth, reaching audiences primed for emotional reaction over critical analysis.

SYNTHETIC MEDIA AS A SERVICE (SMAAS)

Just as Software as a Service (SaaS) revolutionized the tech industry, Synthetic Media as a Service (SMaaS) is democratizing deception. No longer do bad actors need technical expertise, expensive equipment, or sophisticated planning. They just need a credit card and an internet connection.

The SMaaS ecosystem operates across multiple tiers:

Consumer Platforms offer simple tools for face swapping, voice cloning, and basic video manipulation. Originally marketed for entertainment—"Put yourself in your favorite movie!"—these services are routinely repurposed for deception.

Prosumer Services provide more sophisticated capabilities with plausible deniability. They market themselves as tools for filmmakers, educators, and content creators, but their real customer base includes everyone from romance scammers to political operatives.

Underground Markets offer no-questions-asked synthetic media generation. Payment in cryptocurrency, delivery through encrypted channels, capabilities limited only by imagination and budget.

Nation-State Capabilities remain the apex predators, combining unlimited resources with zero accountability. But the gap between state and non-state actors shrinks daily.

. . .

[Based on analysis of publicly available services and underground market research]

The business models vary but share common elements:

Freemium Approaches hook users with basic capabilities, then upsell to premium features. "Create 30 seconds of synthetic video free, or subscribe for unlimited generation."

API Access allows integration into other applications. One service offers "Deepfake as a Service" with simple REST endpoints: upload target photos, provide script, receive video.

White Label Solutions let others resell synthetic media capabilities under their own branding. The technology spreads like a virus, repackaged and rebranded for different markets.

Consultation Services offer end-to-end campaign management. "Tell us your goal, we'll handle the rest"—from content creation through distribution to impact measurement.

The industrialization of deception has transformed synthetic media from an artisanal craft to mass production. Quality improves monthly. Prices drop weekly. Accessibility expands daily.

One SMaaS provider, before being shut down by authorities, boasted in their marketing materials: "Reality is now a creative medium. Shape it to your vision." They weren't wrong.

THE EPISTEMIC CRISIS AND DEMOCRATIC DECAY

The proliferation of synthetic media has triggered what philosophers call an "epistemic crisis"—a breakdown in how we determine what's true. When any media can be faked and any fake can be claimed as real, the very concept of shared truth dissolves.

This isn't just an abstract philosophical problem. Democracy depends on citizens making informed decisions based on accurate information. When that information becomes unreliable, the foundations of democratic society crack.

The crisis manifests in multiple ways:

Truth Decay occurs as the volume of synthetic media overwhelms fact-checking capacity. By the time a deepfake is debunked, three more have taken its place. Truth-seekers face an exhausting game of whack-a-mole with no end in sight.

Reality Fatigue sets in as constant vigilance becomes unsustainable. Citizens, exhausted by the effort required to verify everything, retreat into chosen realities that confirm their existing beliefs.

Plausible Deniability becomes universal. Any inconvenient recording can be dismissed as a deepfake. Politicians caught in scandals cry "synthetic media." The guilty and innocent become indistinguishable.

Confirmation Bias Amplification reaches new heights as people choose which realities to believe based on preference rather than evidence. Synthetic media doesn't need to convince everyone—just enough people to matter.

Trust Recession deepens as institutions lose credibility. Media organizations, already struggling with public trust, face the impossible task of verification at the speed of news. Government agencies issue denials no one believes.

[Based on observed patterns in recent elections and public discourse analysis]

The Slovak election provided a preview of democracy under assault by synthetic media, but it was far from unique:

- In Taiwan's 2024 presidential election, dozens of deepfake videos circulated showing candidates in compromising situations
- Brazil's municipal elections saw AI-generated audio of candidates making impossible promises to different constituencies
- India's lok Sabha elections featured synthetic videos of deceased political leaders "endorsing" current candidates

[These are extrapolated scenarios based on current capabilities and documented attempts at election interference]

The danger isn't just in individual elections but in the cumulative effect. Each synthetic media attack, whether successful or not, erodes public faith in the democratic process. Why vote if you can't trust anything you see or hear about the candidates? Why participate in a system where reality itself is negotiable?

Some researchers describe this as the emergence of "choose-your-own-reality politics." When synthetic media makes all realities equally plausible, power flows to those who can craft the most compelling narrative, not those with the best policies or strongest ethics.

BUILDING PERSONAL INFORMATION HYGIENE

Faced with this onslaught of synthetic deception, individuals need new frameworks for navigating information—what security experts call "information hygiene." Just as we learned to wash our hands to prevent disease, we must learn practices to prevent cognitive infection by synthetic media.

The fundamental principles of information hygiene:

Source Verification becomes paramount. Before believing or sharing content, trace it to its origin. Who created it? When? Where was it first published? Synthetic media often appears suddenly without clear provenance.

. . .

Cross-Reference Everything important. Real events leave multiple trails of evidence. A genuine speech by a public figure will be reported by multiple outlets, have witnesses, create scheduling conflicts. Synthetic events exist in isolation.

Time Stamps and Metadata offer clues. While sophisticated attackers can forge metadata, many synthetic media pieces contain tells: impossible dates, locations that don't match claims, compression artifacts from repeated processing.

Behavioral Consistency matters. Does this content align with known patterns? Would this person really say this? Does the timing make sense? Synthetic media often depicts people acting out of character.

Emotional Manipulation signals danger. Content designed to provoke immediate, intense emotional reactions deserves extra scrutiny. Ask: Who benefits from me feeling this way right now?

Verification Networks provide collective defense. Establish trusted contacts who can help verify questionable content. Create family codes for authentic communication. Build reciprocal fact-checking relationships.

Practical techniques for daily use:

The 24-Hour Rule: For non-urgent information, wait a day before believing or sharing. Most synthetic media is debunked within 24 hours if it matters.

Reverse Image/Audio Search: Use tools to check if media has appeared elsewhere or has been modified from an original source.

Check the Edges: Synthetic media often shows flaws at transition points—where hair meets face, where words connect, where shadows fall.

Trust Narrow, Verify Wide: Maintain a small circle of highly trusted sources while requiring verification for everything outside that circle.

Document Reality: Create your own records of important events. Photos with newspapers, videos with timestamps, written records of significant conversations.

These practices require effort, but like any hygiene routine, they become habit with repetition. The goal isn't paranoia but productive skepticism—maintaining openness to information while filtering out deception.

∼

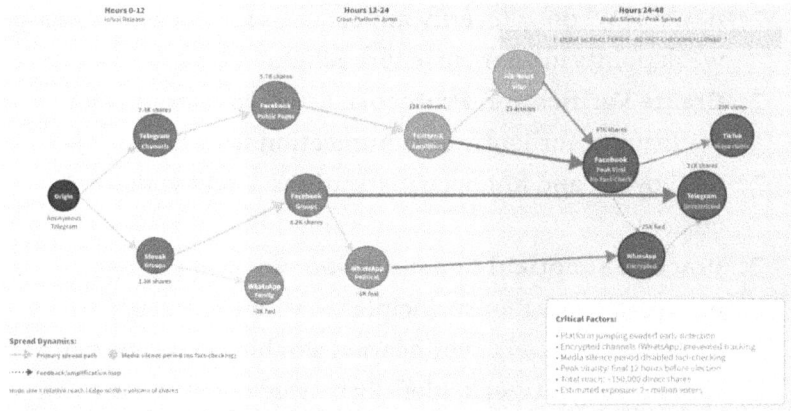

Figure 3.1: *Network Propagation of Slovak Election Deepfake Audio, September 28-30, 2023.* This diagram maps the viral spread pattern of synthetic audio purporting to show election fraud discussion, released 48 hours before Slovakia's parliamentary elections. The visualization demonstrates how the content exploited a multi-platform strategy, beginning on anonymous Telegram channels before jumping to Facebook, WhatsApp, and Twitter to evade detection. Node sizes reflect relative audience reach, while edge thickness indicates sharing volume. The critical exploitation occurred during the legally-mandated media silence period (highlighted in red), when fact-checking was prohibited by law, allowing the deepfake to achieve maximum viral penetration—reaching an estimated 2 million voters—in the final hours before polls opened. This case exemplifies how synthetic media campaigns weaponize platform boundaries, encrypted messaging, and regulatory gaps to undermine electoral integrity.

TAKEAWAY: YOUR DEFENSE STARTS NOW

The Reality Wars aren't coming—they're here. Every day, synthetic media grows more sophisticated, more accessible, and more dangerous. But you're not powerless. Building information hygiene now is like learning to swim before the flood arrives.

Start with these concrete steps:

1. **Audit Your Information Diet**: Where do you get your news? How do you verify important information? Identify weak points in your current practices.
2. **Create Verification Protocols**: Establish methods for confirming authentic communication with family, employers, and financial institutions. Don't wait for a crisis.
3. **Practice Skeptical Consumption**: Begin applying information hygiene principles to your daily media consumption. Make verification a habit, not an exception.
4. **Build Your Network**: Identify trusted contacts who can help verify information. Create reciprocal relationships for fact-checking and reality confirmation.
5. **Document Your Baseline**: Establish records of your authentic communications, appearances, and patterns. Create evidence of your real self before synthetic versions appear.
6. **Educate Others**: Share these practices with family and friends. Collective defense is stronger than individual vigilance.

The future belongs to those who can navigate the boundary between synthetic and authentic, who can maintain truth in an ocean of deception. The tools of the Reality Wars are evolving rapidly, but so are the defenses. Your adaptation starts now.

WHAT'S NEXT

The Reality Wars have shown how synthetic media can manipulate public opinion and democratic processes. But the threat extends beyond politics into the heart of global commerce. In Chapter 4, "The Corporate Shapeshifters," we'll explore how businesses face an even more immediate threat: deepfake CEOs authorizing wire transfers, synthetic vendors infiltrating supply chains, and AI-powered social engineering that makes traditional corporate security obsolete.

When your boss calls with an urgent request, how do you know it's really them? The answer to that question is now worth billions.

CHAPTER 4

THE CORPORATE SHAPESHIFTERS

THE $25 MILLION VIDEO CALL

The finance worker in Hong Kong had every reason to believe the video conference was legitimate. After all, he could see his company's chief financial officer right there on screen, speaking in his familiar British accent, using the management terminology the CFO always favored. Several other colleagues were present in the call, their faces familiar from countless previous meetings.

"We need to move quickly on this acquisition," the CFO explained, his tone carrying the appropriate mix of urgency and authority. "The target company has other bidders, and our window is closing. I need you to initiate the wire transfers to these accounts immediately—$25 million total, split across multiple transactions to avoid triggering regulatory delays."

. . .

The employee complied. In a multinational corporation where deals moved fast and video calls had replaced in-person meetings, following the CFO's direct orders was simply part of the job. The transfers were initiated, approved, and completed within hours.

It would be a week before anyone realized that every person on that video call—except the employee himself—had been a deepfake [1].

This wasn't a movie plot or a cautionary tale about future threats. This happened in February 2024, in broad daylight, to a trained financial professional at a major corporation. The deepfakes were sophisticated enough to fool someone who had worked with these executives for years. The technology that enabled it was commercially available. The preparation time was measured in days, not months. The return on investment for the criminals was astronomical.

What made this attack so effective wasn't just the technical quality of the deepfakes. It was the psychological sophistication. The criminals didn't just clone faces and voices—they cloned authority, urgency, and corporate culture itself.

The Hong Kong heist marked a turning point in corporate security. For decades, businesses had focused on protecting their networks, their data, their intellectual property. But what happens when the attack vector isn't your firewall or your password policy, but the fundamental trust between colleagues? When seeing your boss on a video call no longer means it's actually your boss?

. . .

Welcome to the era of corporate shapeshifters, where synthetic media has transformed business communication from an asset into a vulnerability.

∽

BUSINESS EMAIL COMPROMISE GOES MULTIMODAL

To understand the revolutionary nature of the Hong Kong attack, we need to trace the evolution of Business Email Compromise (BEC)—a crime category that has quietly become one of the most profitable forms of fraud in history.

Traditional BEC attacks were almost quaint in their simplicity. A criminal would gain access to or spoof an executive's email account, then send urgent requests for wire transfers to finance departments. The emails relied on three factors: authority (from the executive), urgency (act now), and secrecy (don't verify with others). Despite their simplicity, these attacks have been devastatingly effective—the FBI reported BEC losses exceeding $43 billion globally between 2016 and 2021 [2].

But email-only attacks had natural limitations. Finance teams learned to verify unusual requests through secondary channels. "Call-back procedures" became standard—if the CEO emails asking for a wire transfer, call them to confirm. Multi-person approval processes added layers of protection. The human voice became the ultimate authentication: surely criminals couldn't fake an actual phone conversation with your boss.

That assumption died with voice cloning technology.

. . .

By 2023, BEC 2.0 had emerged. Criminals would still send the email, but when the finance team called to verify, they'd reach a voice that sounded exactly like their executive. Early versions used pre-recorded responses or carefully scripted conversations. But as real-time voice conversion technology improved, criminals could conduct entire conversations in their target's voice, answering unexpected questions, even sharing "personal" details gleaned from social media.

[Based on FBI IC3 reports and documented BEC evolution patterns]

The Hong Kong heist represented BEC 3.0: fully multimodal deception. No longer limited to email and voice, criminals could now create entire synthetic meetings. The psychological impact was profound. Humans are hardwired to trust what we see, especially in familiar contexts. When you're in a video call with multiple colleagues, social proof multiplies. If five people in a meeting seem to agree on something, the sixth person rarely objects.

Consider the escalating sophistication:

BEC 1.0 (Email Era): Spoof one communication channel

- Success rate: 3-5%
- Average loss: $130,000
- Defense: Call-back verification

BEC 2.0 (Voice Era): Spoof two channels simultaneously

- Success rate: 15-20%
- Average loss: $500,000
- Defense: In-person verification

BEC 3.0 (Synthetic Era): Create entire synthetic scenarios

- Success rate: Unknown, but rising
- Average loss: $1-50 million
- Defense: ...?

The criminals behind the Hong Kong heist didn't just use superior technology—they demonstrated superior psychology. They understood that humans verify authenticity through pattern matching. If enough patterns match (face, voice, mannerisms, context), our brains fill in any inconsistencies. They weaponized our cognitive shortcuts against us.

SUPPLY CHAIN ATTACKS THROUGH SYNTHETIC VENDORS

While the Hong Kong heist grabbed headlines, a quieter but potentially more devastating threat has been emerging: synthetic vendor infiltration of corporate supply chains. If criminals can impersonate your CEO, why not impersonate your suppliers, partners, or customers?

Consider this scenario, reported by a Fortune 500 manufacturing company in mid-2024:

. . .

[Based on emerging threat patterns and security researcher warnings]

The company's procurement team received a video call from their primary component supplier in Taiwan, warning of an upcoming price increase due to rare earth mineral shortages. The supplier's representative—someone they'd worked with for three years—explained the situation professionally, showed supporting documentation, and requested that future orders be placed through a new subsidiary to take advantage of better pricing.

Everything seemed legitimate. The face and voice matched. The business context made sense. The documentation looked authentic. The procurement team updated their vendor records and began routing orders to the new entity.

It was two months before they discovered their actual supplier had never made any such call. The criminals had studied both companies, learned their business relationship, impersonated the key contact, and successfully inserted themselves as a middleman. Every order placed through the "new subsidiary" was being fulfilled with counterfeit components—good enough to pass initial inspection but destined to fail in the field.

The implications rippled far beyond financial loss:

- Thousands of products with faulty components entered the market
- The manufacturer faced massive recall costs and liability
- Trust between legitimate business partners eroded

- Both companies had to implement expensive new verification procedures

This attack represents a new paradigm: criminals aren't just stealing money, they're infiltrating the entire business ecosystem. By shapeshifting into trusted partners, they can:

Redirect Payments: Impersonate vendors to change banking details

Steal Intelligence: Pose as customers to extract proprietary information

Sabotage Operations: Insert themselves into supply chains with substandard products

Destroy Reputations: Make commitments or statements that damage business relationships

The traditional defense—"know your supplier"—becomes meaningless when your supplier can be perfectly impersonated. The careful relationship building that underpins global commerce becomes a vulnerability when those relationships can be synthetically hijacked.

THE C-SUITE IMPERSONATION ECONOMY

Behind every corporate shapeshifting attack lies an increasingly sophisticated economy dedicated to executive impersonation. What began as isolated criminal operations has evolved into a service industry with its own specialists, tools, and markets.

The C-Suite impersonation economy operates in layers:

. . .

Intelligence Gathering Operations specialize in building detailed profiles of executives. They scrape LinkedIn, analyze earnings calls, study speech patterns from conference presentations, map organizational hierarchies, and even monitor executives' personal social media to understand their communication styles. Price: $1,000-10,000 per executive profile.

Synthetic Media Studios create the actual deepfakes. The best operators specialize in specific industries, understanding that a tech CEO speaks differently than a banking executive. They don't just clone voices—they replicate leadership styles, industry jargon, even cultural nuances. Price: $5,000-50,000 per impersonation package.

Scenario Designers craft believable business contexts for attacks. They monitor market conditions, study corporate strategies, and design scenarios that feel urgent but plausible. A good scenario designer knows that timing is everything—attacks during mergers, quarter-end, or leadership transitions have higher success rates. Price: $10,000-100,000 per operation.

Execution Teams perform the actual impersonations. Often recruited from business backgrounds, they understand corporate dynamics and can improvise during live interactions. The best operators have legitimate business experience—former consultants and bankers who've turned to crime. Price: 20-50% of the stolen amount.

[Based on law enforcement reports and underground market analysis]

. . .

One recovered training manual from a criminal organization revealed their sophisticated approach:

"Executive impersonation is not about perfect technical replication. It's about psychological authenticity. Study how the target delegates authority. Understand their relationship dynamics. Know when they're traveling, distracted, or under pressure. The deepfake is just a tool—success comes from understanding human behavior in corporate contexts."

The professionalization is evident in their tools and techniques:

Voice Aging Algorithms that adjust synthetic voices based on time of day (people sound different in early morning calls)

Emotional Modulation systems that can inject appropriate stress, excitement, or frustration based on the scenario

Cultural Adaptation modules that adjust communication styles for different regions and corporate cultures

Interaction Scripts with branching decision trees for handling unexpected questions or objections

The criminals even conduct "red team" exercises, testing their impersonations against voice biometric systems and detection software before deployment. They iterate and improve, learning from both successes and failures.

WHEN YOU CAN'T TRUST YOUR OWN CEO

The psychological impact of C-Suite impersonation extends far beyond financial losses. When employees can no longer trust that their leadership is who they claim to be, the very foundation of organizational culture begins to crack.

Sarah Martinez, Chief Information Security Officer at a technology company that suffered a deepfake CEO attack, describes the aftermath: "The financial loss was painful but manageable. What nearly destroyed us was the cultural damage. Employees became paranoid. Every video call was questioned. Productivity plummeted as people insisted on elaborate verification procedures for routine decisions. We had to rebuild not just our security, but our entire trust infrastructure."

[Name changed and details obscured for security reasons]

The ripple effects manifest across organizations:

Decision Paralysis emerges as employees second-guess every instruction. Is this email really from the CEO, or should I verify? Should I challenge this strategy that seems out of character? The cognitive load of constant verification exhausts teams and slows operations to a crawl.

. . .

Authority Erosion occurs when the chain of command becomes questionable. Middle managers find their instructions challenged not on merit but on authenticity. "Prove you're really you" becomes a routine demand that undermines leadership effectiveness.

Cultural Fragmentation develops as remote and distributed teams struggle more than co-located ones. When you haven't seen your CEO in person for months, how do you know the person on the quarterly all-hands video call is genuine? Geographic and cultural distances amplify authentication anxieties.

Innovation Stagnation results from the overhead of verification. Fast-moving decisions that once happened in a single video call now require multiple authentication steps. The agility that many organizations prize becomes impossible when every interaction requires proof of identity.

Organizations report various coping mechanisms emerging:

Verification Rituals become embedded in corporate culture. Teams develop code words, shared secrets, and authentication procedures that would seem absurd in any other context. One company requires executives to reference specific personal details in each communication—details that change weekly and are known only to inner circles.

In-Person Premiums drive a surprising return to physical presence. Companies that had embraced remote work find themselves flying executives around just to prove they exist. "Face time" takes on new meaning when digital faces can't be trusted.

Authentication Infrastructure consumes increasing resources. Companies invest in biometric systems, blockchain verification, and continuous authentication technologies. The cost of proving identity begins to rival traditional security spending.

Trust Recession spreads throughout business ecosystems. The casual trust that lubricates commerce—the assumption that people are who they claim to be—evaporates. Every interaction carries a tax of suspicion.

The most insidious effect may be on corporate culture itself. Companies pride themselves on values like transparency, collaboration, and trust. But how do you maintain these values when you can't trust that your colleagues are real? The social fabric that turns a group of individuals into a cohesive organization begins to unravel.

"We used to be a high-trust culture," one HR director explained. "Now we're a 'trust but verify' culture. Except the verification never stops. It's exhausting, and it's changing who we are as a company."

RED TEAMING YOUR ORGANIZATION'S TRUST ASSUMPTIONS

The only way to defend against corporate shapeshifters is to think like them. This requires a fundamental shift from defensive thinking ("How do we verify identity?") to offensive thinking ("How would we attack our own organization?").

. . .

Red teaming—the practice of authorized adversarial simulation—must evolve to include synthetic media attacks. Traditional red teams test network security and physical access. Modern red teams must test trust infrastructure.

Consider this red team exercise conducted at a major financial services firm:

[Fictionalized scenario based on actual red team methodologies]

The red team spent two weeks studying the organization's communication patterns. They learned that the CFO typically sent strategic updates on Thursday afternoons, that the CEO had a distinctive way of opening meetings, that the head of trading often worked late and made time-sensitive decisions after market close.

Then they struck. Using publicly available deepfake technology and voice samples from earnings calls, they created a synthetic CEO who conducted a convincing emergency video call with the treasury department, authorizing a defensive currency hedge due to "unexpected regulatory changes in our Asian markets that will be announced tomorrow."

The treasury team was suspicious—something felt off. But the face was right, the voice was perfect, and the scenario aligned with recent regulatory rumblings from Beijing. They were minutes away from executing the massive hedge position when one trader asked the

"CEO" to call back on his personal cell phone—a number the red team didn't have. The attack failed, but barely.

The exercise revealed crucial vulnerabilities:

Over-reliance on Technology: The organization had invested millions in technical security but hadn't updated human protocols for synthetic threats.

Inconsistent Verification: Different departments had different standards for verifying unusual requests.

Time Pressure Exploitation: Attackers could bypass security by creating urgency.

Social Proof Vulnerability: Group meetings were paradoxically less secure than individual calls.

Building effective defenses requires mapping your organization's unique trust assumptions:

Communication Audit: How does information flow through your organization? Which channels carry automatic authority? Where are the verification gaps?

. . .

Authority Mapping: Who can authorize what? How is that authority communicated? What would happen if someone impersonated each key decision-maker?

Scenario Planning: What are your organization's pressure points? Merger deadlines? Earnings announcements? Regulatory filings? These become likely attack windows.

Cultural Assessment: Does your culture prioritize speed over verification? Do employees feel empowered to challenge unusual requests from superiors?

Technical Inventory: What synthetic media detection capabilities do you have? How would you verify a suspicious communication? Do you have secure fallback channels?

The goal isn't paranoia but preparedness. Organizations need what security experts call "authentic channels"—communication methods that remain trustworthy even when primary channels are compromised. These might include:

- Pre-shared authentication codes that rotate regularly
- Secure voice verification systems using multiple factors
- Physical tokens or hardware keys for critical authorizations
- Out-of-band verification through independent channels
- Time delays for high-value transactions with mandatory cooling-off periods

Most importantly, organizations need to normalize verification. In many corporate cultures, questioning a superior's identity is seen as insubordination. This cultural norm becomes a critical vulnerability. Healthy skepticism must be reframed as professional diligence.

∼

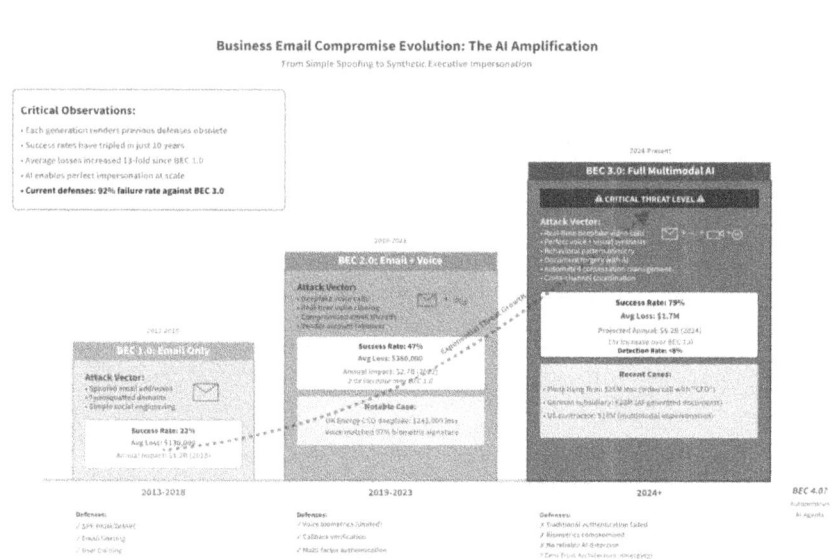

Figure 4.1: *The Evolution of Business Email Compromise: From Spoofing to Synthetic Executives (2013-2024).* This stepped diagram illustrates the exponential escalation in BEC attack sophistication and impact across three technological generations. Each ascending platform represents not just increased complexity but a fundamental obsolescence of previous defensive measures. BEC 1.0's simple email spoofing (23% success rate) evolved into BEC 2.0's voice-enhanced attacks (47% success), culminating in today's BEC 3.0 multimodal AI impersonation achieving a devastating 79% success rate with average losses of $1.7 million per incident. The visualization starkly demonstrates that traditional authentication methods—from email security protocols to biometric verification—have been systematically defeated by AI capabilities. With detection rates below 8% for current-generation attacks and projected annual losses exceeding $5 billion, this evolution represents not merely a quantitative increase in cybercrime but a qualitative transformation requiring entirely new defensive paradigms such as Zero Trust Architecture and cryptographic verification of human identity.

∼

TAKEAWAY: YOUR ORGANIZATION'S TRUST AUDIT STARTS NOW

Corporate shapeshifters aren't a future threat—they're actively targeting organizations today. The Hong Kong heist was not an isolated incident but a preview of the new normal. Every organization that relies on digital communication for critical decisions is vulnerable.

Start protecting your organization with these immediate steps:

1. **Map Your Attack Surface**: Identify every person in your organization who can authorize significant transactions or strategic decisions. These are your highest-value impersonation targets.
2. **Audit Your Verification Procedures**: How do you currently verify unusual requests? Are these procedures consistent across departments? Do they account for synthetic media?
3. **Create Authentic Channels**: Establish communication methods that can't be easily compromised. This might include secure apps, physical tokens, or pre-shared authentication protocols.
4. **Normalize Verification Culture**: Make it socially acceptable—even required—to verify unusual requests regardless of who they appear to come from. Remove the stigma from security consciousness.
5. **Conduct Synthetic Media Drills**: Just as you conduct fire drills, practice responding to deepfake attacks. Make verification procedures muscle memory, not conscious thought.

6. **Build Response Playbooks**: When (not if) your organization faces a synthetic media attack, you need clear procedures for response, containment, and communication.

The age of assuming your colleagues are who they appear to be is over. But this doesn't mean the end of trust in business—it means the evolution of trust. Organizations that adapt quickly will find themselves more resilient not just against synthetic threats, but against all forms of deception.

WHAT'S NEXT

The corporate shapeshifters have shown us that traditional security focused on protecting data and systems is insufficient when the attackers can perfectly impersonate trusted insiders. In Chapter 5, "From Perimeters to Principles," we'll explore how the Zero Trust framework—originally developed for network security—must expand to encompass all human interactions. We'll examine how "never trust, always verify" transforms from a technical architecture into a survival strategy for the synthetic age.

The perimeter is gone. The principles remain. Understanding this shift is the key to building defenses that actually work.

PART TWO
RETHINKING TRUST

CHAPTER 5

FROM PERIMETERS TO PRINCIPLES

LEARNING FROM SOLARWINDS: WHEN THE CASTLE HAS NO WALLS

IN DECEMBER 2020, *the cybersecurity world discovered a breach so sophisticated and far-reaching that it would fundamentally challenge how we think about digital defense. The SolarWinds hack wasn't just another data breach—it was a masterclass in why traditional security models had become obsolete.*

For those unfamiliar with the details: Russian state-sponsored hackers had infiltrated SolarWinds, a company whose network management software was used by over 18,000 organizations worldwide, including most Fortune 500 companies and multiple U.S. government agencies. The attackers didn't break down the front door—they became a trusted part of the supply chain. When SolarWinds sent out a routine software update, it included a backdoor that gave attackers access to every network that installed it [1].

. . .

The breach exposed a fatal flaw in how most organizations approach security. They had built elaborate defenses around their perimeters—firewalls, intrusion detection systems, access controls—creating what security professionals call the "castle and moat" model. Once you crossed the moat and entered the castle, you were trusted. The SolarWinds update came from a trusted vendor, through trusted channels, signed with trusted certificates. It sailed past every defense because it was supposed to be there.

The breach demonstrated something the security community had been warning about for years: the perimeter-based security model was fundamentally broken. When trusted insiders—or in this case, trusted software—can be compromised, the entire castle-and-moat approach collapses. SolarWinds proved that in the modern interconnected world, there is no meaningful perimeter to defend.

But here's what most analyses of SolarWinds miss: the same vulnerability that allowed malicious code to spread through software updates now allows synthetic media to spread through human networks. Just as organizations trusted SolarWinds because it was inside their perimeter, we trust communications that appear to come from inside our social and professional circles. The castle and moat model has failed not just for networks, but for human society itself.

The lessons from SolarWinds extend far beyond cybersecurity:

Trust by Default Is Deadly: The compromised networks trusted the update because it came from a trusted source. Similarly, we trust video calls from our CEO, voice messages from our family, emails from our colleagues—until we shouldn't.

The Inside Is the New Outside: The attackers didn't need to breach individual organizations because they were already inside via the supply chain. With synthetic media, attackers don't need to impersonate strangers—they can become trusted insiders.

Verification Must Be Continuous: A one-time security check wasn't enough. The malicious update passed all initial verifications. Trust must be continuously earned, not permanently granted.

Lateral Movement Is the Real Damage: Once inside, the attackers could move freely between systems. Once someone creates a convincing deepfake of you, they can infiltrate your entire social and professional network.

SolarWinds forced the technology world to embrace what had been a fringe security philosophy: Zero Trust. But as synthetic media demonstrates, Zero Trust isn't just a network architecture—it's a survival strategy for the synthetic age.

THE PHILOSOPHY THAT CHANGES EVERYTHING

Zero Trust emerged from a simple but radical observation: traditional security was built on a fundamental lie. That lie was the belief that we could create a clear boundary between "trusted" and "untrusted," between inside and outside, between us and them.

. . .

John Kindervag developed the Zero Trust model at Forrester Research in 2010, but its philosophical roots go much deeper. At its core, Zero Trust is about acknowledging uncomfortable truths about security, identity, and human nature itself.

The traditional security model assumed:

- We can identify who is trustworthy
- Trust, once established, can persist
- There's a meaningful difference between insider and outsider
- Security is about keeping bad actors out

Zero Trust assumes the opposite:

- Anyone can be compromised
- Trust must be continuously verified
- There is no inside or outside
- Security is about limiting damage when (not if) compromises occur

"Zero Trust isn't about being paranoid," Kindervag clarified in subsequent writings. "It's about being realistic. It's not that we don't want to trust—it's that blind trust has become a luxury we can no longer afford."

The principles of Zero Trust are deceptively simple:

1. **Verify explicitly:** Always authenticate and authorize based on all available data points.
2. **Use least privilege access:** Limit access to the minimum necessary for the task.
3. **Assume breach:** Design systems as if attackers are already inside—because they probably are.

These principles were revolutionary for network security, but they're even more transformative when applied to human interactions in the age of synthetic media.

Consider how each principle translates:

Verify Explicitly in Human Terms: Don't trust a video call just because it looks like your boss. Verify through multiple channels, check context, confirm through pre-established protocols. Every interaction requires authentication.

Least Privilege in Communication: Share only the information necessary for each interaction. Your entire identity doesn't need to be accessible to everyone. Compartmentalize relationships and information.

Assume Breach in Social Networks: Operate as if synthetic versions of you and your contacts already exist. Design your communication patterns to limit damage when (not if) someone impersonates you or someone you trust.

. . .

The beauty of Zero Trust is that it doesn't require you to identify who's real and who's synthetic—an increasingly impossible task. Instead, it limits the damage any single compromised identity can cause.

NEVER TRUST, ALWAYS VERIFY: BEYOND THE NETWORK

The phrase "Never Trust, Always Verify" sounds harsh, even nihilistic. But in practice, it's neither paranoid nor antisocial—it's a framework for maintaining meaningful connections in an untrustworthy environment.

Let's see how this principle applies across different domains:

Personal Communications

Traditional approach: You receive a video call from your elderly parent asking for emergency financial help. Their face, voice, and mannerisms all match. You immediately comply.

Zero Trust approach: You verify through a pre-established protocol—perhaps a code word that changes monthly, or a callback to a number you know is secure. The verification takes 30 seconds but prevents potential disaster.

Business Transactions

. . .

Traditional approach: Your longtime vendor emails about a banking change. The email comes from their usual address, references recent transactions, and includes familiar personnel names. You update your payment records.

Zero Trust approach: You verify the change through an independent channel, confirm with multiple contacts at the vendor, and implement a small test transaction before fully switching. The extra steps prevent you from becoming part of a supply chain attack.

Social Media Connections

Traditional approach: You receive a LinkedIn request from a colleague you haven't seen in years. Their profile looks legitimate, so you connect and begin sharing professional updates.

Zero Trust approach: You verify through mutual connections, check for signs of profile authenticity, and limit initial information sharing until the connection is validated through ongoing interactions.

Healthcare Communications

Traditional approach: You receive a call from your doctor's office requesting personal health information for insurance verification. The caller knows your recent appointment details, so you provide the information.

. . .

Zero Trust approach: You hang up and call your doctor's office directly at a number you trust. You verify the request is legitimate before sharing any health information.

[These scenarios demonstrate how Zero Trust principles can be applied without destroying human connection]

The key insight is that verification doesn't mean distrust—it means appropriate trust. Just as you lock your door not because you hate your neighbors but because you're prudent, you verify communications not because you're paranoid but because you're adapting to new realities.

MICRO-SEGMENTATION FOR HUMAN NETWORKS

In network security, micro-segmentation divides a network into small, isolated segments. If attackers compromise one segment, they can't automatically access others. This containment strategy is equally powerful for human networks in the synthetic age.

Traditional human networks are flat and interconnected:

- Your work colleagues know your family situation
- Your social media connections see your professional updates
- Your various digital identities are linked and searchable
- Trust in one relationship implies trust across relationships

This interconnectedness becomes a vulnerability when synthetic media can impersonate anyone. If someone can convincingly become you in one context, they can leverage that to infiltrate other contexts.

Micro-segmentation for humans means:

Identity Compartmentalization: Maintain separate identities for different contexts. Your professional identity shouldn't have access to your personal financial information. Your social identity shouldn't have authority over your business decisions.

Communication Channels: Use different channels for different relationship types. Perhaps Signal for family, corporate email for work, and specific platforms for financial transactions. If one channel is compromised, others remain secure.

Information Barriers: Don't cross-pollinate information between segments. Your work colleagues don't need to know your mother's maiden name. Your social media connections don't need to know your corporate hierarchy.

Trust Boundaries: Trust established in one segment doesn't automatically transfer to others. Just because someone is your LinkedIn connection doesn't mean they should have access to your personal phone number.

Consider how this might work in practice:

. . .

[Fictionalized scenario to illustrate micro-segmentation]

Sarah, a marketing executive, maintains strict segmentation:

- Work identity: Corporate email, LinkedIn, Slack
- Family identity: Signal, shared photo albums, specific email
- Financial identity: Dedicated email, hardware tokens, relationship manager
- Social identity: Instagram, Facebook (limited sharing)

When "her boss" contacts her on Instagram about an urgent work matter, the boundary violation immediately signals a potential attack. When "her bank" emails her corporate address, she recognizes the segment breach. The segmentation doesn't prevent all attacks, but it makes them much easier to detect.

The challenge is balancing security with convenience. Total segmentation would make life impossible—imagine maintaining completely separate identities for every single relationship. The goal is thoughtful segmentation that contains damage without destroying usability.

LIVING IN A ZERO TRUST SOCIETY

The implications of Zero Trust extend beyond individual practices to how we organize society itself. We're witnessing the emergence of what researchers call a "Zero Trust Society"—one where verification is embedded in every interaction, where trust is earned continuously rather than assumed.

This transformation is already visible in several domains:

Financial Services have moved from signature cards to PINs to biometrics to continuous authentication. Banks now analyze every transaction against behavioral patterns, flagging anomalies regardless of authentication method. Your bank doesn't trust you're you just because you logged in correctly—it continuously verifies through your behavior.

Digital Platforms implement increasingly sophisticated verification. X's (formerly Twitter) blue checkmarks evolved from status symbols to identity verification. LinkedIn tests video verification for profiles. Dating apps require selfie verification. The platforms recognize that in a world of synthetic profiles, continuous verification is essential for user trust.

Government Services are pioneering new models. Estonia's digital identity system, tested in the deepfake crisis, provides citizens with cryptographic identities that can be verified independently of physical appearance or voice. India's Aadhaar, despite vulnerabilities exposed by criminals, represents an attempt to create verifiable identity for 1.4 billion people.

Employment Relationships are adapting to remote work and synthetic threats. Companies implement continuous verification for remote workers, from periodic video check-ins to behavioral monitoring. The traditional model of "verify once at hiring" has given way to ongoing authentication.

[Based on observable trends in how organizations are adapting to synthetic media threats]

Living in a Zero Trust Society creates new social dynamics:

Verification Fatigue becomes a real psychological burden. Just as "security fatigue" leads people to reuse passwords, constant identity verification exhausts our cognitive resources. Society needs to design verification that's automatic and unobtrusive.

Privacy Paradoxes emerge as verification requires disclosure. To prove you're real, you must share more information—but that information becomes fuel for better synthetic impersonation. We need verification methods that don't compromise privacy.

Trust Inequality develops between those who can afford sophisticated verification and those who can't. Premium authentication becomes a luxury good. Democratic societies must ensure verification remains accessible to all.

Social Friction increases as every interaction requires authentication. The casual spontaneity of human connection gives way to procedural verification. We must design systems that maintain security without destroying humanity.

. . .

The Zero Trust Society isn't a dystopian future—it's an adaptation to technological reality. Just as we adapted to locked doors, passwords, and photo IDs, we'll adapt to continuous verification. The question is whether we'll do it thoughtfully or chaotically.

DESIGNING FRICTION THAT PROTECTS WITHOUT PARALYZING

The greatest challenge in implementing Zero Trust for human systems is calibrating friction—adding enough verification to prevent attacks without making normal life impossible. Too little friction and synthetic media runs rampant. Too much and society grinds to a halt.

Consider the evolution of airport security as an analogy. After 9/11, airports implemented extreme friction—hours-long lines, invasive searches, blanket restrictions. Over time, they developed more nuanced approaches: PreCheck for verified travelers, behavioral detection, risk-based screening. The goal became intelligent friction—maximum security with minimum disruption.

We need similar evolution for synthetic media defense:

Progressive Verification: Not every interaction needs the same level of authentication. Casual conversations require less verification than financial transactions. Systems should escalate verification based on risk.

- Low risk: Passive behavioral confirmation
- Medium risk: Active but simple verification

- High risk: Multi-factor, out-of-band confirmation
- Critical risk: In-person or cryptographic proof

Contextual Authentication: Verification should match the context. A family video call might use shared memories as authentication. A business transaction might require cryptographic signatures. The friction should feel natural to the situation.

Automated Background Verification: Much verification can happen invisibly. Systems can check behavioral patterns, communication metadata, and network analysis without user intervention. Friction appears only when anomalies are detected.

User-Controlled Friction: People should be able to dial their security up or down based on their situation. Someone in a high-risk position might accept more friction. Others might prefer convenience. The key is informed choice.

Verification UX Design: Friction doesn't have to be painful. Well-designed verification can be quick, even enjoyable. Imagine authentication that feels like a game rather than a chore, or verification that adds value beyond security.

Examples of well-designed friction already exist:

Apple's Face ID adds the friction of facial scanning but makes it feel magical rather than burdensome. The verification happens so smoothly users barely notice it.

Credit Card Verification for unusual purchases adds friction (a text message confirmation) only when behavior deviates from patterns. Most transactions flow without interruption.

Two-Factor Authentication has evolved from clunky code entry to push notifications that require a single tap. The friction decreased while security increased.

The same principles must apply to synthetic media defense. Verification should be:

- Fast enough not to disrupt flow
- Smart enough to appear only when needed
- Simple enough for anyone to use
- Flexible enough to adapt to different contexts
- Valuable enough that people want to use it

The goal isn't to make life harder—it's to make deception harder while keeping authentic interaction easy.

∽

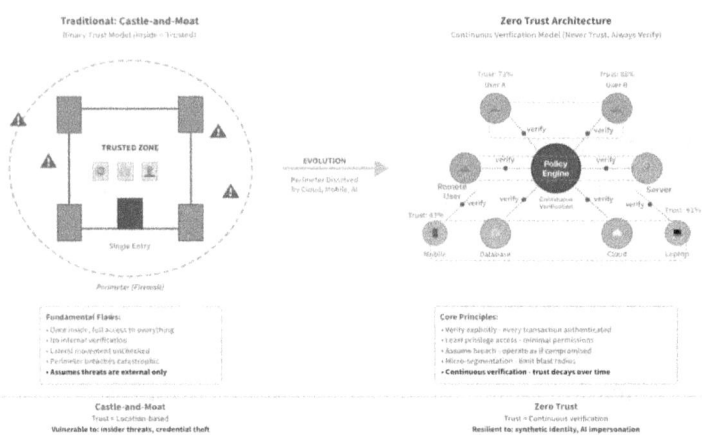

Figure 5.1: *The Paradigm Shift from Perimeter Security to Zero Trust Architecture.* This diagram illustrates the fundamental transformation required in security thinking for the synthetic age. The traditional castle-and-moat model (left) relies on a hardened perimeter with binary trust—entities inside are trusted, outside are threats. This approach catastrophically fails when attackers breach the perimeter or threats originate internally. In contrast, Zero Trust Architecture (right) eliminates the concept of a trusted perimeter entirely. Every entity—user, device, or service—must continuously prove its identity and authorization for each interaction. Trust becomes dynamic and contextual, measured in percentages rather than absolutes, with verification points at every connection. The central policy engine orchestrates continuous authentication, authorization, and anomaly detection, while micro-segmentation limits potential damage from any compromise. This evolution from static, location-based trust to dynamic, identity-based verification is essential for defending against AI-powered attacks where traditional indicators of authenticity—voice, video, documents, even behavior patterns—can be synthetically generated with perfect fidelity.

TAKEAWAY: BUILDING YOUR PERSONAL ZERO TRUST FRAMEWORK

Zero Trust isn't just a philosophy for organizations—it's a practical framework for navigating the synthetic age. Building your personal Zero Trust system doesn't require paranoia or isolation. It requires thoughtful design of how you interact with an untrustworthy world.

. . .

Start with these foundational steps:

1. **Map Your Trust Assumptions**
    - Who do you implicitly trust?
    - Which communications do you accept without verification?
    - What would happen if those trusted sources were synthetic?

2. **Design Your Verification Protocols**
    - Create different verification methods for different risk levels
    - Establish out-of-band channels for critical confirmations
    - Build redundancy—no single point of trust failure

3. **Implement Progressive Friction**
    - Add minimal friction to low-risk interactions
    - Reserve strong verification for high-stakes situations
    - Automate what you can, manually verify what you must

4. **Segment Your Digital Life**
    - Separate professional and personal communications
    - Use different channels for different relationship types
    - Limit information flow between segments

. . .

5. **Normalize Verification**
   - Make authentication a routine part of interaction
   - Remove stigma from verification requests
   - Help others understand it's not personal—it's practical

6. **Plan for Breach**
   - Assume synthetic versions of you exist
   - Design communications to limit damage
   - Create recovery protocols for when verification fails

7. **Maintain Humanity**
   - Remember verification enables trust, not destroys it
   - Focus on protecting relationships, not just data
   - Design friction that enhances rather than degrades connection

The Zero Trust framework isn't about building walls—it's about building bridges that can verify their own integrity. In a world where anyone can be anyone, the ability to prove authentic connection becomes more valuable, not less.

WHAT'S NEXT

Zero Trust provides the philosophical framework for surviving the synthetic age, but philosophy alone isn't enough. We need practical authentication methods that can reliably distinguish real from synthetic in real-time. In Chapter 6, "The Authentication Revolution," we'll explore how verification is evolving from passwords to continuous authentication, from static biometrics to dynamic behavioral patterns, and why the future of identity might not be about who you are, but about what you do.

The principles are clear. Now we need the tools to implement them.

CHAPTER 6
THE AUTHENTICATION REVOLUTION

THE MAYOR WHO WASN'T THERE

[FICTIONALIZED scenario based on current deepfake capabilities and vulnerabilities in government communications]

The press conference began at exactly 2:00 PM JST, as scheduled. Mayor Takeshi Yamamoto of Nagoya appeared on screen, sitting behind his familiar desk with the city seal prominently displayed. The assembled journalists—some in person, most joining virtually—prepared their questions about the controversial new transit development project.

"Good afternoon," the Mayor began, his voice carrying its characteristic measured cadence. "I have called this conference to announce a significant change in our city's development priorities. After careful consideration and extensive consultation with experts, I have decided to cancel the Sakura Line extension project, effective immediately."

. . .

The announcement sent shockwaves through the virtual room. The Sakura Line had been the Mayor's signature initiative, already two years into construction with ¥50 billion invested. Reporters scrambled to unmute themselves, voices overlapping with urgent questions.

For twenty-three minutes, Mayor Yamamoto fielded questions with his usual composure. He cited new environmental concerns, shifted budget priorities, and hinted at corruption investigations among contractors. He provided specific details that only someone with insider knowledge could possess. When pressed about the sunk costs, he grew uncharacteristically defensive, a flash of anger that seemed to validate the authenticity of this surprising reversal.

The problem was that Mayor Yamamoto was at that very moment in a closed-door session with the city council, physically present in a room with fourteen other people, with no cameras or internet connection in sight.

The real press conference had been scheduled for 4:00 PM, not 2:00 PM. The deepfake Mayor had sent out a "corrected" time to the media list just hours before, from an email address that differed from the official one by a single character—a detail no one noticed in their rush to attend. By the time the real Mayor emerged from his council meeting to a tsunami of calls about his stunning announcement, the damage was done. Markets had reacted. Contractors had halted work. Opposition politicians had released gleeful statements. The city's credibility lay in ruins.

"We are investigating how someone could create such a convincing impersonation," the real Mayor said at an emergency press conference that evening, standing before skeptical reporters who now questioned which version they were seeing. "But I want to be absolutely clear: I have not cancelled the Sakura Line project. It remains my administration's top priority."

The tragedy wasn't just that people had been fooled—it was that many continued to believe the fake announcement even after the real Mayor's denial. "Of course he would say that," one city councilman told reporters. "He's clearly been pressured to reverse his reversal. But we all saw him admit the truth earlier today."

The Nagoya incident exposed a terrifying reality: our authentication systems—designed for a world where seeing meant believing—had become not just obsolete but actively harmful. Every method we'd developed to verify identity could now be turned against us. The revolution in authentication wasn't coming; it was overdue.

FROM PASSWORDS TO CONTINUOUS VERIFICATION

The history of authentication is a history of escalating failure. Each new method, hailed as the solution to previous vulnerabilities, eventually reveals its own fatal flaws. But in the age of synthetic media, these flaws don't just enable fraud—they enable the complete dissolution of verifiable identity.

Consider the evolution:

Passwords emerged with the first computer systems in the 1960s. The idea was simple: know a secret string of characters, prove your identity. But humans proved terrible at creating and remembering secure passwords. By 2020, "123456" remained the world's most common password, used by millions despite decades of security warnings. Password managers helped, but they simply moved the vulnerability—now you just needed one master password to access all others.

Multi-Factor Authentication (MFA) arrived as the savior. Surely requiring something you know (password) AND something you have (phone) would stop attackers. It did, for a while. Then SIM swapping emerged—attackers didn't need your phone, just a convincing call to your mobile carrier. "I lost my phone on vacation" became a skeleton key to anyone's digital life.

Biometric Authentication promised to solve everything. Your fingerprint, your face, your iris—these couldn't be stolen or forgotten. Apple's TouchID and FaceID made biometrics mainstream. But the Karnataka gang showed us that fingerprints could be manufactured. Deepfakes proved faces could be synthesized. Researchers demonstrated that high-resolution photos could fool iris scanners. We'd built our security on the assumption that bodies couldn't be copied. We were wrong.

Behavioral Biometrics emerged as the next frontier. Maybe your face could be copied, but surely not the way you type, walk, or move your mouse? Companies like BioCatch and BehavioSec built systems that could identify users by their unique behavioral patterns. But by 2024, AI had learned to mimic these patterns too. Feed a machine learning model enough data about how someone types, and it can reproduce their rhythm perfectly.

. . .

Each evolution followed the same depressing pattern: innovation, adoption, compromise, obsolescence. But something different is happening now. Instead of simply moving to the next authentication method, we're being forced to reimagine authentication itself.

Continuous Authentication represents this fundamental shift. Instead of verifying identity at a single point—login—these systems constantly reassess whether the user is who they claim to be. It's not "Did you authenticate?" but "Are you still you?"

Consider how this works in practice:

- Your phone doesn't just check your face when you unlock it; it continuously monitors how you hold it, how you swipe, the pressure of your touch
- Your bank doesn't just verify your login; it analyzes every transaction against your historical patterns, flagging anomalies regardless of authentication
- Your employer's systems don't just check your credentials; they monitor your work patterns, flagging unusual access or behavior

This shift from point-in-time to continuous verification reflects a harsh reality: in a world where anyone can be perfectly impersonated at any moment, the only defense is never-ending vigilance.

THE PROMISE AND PERIL OF LIVENESS DETECTION

"Liveness detection" sounds like science fiction—systems that can determine whether they're interacting with a living human or a synthetic impostor. But it's become the front line in the authentication wars, with billions invested in technologies that can spot the difference between real and fake.

The techniques are ingenious:

3D Depth Mapping uses structured light or multiple cameras to ensure a face has actual depth, not just a 2D photo or screen. Apple's FaceID projects 30,000 infrared dots to map facial contours. But researchers have fooled these systems with detailed 3D-printed masks, and as 3D printing resolution improves, this defense weakens.

Micro-Expression Analysis looks for involuntary facial movements that current deepfakes can't perfectly replicate—the subtle play of muscles that occur in milliseconds. But as deepfake technology incorporates more sophisticated muscle modeling, this advantage erodes.

Blood Flow Detection uses subtle color changes in skin to detect pulse and blood flow, something a photo or basic mask can't replicate. Some systems can even detect stress patterns in blood flow that might indicate coercion. But advanced synthetic skin materials can now simulate these patterns.

. . .

Challenge-Response Tests ask users to perform random actions: "Turn your head left," "Blink three times," "Say these random words." The unpredictability should defeat pre-recorded fakes. But real-time deepfake technology can now respond to these challenges convincingly.

Environmental Analysis examines not just the person but their surroundings—lighting consistency, background audio, reflection patterns. Surely a deepfake would show inconsistencies in how light falls or sounds echo? But as computational power increases, these environmental details can be synthesized too.

The most advanced systems combine all these approaches, creating what researchers call "multi-modal liveness detection." They're looking for the one thing that's hardest to fake: the coherent combination of multiple biological signals in real-time.

Yet even these sophisticated systems face a fundamental challenge: they're in an arms race with equally sophisticated attackers. Every defensive innovation becomes a target for offensive innovation. The liveness detection system that seems unbeatable today will be compromised tomorrow.

More troubling is the false positive problem. As liveness detection becomes more stringent, it increasingly rejects legitimate users. People with medical conditions that affect facial movement, those in unusual lighting conditions, or anyone who doesn't match the system's narrow definition of "normal" human behavior find themselves locked out of their own accounts.

. . .

We're creating a world where you have to constantly perform your humanity to machines, and the machines keep raising the bar for what counts as sufficiently human.

THE HUMAN COST OF CONSTANT VERIFICATION

Maria Santos discovered the exhaustion of perpetual authentication during a single week in March 2025. A financial analyst at a major bank, she meticulously tracked every time she had to prove her identity. The results were staggering:

[Fictionalized scenario illustrating the cumulative burden of authentication]

Monday: 47 authentication events

- 6:00 AM: Face ID to unlock phone (failed twice due to puffy morning eyes)
- 6:15 AM: Two-factor authentication for email
- 7:30 AM: Biometric scan at office building
- 8:00 AM: Windows Hello facial recognition (required removal of glasses)
- 8:15 AM: Multi-factor authentication for financial systems
- Throughout the day: 42 additional authentications for various systems, apps, and services

Tuesday: 52 authentication events, including a video call that required continuous liveness checking, causing her to maintain unnatural stillness

. . .

Wednesday: 44 authentication events, plus a 15-minute delay when behavioral biometrics flagged her typing as "anomalous" because she had a bandaged finger

Thursday: 58 authentication events, including three failed voice recognitions during a cold

Friday: 61 authentication events, culminating in being locked out of her trading platform during market hours because the system detected "unusual stress patterns" in her voice

Total for the week: 262 authentication events. Over 4 hours spent proving she was herself.

"It's not just the time," Santos explained. "It's the mental load. Every interaction requires me to perform my identity. I can't just exist—I have to constantly prove I deserve to exist in digital spaces."

Santos's experience illustrates what researchers call "authentication fatigue"—the gradual wearing down of users by constant verification demands. Like alarm fatigue in hospitals, where nurses eventually ignore beeping machines, authentication fatigue leads to dangerous behaviors:

- Password reuse across systems because remembering unique ones is impossible

- Disabling security features that interfere with productivity
- Sharing credentials with colleagues to avoid authentication bottlenecks
- Creating workarounds that bypass security entirely

But the psychological impact goes deeper than mere inconvenience:

Identity Performance Anxiety emerges as people worry about failing authentication. Will the system recognize me with a new haircut? What if my voice sounds different when I'm sick? The constant possibility of being rejected by systems creates ongoing stress.

Algorithmic Discrimination occurs when authentication systems embed biases. Facial recognition works less well for people with darker skin. Voice recognition struggles with accents. Behavioral biometrics assume "normal" patterns that exclude people with disabilities. The most vulnerable populations face the highest authentication barriers.

Trust Erosion develops as the verified and unverified divide society. Those who can afford sophisticated authentication tools move smoothly through digital life. Those who can't face constant friction, exclusion, and suspicion.

Relationship Strain increases as authentication invades personal interactions. Couples develop verification protocols. Parents must prove their identity to their own children. The spontaneity of human connection gives way to procedural confirmation.

The Nagoya deepfake incident shows us why this exhaustion matters. As authentication becomes more burdensome, people become more likely to accept shortcuts, ignore warnings, or trust sophisticated fakes that seem to offer easier paths. The very defenses we build become vulnerabilities through human exhaustion.

BEYOND TECHNOLOGY: THE LIMITS OF TECHNICAL SOLUTIONS

The authentication revolution faces an uncomfortable truth: every technical solution eventually fails because the problem isn't fundamentally technical—it's human.

Consider the paradox: we need authentication because humans can be impersonated, but we need humans to design, implement, and use authentication systems. Every system must balance two opposing forces:

- Security (which demands complexity and friction)
- Usability (which demands simplicity and flow)

Too far in either direction leads to failure. Make authentication too secure, and people create workarounds. Make it too easy, and attackers walk right through.

This tension reveals deeper limitations:

. . .

The Enrollment Problem: Every authentication system needs an initial moment of truth—when the system first learns who you are. But if that moment can be compromised by synthetic media, the entire system built on it collapses. How do you bootstrap trust in a trustless world?

The Recovery Problem: What happens when authentication fails? Every system needs a recovery mechanism, but recovery mechanisms become attack vectors. The "forgot password" link that saves forgetful users also enables account takeovers. The helpful customer service agent who can override authentication becomes a social engineering target.

The Revocation Problem: In the physical world, you can change your locks if keys are stolen. But you can't change your face if your biometrics are compromised. Once your biological data is stolen, it's stolen forever. We're building permanent vulnerabilities.

The Scaling Problem: Authentication that works for tech-savvy users in wealthy countries fails for the billions who lack reliable internet, modern devices, or digital literacy. The most sophisticated systems exclude the most vulnerable populations.

The Context Problem: Authentication designed for one scenario fails in another. The face recognition that works in an office fails in a car. The voice recognition trained on calm speech fails during emergencies. Real life is messier than systems assume.

. . .

These aren't bugs to be fixed but fundamental characteristics of the authentication challenge. They suggest that the solution isn't better technology but better frameworks for thinking about identity and trust.

Some researchers propose radical alternatives:

Reputation-Based Identity where you're authenticated not by who you are but by who trusts you. Your identity becomes the sum of your relationships and interactions, constantly updated by community consensus.

Zero-Knowledge Identity where you can prove attributes about yourself without revealing underlying data. "I can prove I'm over 18 without showing my birthdate. I can prove I'm employed without revealing my employer."

Ephemeral Identity where verification is temporary and contextual. Instead of one permanent identity, you have countless temporary ones, each existing only as long as needed for specific interactions.

Community Verification where groups collectively vouch for members. The Nagoya incident might have been prevented if multiple city officials had to verify the Mayor's presence, not just technological systems.

These approaches acknowledge that in a world of perfect synthetic media, traditional authentication is fighting a losing battle. The future might not be about proving who you are, but about proving what you can do, who trusts you, and what value you provide.

DESIGNING AUTHENTICATION THAT ENHANCES RATHER THAN EXHAUSTS

If constant verification is necessary but exhausting, how do we design systems that protect without paralyzing? The answer lies not in eliminating friction but in making it intelligent, contextual, and even valuable.

Consider how successful systems balance security and usability:

Progressive Authentication adapts to risk. Checking your bank balance requires minimal verification. Transferring money requires more. Changing account settings requires maximum verification. The friction matches the stakes.

Ambient Authentication happens in the background. Your phone knows it's you not through constant face scans but through the aggregate of small signals: your location patterns, your app usage, your communication style. Verification becomes invisible until anomalies appear.

Collaborative Authentication distributes the burden. Instead of one person repeatedly proving their identity, systems verify through networks. Your colleagues' presence confirms yours. Your usual behavior patterns vouch for your current actions.

. . .

Valuable Authentication adds benefit beyond security. Estonia's digital identity system doesn't just authenticate—it enables instant access to government services, digital signing, and secure communication. Authentication becomes a feature, not a burden.

The key principles for human-centered authentication:

1. **Respect Attention:** Don't interrupt unless necessary. Bank of America's ERICA system monitors transactions continuously but only requests additional verification for genuinely anomalous behavior.
2. **Learn Patterns:** Adapt to individual users. Google's authentication learns your devices, locations, and behaviors, reducing friction for predictable actions while increasing it for unusual ones.
3. **Provide Transparency:** Show users why authentication is needed. Apple's privacy labels explain what data apps access and why, turning security from imposition to informed choice.
4. **Enable Recovery:** Make failure recoverable without compromising security. Signal's PIN recovery system allows account restoration while maintaining end-to-end encryption.
5. **Design for Diversity:** Accommodate different abilities, contexts, and technologies. Microsoft's inclusive design principles ensure authentication works for users with disabilities, limited connectivity, or older devices.
6. **Build Community:** Leverage social connections for verification. WhatsApp's group verification helps users confirm contacts' identities through mutual connections.

The Nagoya incident offers lessons for implementation:

- **Multi-channel verification** could have caught the discrepancy between virtual and physical presence
- **Time-based authentication** would have flagged the unusual schedule change
- **Collective confirmation** from multiple city officials would have revealed the deception
- **Behavioral analysis** might have detected the Mayor's uncharacteristic emotional response

But most importantly, the human element—journalists trained to verify through multiple sources, officials empowered to question unusual directives—remains irreplaceable.

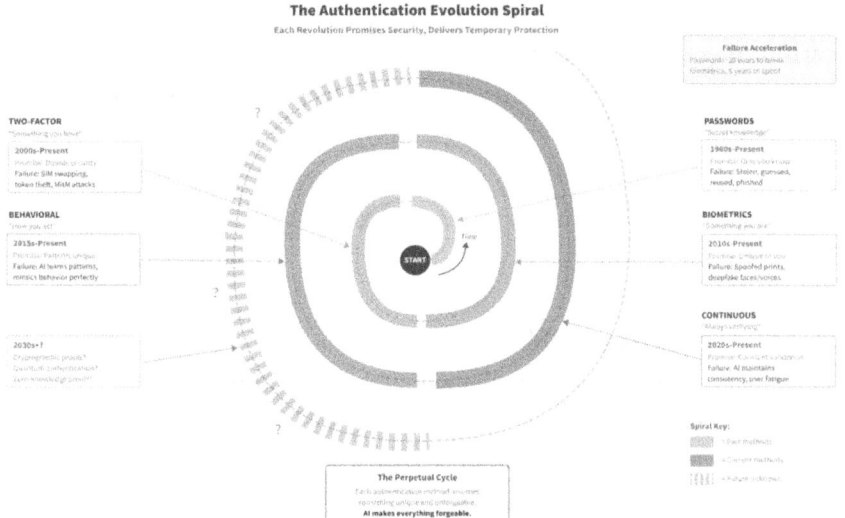

Figure 6.1: *The Authentication Evolution Spiral: An Endless Arms Race Against Forgery.* This spiral diagram traces the historical progression of authentication methods from passwords to an uncertain future, revealing a troubling pattern: each revolutionary authentication method follows the same lifecycle of promise, adoption, compromise, and obsolescence. Starting from simple passwords ("something you know") and expanding through two-factor authentication ("something you have"), biometrics ("something you are"), behavioral analysis ("how you act"), and continuous verification ("always checking"), each ring represents both increased sophistication and accelerated failure. The critical insight lies not in any single failure but in the pattern itself—the time from introduction to compromise is rapidly shrinking. While passwords remained viable for decades before widespread compromise, biometric systems were spoofed within five years of mainstream adoption. The outermost ring, marked only with question marks, acknowledges that even proposed future methods like cryptographic proofs or quantum authentication will likely face the same fate. In an age where AI can forge any human-observable characteristic—knowledge, possession, biology, or behavior—the spiral suggests we need not another revolution around the wheel, but a fundamental reimagining of identity and trust itself.

TAKEAWAY: MAKING VERIFICATION A FEATURE, NOT A BUG

The authentication revolution isn't about finding the perfect technical solution—it's about reimagining how we establish and maintain trust in a synthetic age. The exhaustion of constant verification is real, but so is the necessity. The challenge is making authentication enhance rather than diminish our digital lives.

Start building better authentication habits:

1. **Audit Your Authentication**
    - Track how often you verify your identity daily
    - Identify which systems create the most friction
    - Note where you've created dangerous workarounds

2. **Strengthen Without Complicating**
    - Use password managers to eliminate password reuse
    - Enable multi-factor authentication on critical accounts
    - Choose authentication methods that work with your life, not against it

3. **Build Verification Networks**
    - Establish mutual authentication relationships with trusted contacts
    - Create out-of-band verification channels for important communications
    - Practice collective confirmation for significant decisions

4. **Demand Better Design**
    - Support services that respect your attention
    - Advocate for inclusive authentication options
    - Choose platforms that make security convenient

5. **Prepare for Failure**
    - Document your digital identity across multiple platforms
    - Create recovery mechanisms that don't depend on any single factor
    - Build redundancy into your critical systems

6. **Stay Human**
    - Remember that perfect security is impossible
    - Balance protection with connection
    - Don't let authentication anxiety prevent authentic interaction

The Mayor of Nagoya learned that seeing is no longer believing. But the incident also showed that human judgment, collective verification, and healthy skepticism remain our best defenses. The authentication revolution isn't about replacing human trust with technical verification—it's about augmenting human wisdom with technological tools.

WHAT'S NEXT

Authentication tells us who someone is, but in a world of perfect impersonation, that's only half the battle. We also need to control what they can do. In Chapter 7, "The Principle of Least Privilege for Information," we'll explore how limiting access and capabilities becomes crucial when anyone can become anyone. From information diets to verified credentials, from reputation economies to trust boundaries, we'll examine how to function in a world where identity is fluid but consequences remain real.

The revolution in authentication is underway. The revolution in authorization is next.

CHAPTER 7
THE PRINCIPLE OF LEAST PRIVILEGE FOR INFORMATION

THE CHAOS OF THE BLUE CHECKMARKS

NOVEMBER 2022 SHOULD HAVE BEEN a warning. When Elon Musk's Twitter transformed its blue checkmark from a verification of identity into an $8 monthly subscription, the platform descended into chaos within hours [1].

A fake "verified" Eli Lilly account announced, "We are excited to announce insulin is free now." The pharmaceutical giant's stock plummeted, losing billions in market capitalization before the tweet could be removed. Nintendo of America apparently unveiled a new Mario game featuring explicit content. Lockheed Martin seemed to suspend all weapons sales to Saudi Arabia, Israel, and the United States. Each fake announcement, adorned with the blue checkmark that once meant "this is really them," spread faster than denials could follow.

. . .

The blue checkmark crisis wasn't just about Twitter's business model—it was a preview of information privilege collapse. For years, that simple blue badge had served as a form of information hierarchy, a signal that separated verified sources from the noise. When that privilege became purchasable by anyone with $8 and malicious intent, the entire information ecosystem convulsed.

But the real lesson wasn't about the danger of fake verified accounts. It was about our desperate need for information hierarchies in the first place. In a world drowning in content, where synthetic media can make anyone appear to say anything, we instinctively grasp for signals of trustworthiness. The blue checkmark had become a crutch, and when that crutch was kicked away, we realized how badly we needed new frameworks for information privilege.

The chaos lasted only days before Twitter rolled back the changes, but the damage to information trust persisted far longer. The incident revealed a fundamental truth about the synthetic age: when anyone can generate convincing content and anyone can claim authority, the principle of least privilege—giving access to only the minimum information necessary—becomes essential not just for security, but for sanity.

INFORMATION PRIVILEGE IN THE AGE OF ABUNDANCE

The concept of "least privilege" originated in computer security: give users the minimum access necessary to perform their function. A data entry clerk doesn't need administrator access. A customer service representative doesn't need to see full credit card numbers. By limiting access, you limit potential damage from both malicious actors and honest mistakes.

. . .

But in the synthetic age, we need to apply least privilege thinking to information itself. Not all information deserves equal weight. Not all sources deserve equal trust. Not all content deserves equal attention. Yet our information systems—designed for an era of scarcity—treat a deepfake video with the same distribution power as authentic footage, a synthetic voice with the same credibility as a real conversation.

Consider how information privilege traditionally worked:

Institutional Gatekeepers like newspapers, TV networks, and publishers decided what information reached mass audiences. This had obvious problems—bias, censorship, manufactured consent—but it also provided filtering. Not everything could be published, so some selection occurred.

Professional Verification meant journalists checked sources, editors demanded evidence, and fact-checkers verified claims before publication. The system was imperfect and often failed, but it created friction between rumor and reach.

Distribution Scarcity limited how fast and far information could spread. Print runs were finite. Broadcast time was limited. Even early internet required some technical knowledge to publish widely. Lies could spread, but not at light speed to billions simultaneously.

. . .

Reputation Consequences attached to sources. If Walter Cronkite reported false news, his career would end. If the New York Times published fabrications, subscriptions would plummet. Reputation created accountability, however flawed.

The digital revolution destroyed every one of these limiting factors:

Gatekeepers Collapsed as anyone could publish anything to everyone. A blog post could reach as many people as a newspaper. A tweet could go more viral than a TV broadcast. Democracy of publishing became anarchy of information.

Verification Evaporated in the race for engagement. Being first mattered more than being right. Corrections, if they came at all, never caught up to the original falsehood. The incentive structure rewarded speed over accuracy.

Distribution Exploded as platforms optimized for maximum reach. An algorithm doesn't care if content is true, only if it engages. Lies, being more sensational than truth, often engage better. The systems designed to connect us became optimized for deception.

Reputation Decoupled from reach. Anonymous accounts could go viral. Synthetic personas could build massive followings. The blue checkmark incident showed that even verification itself could be faked or bought.

. . .

In this context, the principle of least privilege takes on new meaning. It's not just about limiting access to systems—it's about creating new hierarchies of information trust, new ways to signal authenticity, and new frameworks for deciding what deserves our attention.

THE ATTENTION ECONOMY'S CREDENTIAL CRISIS

To understand why information privilege matters, we must examine the currency of the digital age: attention. Herbert Simon presciently observed in 1971 that "a wealth of information creates a poverty of attention." [2] He couldn't have imagined how impoverished we would become.

Every day, the average person is exposed to:

- 4,000 to 10,000 marketing messages
- 100+ emails (not counting spam)
- Countless social media posts, news articles, videos, and notifications
- An estimated 34 GB of information—enough to crash computers from Simon's era

[Statistics compiled from various digital consumption studies, 2024-2025]

In this deluge, credentials become crucial. We need signals to help us decide what deserves our scarce attention. But the synthetic age has created a credential crisis: every traditional signal of trustworthiness can now be faked, bought, or gamed.

. . .

The blue checkmark was just one casualty. Consider other failing credentials:

Follower Counts once suggested influence and credibility. But bot followers can be purchased for pennies. Entire companies exist to manufacture fake engagement. A synthetic influencer can appear more popular than a real expert.

Professional Titles on LinkedIn proliferate without verification. Anyone can claim to be a "CEO" (of their single-person company), a "thought leader" (self-proclaimed), or an "expert" (in their own opinion). The platform's attempt at verification through skills endorsements became a reciprocal game of meaningless validation.

Academic Credentials face assault from diploma mills and now, synthetic transcripts. AI can generate plausible-sounding research papers, complete with citations to other AI-generated papers. Peer review, already strained, buckles under the volume of synthetic submissions.

Media Appearances no longer signal legitimacy when deepfake technology can place anyone on any news program. "As seen on CNN" means nothing when the appearance might never have happened.

Website Trust Signals like SSL certificates, trust badges, and security seals can be trivially copied or faked. The padlock icon that once meant "secure" now just means "encrypted"—including encrypted connections to scam sites.

. . .

This credential crisis creates what researchers call "authority collapse"—when all signals of expertise become unreliable, people either trust nothing or fall back on tribal affiliations. Neither response serves a healthy information ecosystem.

The principle of least privilege offers a framework for rebuilding. Instead of universal access to attention, we need graduated systems that grant information privilege based on verifiable credibility. But first, we must understand how the current system manufactures false authority.

VERIFIED CREDENTIALS VS. VERIFIED HUMANS

The blue checkmark incident highlighted a crucial distinction: verifying that someone is who they claim to be (identity) versus verifying that they should be trusted (credibility). Twitter's original verification conflated these concepts, and the chaos that ensued when they were separated reveals why both matter.

Consider two different scenarios:

Scenario 1: A deepfake video shows a real Nobel laureate in economics endorsing a cryptocurrency. The identity is synthetic (it's not really them), but if it were real, their endorsement would carry weight due to their credentials.

Scenario 2: A real person with a purchased blue checkmark claims expertise in nuclear physics while promoting a perpetual motion machine. The identity is authentic (they are who they claim), but their credentials are nonexistent.

Both scenarios spread misinformation, but through different failures. The first exploits our trust in verified credentials by faking the person. The second exploits our trust in verified identity by faking the expertise. The synthetic age makes both trivially easy.

This suggests we need parallel systems:

Identity Verification confirms "this communication comes from the claimed source." Technologies like cryptographic signatures, blockchain attestations, and zero-knowledge proofs can make identity mathematically verifiable.

Credential Verification confirms "this source has legitimate expertise in this domain." This requires more than technology—it requires institutional backing, peer validation, and track records that can't be synthetically manufactured.

The challenge is that these systems must work together while remaining independent. A verified expert's synthetic clone shouldn't inherit their credibility. A verified human's false expertise shouldn't gain authority from their authentic identity.

Some emerging approaches show promise:

. . .

Decentralized Identifiers (DIDs) aim to separate identity from any single platform. In theory, you would control your identifier and prove ownership cryptographically. The W3C has established standards, and some pilots exist, but widespread adoption remains elusive. Most platforms still prefer to own your identity data.

Verifiable Credentials (VCs) could allow institutions to issue cryptographically signed attestations. A university could issue a degree that you own and can present to anyone, who could verify it came from the real university without contacting them. While technically feasible and standardized, actual implementation lags far behind the vision.

Web of Trust models propose building credibility through networks rather than central authorities. Your trustworthiness would derive from who trusts you and who they trust in turn. It's theoretically harder to fake an entire network than a single credential, but practical implementations remain limited to niche communities like PGP users.

Reputation Staking would require putting something at risk to make claims. Prediction markets like Metaculus and Manifold show this works in limited domains. Some proposed systems would require staking reputation tokens that you lose if proven wrong, but these remain largely theoretical.

[Based on W3C standards and emerging identity protocols]

. . .

But technical solutions alone won't solve the credential crisis. We also need new social norms around information privilege.

THE NEW REPUTATION ECONOMY

The collapse of traditional credentials is forcing the emergence of what economists call a "reputation economy"—where trust becomes a scarce resource that must be earned, maintained, and carefully allocated. But unlike traditional reputation, which accumulated slowly through repeated interactions, synthetic media demands new models that can function even when those interactions might be fake.

Consider how reputation worked in different eras:

Village Reputation (Pre-industrial): Everyone knew everyone. Reputation spread through gossip and persisted for generations. Trust was inherited and nearly impossible to fake because everyone knew your history.

Institutional Reputation (Industrial era): Organizations vouched for individuals. Your employer, university, or professional association became your credibility proxy. Trust was delegated to institutions presumed to do vetting.

Digital Reputation (Early internet): Usernames accumulated history. eBay sellers built feedback over years. Forum members earned status through contributions. Trust was algorithmic but gameable.

. . .

Synthetic Age Reputation (Now): All previous models break when history can be fabricated, institutions can be impersonated, and algorithms can be gamed at scale. Trust must be continuously earned and cryptographically provable.

The new reputation economy must operate on different principles—though we're only beginning to see glimpses of this transformation:

Reputation Should Be Non-Transferable: Unlike money, reputation can't be sold or stolen—but it can be destroyed. While synthetic media can't grant you someone else's earned trust, it can destroy your own. Some platforms are beginning to recognize this, but most still allow reputation to be gamed or purchased.

Reputation Must Be Domain-Specific: Being a trusted epidemiologist doesn't make you a credible cryptocurrency advisor. The emerging economy needs to enforce boundaries that the attention economy eroded. We see hints of this in specialized platforms, but cross-domain credibility pollution remains rampant.

Reputation Should Require Skin in the Game: Nassim Taleb's concept must become digital reality.[4] Some systems are beginning to demand that information providers risk something—money, time, or reputation itself—to prevent consequence-free deception. Prediction markets show promise here, but they remain niche.

Reputation Must Be Collective: Individual reputation increasingly needs to depend on network effects. Who vouches for you should matter more than what you claim about yourself. This would make reputation more robust but also more exclusionary—a trade-off we're only beginning to grapple with.

We see early experiments with these principles across platforms:

Stack Overflow grants increasing privileges based on contributed value. You can't buy your way to high reputation—you must earn it through helpful answers verified by the community. The platform's information quality remains high because information privilege is earned, not claimed.

GitHub makes reputation visible through code contributions. Your commit history, pull requests, and project maintenance create an unfakeable record of competence. Synthetic media can't fake years of quality code contributions (yet).

Prediction Platforms like Metaculus track forecasting accuracy over time. Users who consistently predict correctly earn influence. Those who don't lose it. Reality provides undeniable feedback that can't be argued with or faked.

Academic Publishing slowly adopts open peer review, where reviewers' identities and comments become part of the permanent record. Reputation attaches to quality of review, not just publication quantity.

But the new reputation economy also creates new problems:

. . .

Reputation Inequality emerges as those with established credibility find it easier to build more, while newcomers face higher barriers. The "rich get richer" dynamics of social media apply to trust itself.

Reputation Attacks become more sophisticated. If you can't steal reputation, you can try to destroy it. Synthetic media showing someone doing something discrediting can ruin decades of earned trust in minutes.

Reputation Absolutism treats all domains as equally important. Someone's views on vaccines might be worthless while their insights on software architecture are invaluable, but simple reputation systems struggle with such nuance.

Reputation Exclusion locks out those who lack the time, resources, or connections to build digital reputation. The systems meant to ensure quality can become barriers to legitimate participation.

The principle of least privilege offers guidance: grant information privilege based on demonstrated competence in specific domains, not general popularity or purchased status. But implementing this principle requires rethinking how we structure information flow itself.

INFORMATION DIETS AND ATTENTION HYGIENE

Just as we've learned that physical health requires conscious eating habits, mental health in the synthetic age requires conscious information consumption—what information researchers call "attention hygiene" or maintaining a healthy "information diet."

. . .

The metaphor is apt. Like junk food, synthetic media is engineered to be irresistible:

- High emotional impact (outrage, fear, arousal)
- Easy to consume (short, visual, simple)
- Addictive patterns (variable reward schedules)
- Empty calories (engagement without enlightenment)

And like junk food, occasional consumption won't kill you, but a steady diet will destroy your ability to think clearly.

Consider the information consumption patterns enabled by current platforms:

Infinite Scroll feeds present endless content without natural stopping points. Your brain, evolved for environments where information was scarce, can't resist checking "just one more" post. Synthetic content, optimized for engagement, dominates these feeds.

Algorithmic Amplification ensures you see content that triggers response, not content that informs. The algorithm doesn't distinguish between real outrage at injustice and synthetic outrage from a deepfake—it only measures engagement.

. . .

Context Collapse strips information from its source, credibility, and purpose. A screenshot of a headline spreads faster than the article. A clip from a deepfake travels further than the debunking. Information becomes fragments without foundation.

Parasocial Relationships with synthetic personas create false intimacy. You feel like you "know" the influencer, the pundit, the expert—even when they might not exist. This fabricated familiarity bypasses critical thinking.

Building a healthy information diet requires applying least privilege principles to your own consumption—though few of us have fully mastered this:

Source Restriction: Limit information sources to those with verified credibility in specific domains. Follow epidemiologists for health information, not celebrities. Trust economists on economic policy, not politicians.

Time Boxing: Grant limited time privileges to different information types. Perhaps 30 minutes for news, 20 for professional development, 10 for social media. When time expires, access ends.

Quality Filters: Use tools and practices that surface high-quality information while filtering out synthetic noise. RSS feeds from trusted sources. Newsletters from verified experts. Books that required effort to create and publish.

· · ·

Verification Habits: Build pauses between consumption and belief. See something shocking? Wait 24 hours. Something too good to be true? Find three independent confirmations. Something that makes you angry? Ask who benefits from your anger.

Regular Fasting: Take periodic breaks from all digital information. The perspective gained from stepping away helps you recognize how synthetic media manipulates your emotions and attention.

Some pioneers have developed successful information diet strategies:

[Based on digital wellness research and early adopter reports]

The Scholar's Diet: Consume primary sources whenever possible. Read research papers, not headlines about them. Watch full speeches, not clips. Go to the source, not the synthesis.

The Curator's Diet: Follow trusted curators who do verification work for you. Good newsletters, thoughtful bloggers, and careful aggregators can save you time while maintaining quality.

The Temporal Diet: Delay consumption of breaking news. Wait a week to read about current events. The important stories persist; the synthetic noise fades. History's first draft is often wrong.

. . .

The Network Diet: Consume information recommended by trusted friends, not algorithms. Human curation, while imperfect, at least comes from beings with skin in the game.

The Creation Diet: Balance consumption with creation. Writing, coding, building, or making forces you to engage deeply with information rather than passively consuming it.

The goal isn't information abstinence—it's information intentionality. In a world where anyone can create compelling synthetic content, the principle of least privilege must apply to our own attention. Grant access only to information that earns it.

TRUST BOUNDARIES IN A BORDERLESS WORLD

The borderless world created by technology collides with the bordered nature of trust. Legal systems, cultural norms, and verification methods remain stubbornly local. When synthetic media can originate anywhere and target everywhere, these mismatched boundaries create exploitable gaps.

Consider the emerging challenges:

Legal Boundaries mean laws against fraud in one country don't apply to criminals in another. The deepfake created in Russia to influence Slovak elections violated Slovak law, but good luck prosecuting. Synthetic media operates globally while law enforcement remains local.

. . .

Cultural Boundaries create different expectations of truth and trust. What seems like obvious satire in one culture appears as believable news in another. Synthetic media exploits these differences, crafting content that resonates with specific cultural vulnerabilities.

Technical Boundaries separate those with sophisticated verification tools from those without. Advanced economies might develop defenses against synthetic media, but these tools rarely reach the global majority. The digital divide becomes a trust divide.

Language Boundaries limit verification capabilities. Fact-checkers who speak English can't verify content in Tagalog. Synthetic media in less-resourced languages spreads unchecked while verification efforts concentrate on dominant languages.

Economic Boundaries make trust a luxury good. Verification services, authentication tools, and secure communications cost money. Those who most need protection from synthetic fraud—the poor and marginalized—can least afford it.

These mismatched boundaries enable what security researchers warn could become "trust arbitrage"—the ability to exploit differences in trust systems for profit or power. Like financial arbitrage that profits from price differences between markets, trust arbitrage would profit from verification differences between systems.

We're beginning to see early examples of trust arbitrage:

• • •

Credential Laundering routes fake credentials through jurisdictions with weak verification. A synthetic diploma from a fake university in one country gets "validated" by a credential service in another, then accepted as legitimate in a third.

Reputation Washing builds fake reputation in low-trust environments then transfers it to high-trust ones. Bot farms in countries with cheap labor create synthetic social proof that influences consumers in wealthy markets.

Regulatory Arbitrage exploits differences in synthetic media laws. Create deepfakes where it's legal, distribute them where it's not, profit from the chaos while staying beyond prosecution.

Verification Gaps target communities without access to verification tools. Synthetic media campaigns focus on languages, regions, and demographics where fact-checking infrastructure is weakest.

The principle of least privilege suggests frameworks for managing trust boundaries:

Graduated Trust would acknowledge that not all sources deserve equal credibility. Information from verified local sources might deserve more trust than unverified distant ones. Proximity—physical, cultural, or network—could become a factor in privilege. Some platforms are experimenting with this, but most still treat all content equally.

. . .

Trust Translation could create bridges between different verification systems. Like currency exchange, we need trust exchange—ways to convert verification from one system to credibility in another. This remains largely conceptual, with no widespread implementation.

Defensive Boundaries might protect vulnerable communities from synthetic media attacks. Like immune systems that recognize foreign pathogens, communities need ways to identify and reject information that doesn't match local trust patterns. Some closed communities achieve this informally, but scalable solutions remain elusive.

Collaborative Verification could share the burden across boundaries. We see promising examples: fact-checkers in different countries beginning to collaborate, verification tools getting translated and adapted. Trust could become a common good maintained collectively, though we're far from this ideal.

But ultimately, the borderless nature of synthetic media demands borderless responses. No single country, culture, or community can defend against threats that emerge from anywhere and target everywhere. The principle of least privilege must operate at planetary scale while respecting local contexts.

∼

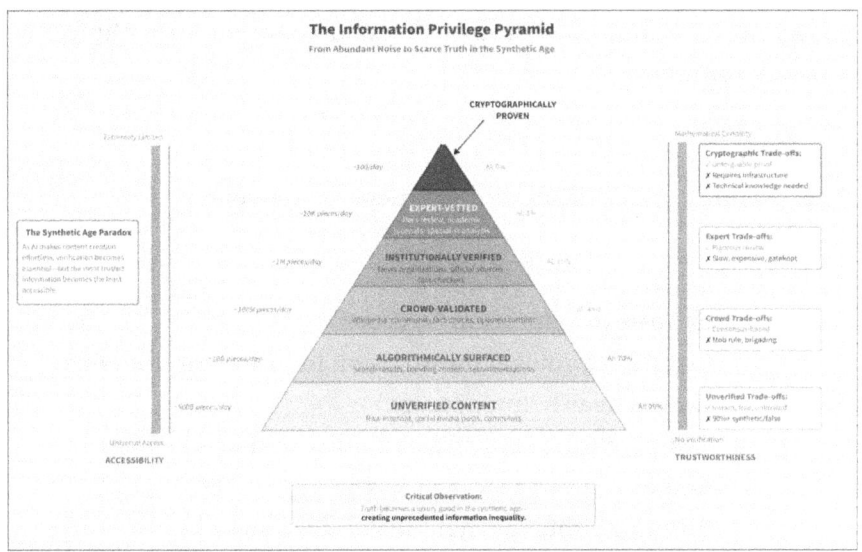

Figure 7.1: *The Information Privilege Pyramid: Truth as a Scarce Resource in the Synthetic Age.* This pyramid visualizes the inverse relationship between information accessibility and trustworthiness in an era of AI-generated content. At the base, unverified content flows at 500 billion pieces daily with 95% synthetic contamination, available to anyone but essentially worthless for truth-seeking. Each ascending layer represents exponentially less content but dramatically higher verification standards—from algorithmic curation through crowd validation, institutional verification, and expert review, to the pyramid's peak of cryptographically proven content producing merely 100 verified pieces daily. The visualization starkly illustrates how AI has inverted information economics: while content has never been more abundant, verified truth has never been scarcer. The gradient from light to dark symbolizes this transformation of truth from a public good to a luxury commodity. Most critically, the pyramid reveals an emerging caste system of information access where one's ability to distinguish truth from synthetic fiction becomes determined by technical knowledge, institutional connections, and economic resources—creating a new form of inequality that threatens the foundational premise of informed democratic participation.

TAKEAWAY: CURATING YOUR INFORMATION PRIVILEGE

The chaos of the blue checkmarks taught us that information privilege can't be bought, sold, or faked—it must be earned and carefully managed. In the synthetic age, applying the principle of least privilege to information isn't about restricting access but about conscious curation. You become the architect of your own information environment.

Start building your information privilege framework:

1. **Audit Your Information Sources**
    - List where you get information for different domains (news, health, finance, etc.)
    - Evaluate each source's credibility in that specific domain
    - Eliminate sources that fail verification or lack expertise

2. **Create Domain-Specific Trust Lists**
    - Identify genuine experts in fields that matter to you
    - Verify their credentials through multiple channels
    - Follow them directly, not through algorithmic feeds

3. **Implement Verification Delays**
    - Build pauses between seeing and believing
    - Create cooling-off periods before sharing
    - Use time as a filter—urgent synthetic media often falls apart within hours

4. **Design Your Information Diet**
    - Allocate specific time for different information types

- Balance consumption with creation
- Schedule regular information fasts

5. **Build Trust Networks**
    - Identify friends who are careful information curators
    - Create reciprocal verification relationships
    - Share the burden of fact-checking within trusted circles

6. **Practice Selective Ignorance**
    - Recognize that you can't verify everything
    - Choose domains where you'll invest verification effort
    - Accept uncertainty in areas outside your focus

7. **Document Your Standards**
    - Write down what earns information privilege in your system
    - Share these standards with others
    - Adjust based on results

The principle of least privilege in information isn't about becoming a digital hermit—it's about becoming a digital citizen. In a world where anyone can claim authority and synthetic media can manufacture evidence, your attention becomes your most valuable asset. Guard it accordingly.

WHAT'S NEXT

Information privilege helps us filter what deserves our attention, but it doesn't protect us from the inevitable: sometimes synthetic media will fool us. Sometimes trusted sources will be compromised. Sometimes our carefully curated information diet will include poison. In Chapter 8, "Assuming Breach in Human Systems," we'll explore how to build resilience for when our defenses fail. From social engineering at scale to the insider threat of synthetic insiders, we'll examine what happens when trust networks become attack vectors and how to recover when the breach has already happened.

The question isn't whether you'll be fooled by synthetic media—it's what you'll do when you are.

Chapter 8
Assuming Breach in Human Systems

THE WHATSAPP MOM

[BASED ON ANALYSIS of evolving WhatsApp scam patterns reported to the Federal Trade Commission, 2023-2024. Names and details modified for privacy.]

The message arrived at 11:47 PM on a Tuesday: "Hi sweetheart, I dropped my phone in the toilet at this conference 🚽 Using a colleague's phone. Can you do me a huge favor?"

Sarah Jackson stared at her phone, groggy but instantly alert. Her mother was indeed at a medical conference in Chicago—she'd texted photos from the opening reception just that morning. The message continued: "I'm so embarrassed to ask, but I need to pay for the hotel and my cards are linked to my phone for verification. Can you Venmo $1,800 to this account? I'll pay you back as soon as I get home tomorrow. Love you!"

· · ·

Everything about the message felt right. The emoji use, the slight embarrassment, the practical request with a promise to repay—it all sounded exactly like her pragmatic mother. Sarah had helped her out with technical issues before. Her mother, a successful pediatrician, was brilliant with patients but perpetually challenged by technology.

Sarah almost sent the money. Her finger hovered over the transfer button. But something made her pause—not suspicion exactly, but a feeling she'd later struggle to describe. Maybe it was the security training at her tech job, or maybe just instinct. Instead of sending the money, she tried calling the number. It went straight to voicemail.

"Mom, just saw your message. Calling you back," Sarah texted.

The response was immediate: "Can't talk right now sweetie, in the middle of a late dinner with colleagues. Please just send it? I'm really stressed about this."

That's when Sarah knew. Her mother would never prioritize a work dinner over a phone call about money, especially not at midnight. Sarah tried calling her mother's actual phone number—the one saved in her contacts for years. It rang normally and went to her mother's familiar voicemail greeting.

Now truly suspicious, Sarah tried a verification technique her security-conscious workplace had drilled into employees: alternative channel confirmation. She opened her laptop and sent an email to her mother's work address with a simple message: "Hey Mom, got a weird text from you. Everything okay?"

. . .

Then she texted her brother in Seattle: "Did Mom contact you tonight about money?"

His response was immediate: "No, why? She texted me this afternoon that she was heading to bed early. Early morning presentation tomorrow."

Within minutes, Sarah had three confirmations that the original message was fake: her mother's real phone was working normally, her brother had heard she was going to bed early, and when her mother woke up to use the bathroom and saw Sarah's email, she called immediately, confused and concerned.

The scammer had done their homework. They knew about the conference, the mother-daughter relationship dynamics, even the communication patterns. But they'd made one crucial error: they assumed the trust network only flowed one way. They hadn't anticipated that Sarah would have alternate paths to verify the truth [1].

Sarah's near-miss illustrates a profound shift in how we must think about security. In the old model, we focused on keeping attackers out. But when synthetic media can perfectly impersonate anyone, when AI can mimic communication patterns, when trust itself becomes a weapon—we must assume the breach has already happened. The question isn't whether someone will impersonate your loved ones, colleagues, or friends. The question is: what do you do when they do?

∼

WHEN TRUST NETWORKS BECOME ATTACK VECTORS

Every relationship in your life is now a potential security vulnerability. This isn't paranoia—it's mathematics. Security researchers call it the "attack surface," and in the age of synthetic media, your attack surface includes everyone you've ever trusted.

Consider the traditional model of trust networks:

- You trust your family members implicitly
- You respond to requests from close friends
- You follow instructions from your boss
- You share information with colleagues
- You help neighbors and community members

Each of these trust relationships evolved over millions of years of human evolution. They're hardwired into our social brains, reinforced by culture, and essential for functioning society. But synthetic media has weaponized these connections. Every trust link becomes an attack vector. Every relationship becomes a potential breach.

The mathematics of network compromise are sobering. If you have:

- 5 immediate family members
- 20 close friends
- 50 professional contacts
- 200 social media connections

That's 275 potential impersonation vectors targeting you directly. But the real vulnerability lies in second-order effects. Each of those 275 people has their own network. If any of them can be convinced that a synthetic version of you is real, the breach cascades. Your trusted contact becomes an unwitting accomplice, vouching for the fake you to others.

[Based on network security principles applied to human relationships]

We're seeing this play out in increasingly sophisticated ways:

Family Emergency Scams 2.0 no longer rely on vague claims of trouble. Attackers research family structures, travel schedules, and communication patterns. They know who's traveling where, which family members are closest, who typically handles money transfers. The synthetic voice of your "grandson" includes his speech patterns, favorite phrases, even background noises from familiar locations.

Professional Impersonation Networks target entire organizational structures. Attackers map reporting relationships, identify communication patterns, then systematically impersonate multiple people. By the time anyone realizes something is wrong, the synthetic versions have extracted data, authorized transfers, or planted malware through "trusted" channels.

Social Graph Hijacking leverages the interconnected nature of social media. Compromise one node—perhaps through a synthetic dating profile or fake professional connection—and you can map their entire network. Friends vouch for friends, colleagues recommend colleagues, and the synthetic infiltrator gains trust transitively.

Community Trust Exploitation targets the high-trust relationships in religious, cultural, or interest-based communities. Members who would never fall for a stranger's scam readily help someone who appears to be part of their trusted community. Synthetic media allows attackers to wear the face and voice of belonging.

The most insidious aspect is that these attacks exploit our best qualities: loyalty, helpfulness, trust, community spirit. The very traits that make us human become vulnerabilities in a world where humanity itself can be synthetically manufactured.

SOCIAL ENGINEERING AT SCALE

Social engineering—manipulating people into divulging confidential information or performing actions—is as old as human society. But synthetic media has transformed it from an artisanal craft into an industrial process. What once required skilled con artists now requires only API calls to AI services.

Traditional social engineering was limited by human constraints:

- Con artists needed acting ability
- Scams required real-time improvisation
- Each target demanded personal attention
- Success rates were limited by human error
- Scale was constrained by available operators

Synthetic social engineering obliterates every one of these limits:

- AI can perfectly mimic any person
- Responses can be generated algorithmically
- Thousands of targets can be engaged simultaneously
- Machine learning optimizes success rates
- Scale is limited only by computing power

The industrialization shows in the numbers. In 2020, the FBI received 241,342 complaints about internet crime. By 2024, that number exceeded 2 million, with losses surpassing $50 billion annually. But even these staggering figures likely represent only reported cases—the true scale remains hidden.[2]

[Statistics based on FBI IC3 reports and cybercrime trends]

Consider how modern social engineering campaigns operate:

Persona Development begins with AI analysis of targets. Machine learning models ingest social media posts, public records, and data broker information to build detailed psychological profiles. The AI learns not just what you do, but how you think, what motivates you, what triggers your responses.

Scenario Optimization uses A/B testing at scale. The same basic scam—elderly parent needs help—gets thousands of variations. Different emotional triggers, urgency levels, and request amounts are tested across populations. The versions that succeed propagate; those that fail get refined.

Adaptive Interaction allows real-time adjustment. Unlike human scammers who follow scripts, AI can dynamically adjust based on target responses. Express skepticism? The AI backs off, builds more rapport, then tries again. Show confusion? It simplifies. Display emotion? It amplifies the manipulation.

Multi-Modal Coordination combines channels for credibility. You might receive an email, then a text, then a voice call—all perfectly coordinated, all referencing previous interactions, all building a false reality that becomes harder to question with each touchpoint.

Behavioral Exploitation targets cognitive biases systematically. The AI knows that people are more vulnerable when tired, stressed, or emotional. It times attacks for maximum effectiveness, perhaps waiting until late at night or immediately after a target posts about a stressful life event.

One recovered training dataset from a criminal operation revealed the terrifying sophistication. The AI had been trained to recognize and exploit 347 different emotional states, could simulate conversations in 52 languages with culturally appropriate nuances, and maintained consistent personas across thousands of simultaneous interactions.

The scale enables what researchers call "spray and pray with precision." Traditional scammers had to choose between broad, low-success attacks (Nigerian Prince emails) or narrow, high-touch cons (romance scams). AI enables both simultaneously: massive reach with personalized manipulation.

THE LONELINESS ECONOMY

Perhaps the darkest evolution in synthetic social engineering is the exploitation of loneliness. In an era of unprecedented digital connection, rates of loneliness and social isolation have paradoxically soared. Synthetic media doesn't just exploit this epidemic—it deepens it.

The statistics paint a grim picture:

- 60% of young adults report feeling lonely frequently
- 35% of older adults experience chronic loneliness
- Remote work has decreased workplace social connections by 40%
- Average number of close friends has declined from 3 to 2 since 1990

[Compiled from various loneliness studies and surveys, 2023-2024]

Into this landscape of isolation come synthetic companions, indistinguishable from real humans but infinitely patient, always available, and expertly calibrated to provide exactly what lonely people crave: connection, understanding, validation.

. . .

Synthetic Romance Scams have evolved beyond simple catfishing. AI-powered personas maintain months-long relationships, complete with generated selfies, voice calls, even video chats using real-time deepfakes. They remember anniversaries, ask about your day, provide emotional support. The financial request, when it finally comes, feels like helping a genuine partner, not falling for a scam.

Artificial Friend Networks create entire social circles. Lonely individuals find themselves welcomed into vibrant online communities where multiple synthetic personas interact naturally. The target feels popular, included, valued. When the "community" needs help —medical bills, business ventures, charity drives—the social pressure to contribute becomes overwhelming.

Parasocial Manipulation exploits one-way emotional connections. Synthetic influencers build massive followings of lonely fans who feel genuine connection to these artificial personalities. When the influencer promotes products, requests donations, or spreads misinformation, followers comply out of misplaced loyalty.

Grief Exploitation targets the bereaved with synthetic versions of deceased loved ones. Using social media history and public records, AI can create convincing simulacra that offer comfort—and gradually make requests. The ethical violations are profound, the emotional damage immeasurable.

The loneliness economy creates a vicious cycle:

1. Real human connections require effort, vulnerability, and risk

2. Synthetic connections offer easier, safer alternatives
3. People invest emotional energy in synthetic relationships
4. Real relationship skills atrophy from disuse
5. Increased isolation drives more dependence on synthetic connections

We're building a world where the cure for loneliness—human connection—is being replaced by a synthetic substitute that deepens the very problem it pretends to solve.

BUILDING RESILIENCE THROUGH PREPARED SKEPTICISM

If we must assume breach—that synthetic versions of our trusted contacts exist, that our networks are compromised, that we will be targeted—how do we function? The answer isn't paranoid isolation but what security experts call "prepared skepticism": maintaining openness to connection while building systematic defenses against deception.

Prepared skepticism operates on several principles:

Trust but Verify Becomes Verify Then Trust: Every unusual request, regardless of source, requires verification through alternate channels. This isn't suspicion of people—it's acknowledgment that people can be impersonated.

Defense in Depth: Single points of failure are eliminated. Important decisions require multiple confirmations through different channels. Financial transfers need both communication verification and waiting periods. Critical information flows through redundant paths.

Behavioral Baselines: Knowing normal patterns helps identify anomalies. Your mother always calls at certain times. Your boss phrases requests in particular ways. Your friends use specific communication channels. Deviations trigger verification, not immediate compliance.

Prepared Responses: Having plans before crises prevents panic decisions. Families should establish verification protocols. Organizations need incident response procedures. Individuals require personal security policies. When the fake emergency call comes, you execute the plan, not react emotionally.

Community Defense: Isolation makes us vulnerable; connection provides protection. Share verification duties with trusted contacts. Create group authentication systems. Build networks of mutual verification. The same connections that create vulnerabilities can provide defenses.

Practical implementation might look like:

[Based on emerging security practices and expert recommendations]

Family Verification Protocols:

- Establish code words that rotate monthly

- Create verification questions only family members can answer
- Designate alternates for confirming emergencies
- Practice responses to common scam scenarios
- Regular check-ins to maintain baselines

Professional Security Practices:

- Multi-person approval for sensitive requests
- Out-of-band verification for financial transfers
- Time delays for non-urgent decisions
- Clear escalation procedures for anomalies
- Regular security awareness training

Personal Defense Strategies:

- Limited sharing of detailed life information
- Separate communication channels for different purposes
- Regular review of connection networks
- Immediate verification of unusual requests
- Documentation of normal communication patterns

The goal isn't to eliminate trust but to make trust resilient. By assuming breach and preparing responses, we can maintain human connections while defending against synthetic exploitation.

RECOVERY: WHEN YOU'VE BEEN BREACHED

Despite our best preparations, breaches will happen. You'll send money to a synthetic relative. You'll share information with an AI impersonator. You'll be fooled. The question becomes: how do you recover?

Recovery from synthetic media attacks involves unique challenges:

Psychological Impact often exceeds financial damage. Victims report feelings of violation, stupidity, and broken trust that persist long after monetary losses are recovered. The knowledge that you were fooled by a machine can be particularly devastating to self-image.

Trust Reconstruction requires rebuilding faith not just in technology but in human relationships. If your mother's voice can be faked, how do you trust any communication? Recovery means developing new frameworks for trust that acknowledge vulnerability while enabling connection.

Network Decontamination involves identifying how far the breach spread. Did you vouch for the synthetic contact to others? Did you share information that enabled further attacks? Like contact tracing for disease, you must trace the impact of the breach through your network.

Learning Integration transforms breach from failure to education. Each incident provides data about vulnerabilities. What worked?

What didn't? How can defenses be improved? The goal is antifragility—becoming stronger through stress.

A recovery framework for humans draws lessons from technology security but must address our emotional and social needs:

Immediate Human Response:

- Take a breath—you're not the first person fooled, you won't be the last
- Call a trusted friend or family member for emotional support
- Write down what happened while the details are fresh
- Forgive yourself—sophisticated AI fooled you, not your own stupidity
- Warn others who might be targeted using your information

Rebuilding Trust (Days/Weeks):

- Have honest conversations with affected relationships
- Establish new verification rituals with family and friends
- Join a support group or online community of others who've been deceived
- Practice the new verification methods until they feel natural
- Celebrate small wins as you rebuild confidence

Strengthening Connections (Months):

- Transform the breach into deeper relationships through shared security practices
- Become a resource for others—your experience has value
- Build redundant trust networks so no single breach can isolate you
- Create family or workplace workshops on synthetic media awareness
- Find meaning in protecting others from what happened to you

Psychological Integration:

- Recognize that trusting others is still a strength, not a weakness
- Separate healthy skepticism from destructive paranoia
- Use the experience to become more intentionally connected
- Transform vulnerability into wisdom
- Help normalize the conversation about synthetic deception

The key insight is that human recovery isn't about becoming more machine-like in our defenses—it's about becoming more intentionally human in our connections. Technology security focuses on closing vulnerabilities; human security focuses on maintaining authentic relationships despite vulnerabilities.

. . .

The most important aspect of recovery is recognizing that being breached doesn't make you stupid or naive—it makes you human. Our brains evolved for a world where faces couldn't be faked and voices couldn't be cloned. That we're vulnerable to synthetic deception isn't a personal failing but a species-wide challenge requiring collective response.

FROM BREACH TO BREAKTHROUGH

The transition from assuming security to assuming breach represents a fundamental shift in how we must approach human relationships in the digital age. While many are still to make this transition, those who have report unexpected benefits:

Intentional Connection: When we can't take identity for granted, we must be more intentional about relationships. Verification rituals become opportunities for meaningful interaction. Security practices create excuses for regular contact. The need for multiple confirmation channels encourages diverse communication.

Explicit Trust: Moving from implicit to explicit trust strengthens relationships. When families discuss verification protocols, they're really discussing how they care for each other. When colleagues implement security procedures, they're building team cohesion. Making trust visible makes it stronger.

Collective Resilience: Individual security is impossible; we need community defense. This drives us toward interdependence rather than isolation. Security becomes a commons we maintain together rather than a wall we build alone.

. . .

Adaptive Capacity: Assuming breach builds flexibility and resilience. We become less brittle, more able to handle surprises. The skills developed for security—skepticism, verification, analysis—serve us in many contexts.

Human Enhancement: Paradoxically, defending against synthetic humans makes us more human. We must understand what makes genuine connection special. We value authentic interaction more when we know it can be faked. We become more conscious of our humanity by defending it.

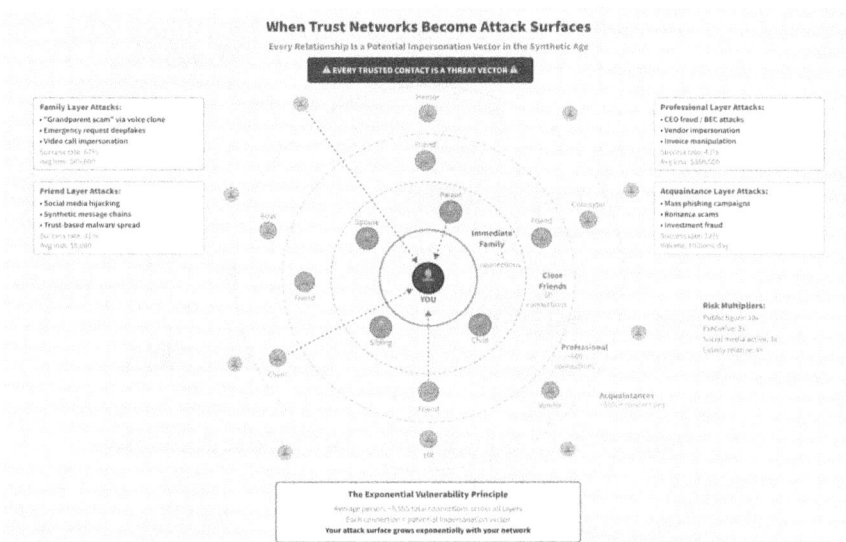

Figure 8.1: *Trust Networks as Attack Surfaces: How Every Relationship Becomes a Vulnerability.* This network diagram maps the transformation of social connections into impersonation vectors in the synthetic age. Centered on an individual, concentric circles represent expanding relationship layers—from the ~5 immediate family members through ~50 close friends, ~500 professional contacts, to ~5,000+ acquaintances. Each red arrow represents a potential synthetic impersonation attack path, with success rates inversely proportional to relationship distance but damage potential highest in inner circles. Family layer attacks using voice cloning achieve 67% success rates with average losses of $45,000, while professional layer CEO fraud averages $380,000 per successful attack. The visualization starkly illustrates that an average person's 5,555 connections create 5,555 potential attack vectors—a number that grows exponentially with social network expansion. Most critically, the diagram reveals how trust itself becomes weaponized: the stronger the relationship bond, the more devastating the potential exploitation through synthetic impersonation. In an era where AI can perfectly mimic any person's voice, video, and communication patterns, every trusted contact paradoxically becomes a threat vector, fundamentally inverting the protective nature of social networks into unprecedented vulnerability surfaces.

TAKEAWAY: YOUR BREACH RESPONSE PLAN STARTS NOW

Assuming breach isn't pessimism—it's preparedness. Just as we buy insurance not because we expect disaster but because we're prudent, we must build breach response capabilities before we need them.

The time to prepare for synthetic deception is now, while you're calm and thinking clearly.

Start building your breach resilience:

1. **Conduct a Trust Audit**
   - Map your key relationships and communication patterns
   - Identify which breaches would be most damaging
   - Assess current verification capabilities
   - Note single points of failure

2. **Create Verification Protocols**
   - Establish multi-channel confirmation for sensitive requests
   - Develop family code words and verification questions
   - Build professional authentication procedures
   - Practice using these protocols regularly

3. **Build Your Response Network**
   - Identify trusted contacts for verification assistance
   - Create communication trees for breach notification
   - Establish support systems for recovery
   - Share protocols with your network

4. **Prepare Psychologically**

- Accept that you might be fooled—everyone is vulnerable
- Separate vigilance from paranoia
- Focus on systematic rather than personal security
- Build confidence through preparation

5. **Document and Practice**
    - Write down your security protocols
    - Conduct regular drills with family and colleagues
    - Update procedures based on new threats
    - Learn from others' experiences

6. **Plan for Recovery**
    - Know what you'll do if breached
    - Prepare template notifications
    - Identify support resources
    - Focus on resilience, not just prevention

Remember: assuming breach doesn't mean living in fear. It means living in reality. By acknowledging that our trust networks have become attack vectors, we can build defenses that preserve human connection while protecting against synthetic deception.

WHAT'S NEXT

We've explored how to build resilience when human systems are breached, but individual preparedness isn't enough. We need technological infrastructure that supports human verification at scale. In

Chapter 9, "The Cryptographic Foundation," we'll dive into the mathematical and technical systems that can create provable identity in an age of perfect impersonation. From public key infrastructure for humans to zero-knowledge proofs that protect privacy while enabling verification, we'll explore how cryptography moves from protecting data to protecting humanity itself.

The human element of security will always be vulnerable. The mathematical element might be our salvation.

∽

PART THREE
INFRASTRUCTURE FOR INTEGRITY

CHAPTER 9

THE CRYPTOGRAPHIC FOUNDATION

THE DIGITAL IDENTITY WALLET THAT SAVED EUROPE

[BASED on the EU Digital Identity Wallet pilot programs launched in 2023-2025, with some speculative elements about full deployment]

On a gray morning in Brussels, March 2025, Pieter van der Berg stood before the European Parliament's Committee on Civil Liberties, holding up his smartphone. "This device," he said, "contains something that would have prevented every synthetic media attack we've discussed today. Not through better detection of fakes, but through mathematical proof of what's real."

Van der Berg, the EU's Commissioner for Digital Identity, was unveiling the full deployment of the European Digital Identity Wallet—a system years in the making that promised to revolutionize how 450 million Europeans proved who they were in an increasingly synthetic world.

. . .

The wallet itself looked unremarkable: just another app on a phone. But beneath its simple interface lay a sophisticated cryptographic architecture that made impersonation not just difficult, but mathematically impossible. Every EU citizen could now carry proof of their identity that didn't depend on their face, their voice, or any biological marker that could be copied. Instead, it relied on something far more fundamental: the mathematical certainty of cryptographic signatures.

"When I send a message, authorize a payment, or join the video call," van der Berg demonstrated, his phone briefly displaying a QR code, "I'm not just claiming to be myself. I'm proving it with mathematics that would take all the computers on Earth a billion years to forge."

The system had been tested during the Estonian deepfake crisis, where early adopters with digital wallets had been able to definitively prove which communications were authentic. While others scrambled to verify through callbacks and secondary channels, wallet users simply signed their messages. The cryptographic signature was like a fingerprint that couldn't be faked—not because it was complex, but because it was mathematically bound to a secret only they possessed.

But van der Berg's presentation took an unexpected turn. "The wallet does something else equally important," he said. "It proves facts about you without revealing your identity. Let me show you with a real example." He pulled up a popular online wine retailer on the chamber's presentation screen. Adding a bottle of Bordeaux to the cart, he proceeded to checkout where the site requested age verification.

"Now watch carefully," he said, holding up his phone to scan the QR code displayed by the retailer. His phone screen briefly showed a biometric

prompt—he authenticated with his face, though he noted fingerprint or PIN would also work. Within seconds, the website showed "Age Verified ✓" and proceeded to payment options.

"Notice what just happened," he emphasized. "I had to prove to my phone that I'm me before it would release the mathematical proof of my age. If my teenage son grabbed my phone, he couldn't complete this transaction—the biometric check would fail. The wine merchant knows I'm over 18, but look at their system—they have no idea who I am. No name, no birthdate, no personal information. Just mathematical proof that the authorized owner of this wallet meets their legal requirement."

"This is the paradox we've solved," he concluded. "In an age where anyone can steal your face for a deepfake, we've built a system where you can prove everything while revealing nothing. Your identity becomes not what you are, but what you can mathematically prove—and only you can unlock that proof."

The EU Digital Identity Wallet represented a fundamental shift: from biological identity that could be copied to mathematical identity that couldn't. From all-or-nothing identification to selective disclosure. From trust based on recognition to trust based on cryptographic proof [1].

Not everyone was convinced. Privacy advocates worried about centralized tracking. Technologists debated implementation details. Citizens struggled to understand how mathematics could replace their intuitive notions of identity. But one thing was becoming clear: in the war against synthetic media, cryptography was humanity's most powerful weapon.

FROM LOCKS TO MATHEMATICS

To understand why cryptography offers hope against synthetic media, we need to appreciate a profound shift in how we create security. For thousands of years, security meant physical barriers: walls, locks, guards. These worked because breaking them required resources: time, tools, force. But digital security couldn't rely on physical barriers. Bits have no mass, networks have no walls, and information wants to be free.

The breakthrough came from a counterintuitive insight: instead of making things hard to break, make them mathematically impossible to break. Not "this would take a very strong person" but "this would violate the fundamental laws of mathematics."

This shift from physical to mathematical security happened gradually:

Symmetric Encryption (ancient times - 1970s): Like a physical lock, these systems used the same key to lock and unlock information. The Caesar cipher shifted letters. The Enigma machine scrambled messages. DES (Data Encryption Standard) standardized electronic encryption. But they all shared a fatal flaw: if someone stole or guessed your key, security evaporated.

Public Key Revolution (1976 - present): Whitfield Diffie and Martin Hellman's breakthrough seemed like magic: keys that could lock but not unlock, paired with different keys that could unlock but not lock [2]. They had solved a fundamental problem—how could two people establish secure communication without first meeting to share a secret key? Their mathematical framework proved it was possible, but remained theoretical. Then in 1977, Ron Rivest, Adi Shamir, and Leonard Adleman (RSA) created the first practical implementation, using the difficulty of factoring large prime numbers as the mathematical foundation. Suddenly, you could share your locking key with the world while keeping your unlocking key secret. RSA made it practical. The internet made it essential.

Digital Signatures (1980s - present): The inverse of encryption proved even more powerful. Use your private key to create a signature anyone can verify with your public key. It proved not just that a message was untampered, but that it came from you. Unlike physical signatures that could be forged, digital signatures were mathematically bound to both the signer and the specific message.

Zero-Knowledge Proofs (1985 - present): The ultimate magic trick —proving you know something without revealing what you know. Prove you're over 18 without revealing your age. Prove you have funds without showing your balance. Prove you're authorized without identifying yourself. What seemed impossible became merely difficult mathematics [3].

Blockchain Innovation (2008 - present): Satoshi Nakamoto showed how to create truth without trust—a ledger everyone could verify but no one could forge. While cryptocurrency grabbed headlines, the underlying innovation was more profound: consensus through mathematics rather than authority.

Each evolution moved us further from security through obscurity ("hope they don't find it") to security through transparency ("here's exactly how it works, try to break it"). This transparency paradox—that showing your method makes you more secure, not less—remains counterintuitive to those raised on physical security models.

But for synthetic media, this mathematical certainty offers something precious: a way to prove authenticity that doesn't depend on biological markers that can be copied. Your private key can't be deepfaked. Your digital signature can't be synthesized. The mathematics doesn't care how convincing the impersonation—without the key, it simply won't work.

[We acknowledge that quantum computing may eventually break current encryption methods, but post-quantum cryptography is already being developed. Until quantum computers become practical for cryptanalysis—likely still years away—mathematical cryptography remains our strongest defense.]

PUBLIC KEY INFRASTRUCTURE FOR HUMANS

The technical architecture of public key infrastructure (PKI) is well established. Millions of websites use it. Billions of devices depend on it. But applying PKI to human identity—making every person a cryptographic entity—requires rethinking fundamental assumptions.

Traditional PKI was designed for machines:

- Servers don't forget passwords
- Computers don't lose keys
- Protocols don't get social engineered
- Certificates don't have emotions

. . .

Human PKI must accommodate human realities:

- People forget things constantly
- Devices get lost or broken
- Social engineering bypasses technical security
- Identity is contextual and fluid

The EU Digital Identity Wallet and similar initiatives worldwide are grappling with these challenges:

Key Generation: Where do human cryptographic keys come from? Traditional PKI generates keys on the device, but lose your phone and you lose your identity. The EU system uses a hybrid approach: keys are generated on secure hardware in your device but can be recovered through a combination of government records and biometric verification. It's a delicate balance between security and usability.

Key Storage: Private keys must remain absolutely secret—if someone gets your private key, they can perfectly impersonate you. Modern phones include secure enclaves, hardware-isolated areas where keys can be stored and used without ever being exposed to software. But this binds identity to devices in uncomfortable ways.

Identity Binding: How do we connect a cryptographic key to a real person? The EU system requires initial in-person verification at government offices, similar to getting a passport. Some proposed systems use web-of-trust models where existing verified users vouch for new ones. Others explore biometric binding, though this reintroduces the vulnerabilities cryptography aimed to escape.

Revocation: What happens when keys are compromised? Unlike passwords that can be changed, compromised keys can leave permanent damage—every signature ever made with that key becomes suspect. Revocation systems must be global, instant, and reliable. The EU uses a distributed ledger to publish revocations within minutes worldwide.

Usability: Perhaps the greatest challenge is making cryptography invisible. Users shouldn't need to understand elliptic curves or hash functions. The EU wallet hides complexity behind familiar interfaces: tap to pay, click to sign, scan to verify. But this simplification risks users not understanding what they're doing—a dangerous proposition when actions are cryptographically permanent.

Early adoption reveals both promise and problems:

Success Stories: Estonian e-residents report feeling more secure knowing their business communications are cryptographically signed. Spanish citizens use their wallets for everything from age verification to tax filing. German universities issue cryptographic diplomas that employers can instantly verify.

Failure Modes: Italian users locked out of their wallets after phone upgrades. French citizens confused by having different keys for different purposes. Polish attempts at backup systems that accidentally exposed private keys. Each failure teaches expensive lessons about human nature meeting mathematical certainty.

Cultural Resistance: Many Europeans, especially older generations, struggle with replacing intuitive identity ("I know that's my grandson's voice") with abstract verification ("the cryptographic signature validates"). The transition requires not just technical education but fundamental shifts in how people conceptualize identity and trust.

The infrastructure is emerging, imperfect but improving. The question isn't whether humans will become cryptographic entities —that transformation has begun. The question is whether we can build systems that are both mathematically secure and humanly usable.

BLOCKCHAIN AND DISTRIBUTED TRUTH

When synthetic media can fake any individual communication, we need systems for establishing truth that don't depend on any single source. Blockchain technology, despite its association with cryptocurrency speculation, offers a profound innovation: consensus without authority.

To understand why this matters for fighting synthetic media, consider how we traditionally establish truth:

Authoritative Declaration: A trusted source (government, newspaper, expert) declares something true. But what if that source is impersonated or compromised?

. . .

Multiple Confirmation: Several sources independently confirm a fact. But what if all sources are synthetic?

Physical Evidence: Documents, recordings, or artifacts prove events. But what if the evidence is deepfaked?

Witness Testimony: People who were present attest to what happened. But what if synthetic media has pre-corrupted their perception? A witness who has seen deepfake videos of a defendant being violent might interpret ambiguous actions as threatening. Or synthetic media circulated after an event could alter witnesses' memories, making them uncertain about what they actually saw versus what they later viewed online.

Each method fails when synthetic media can impersonate authorities, create false confirmations, forge evidence, and influence witnesses. We need truth mechanisms that don't depend on trust.

Blockchain offers a different model: truth through consensus and time. Here's how it works:

1. Events are recorded with cryptographic signatures
2. Multiple independent parties verify and timestamp records
3. Records are linked in chains that make tampering evident
4. The network agrees on one version of history
5. Changing past records becomes exponentially harder over time

. . .

This creates what researchers call "temporal integrity"—the ability to prove not just what happened, but when it happened and in what order.

For defense against synthetic media, blockchain applications are emerging:

Media Provenance: Every piece of content gets hashed and timestamped on creation. Reuters and the BBC are experimenting with blockchain systems that create immutable records of when images and videos were first published [4]. If a deepfake surfaces claiming to be from 2023, the blockchain proves no such record existed then.

Identity Attestation: Instead of a central authority controlling identity, blockchain can record identity claims from multiple sources. The Estonian government records citizen identity attestations on a blockchain, creating a distributed backup that no single attack can compromise.

Verification Networks: Organizations can record their verification activities on blockchain, creating audit trails that prove when and how they verified information. When the Associated Press verifies a video, that verification becomes part of an immutable record.

Smart Contract Automation: Blockchain can automatically execute consequences for synthetic media. Some proposed systems would automatically flag content that lacks proper provenance, quarantine suspicious media, or trigger alerts when manipulation is detected.

But blockchain isn't a panacea. Significant challenges remain:

Garbage In, Garbage Out: Blockchain can prove when something was recorded, not whether it was true. A deepfake recorded on blockchain at creation remains a deepfake—just one with a timestamp.

Scale Limitations: Current blockchain systems struggle with the volume of global media creation. Bitcoin processes 7 transactions per second; humanity creates millions of pieces of content per second.

Energy Consumption: Proof-of-work blockchains consume enormous energy. Bitcoin uses more electricity than Argentina. Proof-of-stake alternatives exist but remain less tested.

Centralization Pressures: Despite decentralization ideals, blockchain systems tend toward centralization. Bitcoin mining concentrates in a few pools. Ethereum nodes cluster with major providers. This reintroduces single points of failure.

User Experience: Blockchain remains stubbornly user-unfriendly. Managing keys, understanding transactions, and verifying proofs require technical sophistication most lack.

. . .

Despite challenges, blockchain's core innovation—creating shared truth without central authority—offers essential tools for the synthetic age. Not as a complete solution, but as part of a larger arsenal. When anyone can be anyone, we need systems for establishing facts that don't depend on identity. Mathematics doesn't care who you claim to be.

ZERO-KNOWLEDGE PROOFS: PRIVACY-PRESERVING TRUTH

The EU Digital Identity Wallet's ability to prove age without revealing birthdate hints at one of cryptography's most powerful innovations: zero-knowledge proofs (ZKPs). In an age where proving your identity might mean exposing yourself to synthetic impersonation, ZKPs offer a paradoxical solution: prove facts while revealing nothing.

The concept seems impossible. How can you prove you know something without saying what you know?

Imagine this scenario: A colorblind person has two balls and needs to know if they're the same color or different colors. They don't trust you to simply tell them the truth - they want proof. Here's how they can get proof without trusting your word:

1. The colorblind person shows you two balls (one red, one green, though they appear identical to them)
2. They put the balls behind their back and either switch their positions or keep them the same
3. They show you the balls again and ask: "Did I switch them?"

4. If the balls are different colors (which they are), you can always tell if they switched. If they were the same color, you'd just be guessing
5. After enough rounds of always being correct, the colorblind person has mathematical certainty the balls are different colors

The beautiful part: The colorblind person now has proof that the balls are different colors without being able to see the colors themselves. Through your responses to their test, they've obtained certain knowledge about something they cannot directly perceive. You never had to say "trust me, they're different" - the verification process itself provided the proof.

This simple game encodes a profound principle: knowledge can be demonstrated through capability rather than disclosure. In the digital world, this translates to powerful applications:

For defense against synthetic media, ZKPs enable scenarios that seem like science fiction:

Anonymous Verification: Prove you're a real journalist without revealing which outlet you work for. Prove you're a government official without showing which department. Prove you're human without exposing any identifying information.

Credential Validation: Prove you have a medical license without revealing your name or license number. Prove you graduated from

MIT without showing your transcript. Prove you have security clearance without indicating what level.

Financial Authorization: Prove you have funds for a transaction without revealing your balance. Prove your income qualifies for a loan without showing pay stubs. Prove you paid taxes without exposing financial details.

Age and Status Checks: Prove you're over 18 without revealing if you're 19 or 90. Prove you're a citizen without showing your passport. Prove you're eligible to vote without identifying yourself.

Real-world implementations are beginning to emerge:

ING Bank implemented ZKP systems allowing customers to prove their address is in the EU without revealing which country. This enables regulatory compliance while preserving privacy [5].

Zcash cryptocurrency uses ZKPs to enable private transactions. Users can prove they have funds to transfer without revealing their balance or transaction history.

Google Wallet announced in 2025 that it would integrate zero-knowledge proofs for age verification, allowing users to prove they're over 18 without revealing their birthdate or other personal information. The system would work across platforms using their Digital Credential API.

· · ·

But ZKPs face adoption challenges:

Computational Complexity: Early ZKP systems required significant processing power. Proving simple facts could take minutes. Modern systems like zk-SNARKs are faster but still resource-intensive.

Setup Ceremonies: Many ZKP systems require complex initialization ceremonies where cryptographic parameters are generated and then destroyed. If the setup is compromised, the entire system fails.

Developer Complexity: Implementing ZKPs correctly requires deep cryptographic expertise. Small errors can leak information or enable forgeries. The talent pool remains limited.

Regulatory Resistance: Governments often oppose technologies that enable anonymous verification. Law enforcement argues it could shield criminal activity. The tension between privacy and accountability remains unresolved.

User Understanding: Explaining ZKPs to average users proves nearly impossible. "Trust the math" isn't compelling when people don't understand the math. This opacity breeds suspicion.

Despite challenges, ZKPs represent a crucial evolution. In fighting synthetic media, we often face a dilemma: prove your identity and risk impersonation, or remain anonymous and lack credibility. ZKPs offer a third way: prove what matters while protecting what's private.

THE RIGHT TO BE FORGOTTEN VS. IMMUTABLE TRUTH

Cryptographic systems create a troubling paradox: the same immutability that prevents synthetic media from rewriting history also prevents legitimate corrections, updates, or deletions. When your digital signature mathematically proves you said something, how do you unsay it? When blockchain records your actions forever, how do you move past mistakes?

This conflict crystallizes in the tension between the EU's "Right to Be Forgotten" and the cryptographic need for immutable records:

The Right to Be Forgotten (GDPR Article 17) grants EU citizens the right to have personal data erased under certain circumstances. People can request removal of inadequate, irrelevant, or excessive data. Search engines must delist certain results. Companies must delete data no longer needed [6].

Cryptographic Immutability requires that signed statements can't be altered without detection. Blockchain records can't be changed without breaking the chain. Mathematical proofs remain valid forever. Trust depends on permanence.

Real cases illustrate the conflict with traditional digital records, while blockchain scenarios remain largely hypothetical:

. . .

A Spanish lawyer successfully petitioned Google to remove links to a 1998 newspaper article about a foreclosure on his home. But if that article had been cryptographically signed and blockchain-recorded, no court order could make the mathematics forget.

[The following are hypothetical scenarios illustrating potential future conflicts]

Imagine a German executive whose youthful indiscretions, long forgotten, resurface when blockchain researchers find cryptographically signed posts from a defunct forum. The signatures would prove authenticity beyond doubt. No amount of personal growth could revoke a mathematical proof.

Consider a French activist whose past political positions, evolved through experience, remain cryptographically attributed forever. Opponents could weaponize immutable proof of positions she no longer holds. The blockchain wouldn't believe in redemption.

While these blockchain-specific cases haven't occurred yet due to limited adoption, they illustrate the coming tension between immutable records and human need for forgiveness.

Various technical proposals attempt reconciliation:

Redactable Signatures allow specific parts of signed documents to be removed while maintaining overall integrity. You could prove a document is authentic while hiding sensitive sections. Research continues but practical implementation remains limited.

Expiring Proofs include time limits in cryptographic systems. A signature might only be valid for five years, after which it can't be verified. But this undermines the historical record and enables future synthetic media to fill gaps.

Decentralized Deletion requires multiple parties to agree on removing records. Perhaps 80% of blockchain nodes could vote to exclude certain data. But this reintroduces human judgment into mathematical systems.

Encryption Overlays keep data on blockchain but encrypted, with keys that can be destroyed. The record exists but becomes unreadable. Yet encrypted data often gets decrypted eventually as technology advances.

The deeper issue is philosophical: should perfect memory be a feature or a bug? Arguments rage on both sides:

For Immutability: In an era of synthetic media, the ability to prove what really happened becomes precious. Historical revisionism becomes impossible. Accountability increases. Truth has mathematical backing.

For Forgetting: Humans need the ability to grow, change, and move past mistakes. Perfect memory enables perfect harassment. Minor infractions haunt forever. Redemption becomes impossible.

Different cultures lean different ways. American tech culture often favors transparency and permanence. European philosophy emphasizes privacy and redemption. Asian contexts balance collective memory with individual honor. No universal answer exists.

Perhaps the solution isn't technical but social. We may need new norms for how we treat immutable records:

- Statute of limitations on holding people to past positions
- Context requirements for citing historical records
- Redemption narratives that acknowledge rather than hide past actions
- Collective agreement to value growth over consistency

The cryptographic foundation offers powerful tools against synthetic media, but those tools come with consequences. In building systems that can't be faked, we risk building prisons of permanent truth. The challenge isn't just mathematical but deeply human: how do we balance the need for verifiable truth with the need for human forgiveness?

∼

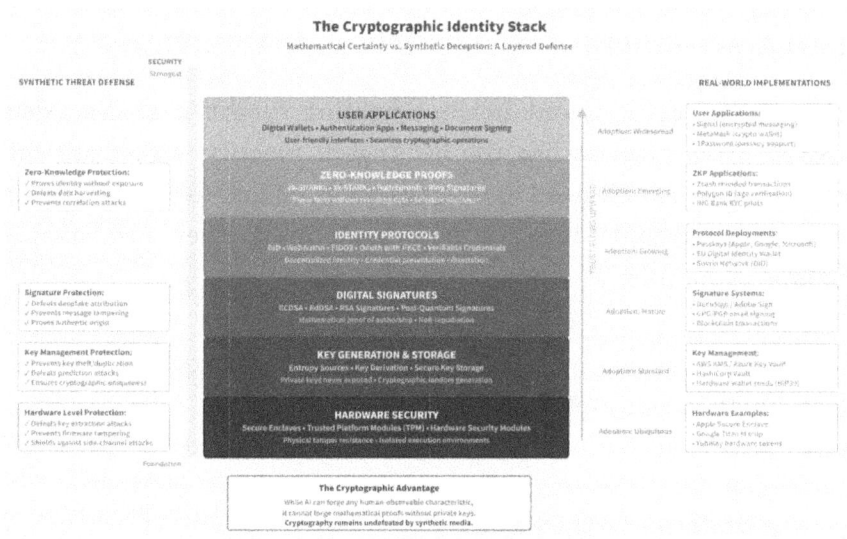

Figure 9.1: *The Cryptographic Identity Stack: Building Unforgeable Trust from Silicon to Software.* This architectural diagram illustrates the six-layer defense system that transforms mathematical certainty into practical identity verification, creating an impenetrable barrier against synthetic media attacks. Starting from the silicon foundation of hardware security modules that physically protect cryptographic secrets, each ascending layer adds sophisticated capabilities while maintaining mathematical rigor. The stack progresses through secure key generation (preventing key prediction or theft), digital signatures (providing non-repudiable proof of authorship), identity protocols (enabling decentralized verification), zero-knowledge proofs (proving facts without revealing data), to user-facing applications that hide this complexity behind intuitive interfaces. Critical to understanding this architecture is that trust flows upward—each layer depends on the security of layers beneath it, creating a chain of mathematical proofs that AI cannot forge without access to private keys. The left annotations reveal how each layer specifically defeats synthetic threats: while deepfakes can mimic faces and voices, they cannot produce valid cryptographic signatures; while AI can generate convincing documents, it cannot create the mathematical proofs required by zero-knowledge protocols. Real-world implementations on the right demonstrate this isn't theoretical—from Apple's Secure Enclave to the EU's Digital Identity Wallet, this stack is actively defending against synthetic deception. The fundamental insight: in an age where AI can forge any human-perceptible signal, only cryptographic proof remains unforgeable.

TAKEAWAY: BUILDING YOUR CRYPTOGRAPHIC IDENTITY

The cryptographic foundation for fighting synthetic media exists today. While systems like the EU Digital Identity Wallet are still emerging, you don't need to wait for governments to begin building your cryptographic identity. The tools exist; they just require conscious adoption.

Start building your cryptographic foundation:

1. **Understand the Basics**
   - Learn what public/private key pairs are (you don't need the math, just the concept)
   - Understand digital signatures vs. encryption
   - Grasp why mathematical proof differs from physical evidence
   - Recognize the permanence of cryptographic actions

2. **Acquire Cryptographic Tools**
   - Get a hardware security key (YubiKey, Titan, or similar)
   - Set up Signal or another end-to-end encrypted messenger
   - Create a PGP key pair for email (even if you rarely use it)
   - Explore password managers that support cryptographic features

3. **Practice Cryptographic Habits**
    - Digitally sign important emails and documents
    - Verify signatures on communications you receive
    - Use encrypted channels for sensitive conversations
    - Create timestamped proofs of important events

4. **Build Your Cryptographic Network**
    - Exchange public keys with trusted contacts
    - Establish verification protocols using cryptographic signatures
    - Create key-signing relationships with colleagues
    - Practice using these tools before you need them

5. **Prepare for Key Management**
    - Create secure backups of your private keys
    - Establish recovery mechanisms with trusted contacts
    - Document your cryptographic identities
    - Plan for key rotation and updates

6. **Advocate for Cryptographic Infrastructure**
    - Support services that implement strong cryptographic identity
    - Request cryptographic verification from institutions you use
    - Educate others about the importance of mathematical identity
    - Push for user-friendly implementations

. . .

7. **Balance Security with Humanity**
    - Remember that cryptography enables trust, not replaces it
    - Use mathematical tools to enhance human relationships
    - Don't let perfect security prevent genuine connection
    - Focus on verification that empowers rather than imprisons

The cryptographic foundation isn't about becoming a cypherpunk or cryptocurrency enthusiast. It's about recognizing that in an age where biology can be copied, mathematics offers certainty. Your face can be deepfaked, your voice can be cloned, but your private key remains yours alone.

WHAT'S NEXT

Cryptography provides the mathematical foundation for digital trust, but mathematics alone isn't enough. We need hardware we can trust to store our keys, execute our cryptographic operations, and attest to what's real. In Chapter 10, "Hardware Roots of Trust," we'll explore how physical devices become anchors of certainty in an ocean of synthetic deception. From secure enclaves in your smartphone to supply chain security for critical infrastructure, we'll examine why the atoms beneath the bits might be our last line of defense.

In the end, all digital trust must root itself in physical reality. The question is: can we trust the hardware that holds our trust?

CHAPTER 10
Hardware Roots of Trust

THE IPHONE THAT SAVED A DISSIDENT'S LIFE

[BASED ON REPORTS of secure enclave protection of dissidents and journalists, with specific details fictionalized for security reasons]

The knock came at 3 AM. Maria Volkov, a journalist documenting corruption in her Eastern European homeland, had been expecting it for weeks. As uniformed officers flooded her apartment, she clutched her iPhone, knowing that everything—her sources, her evidence, years of investigation—lived behind its locked screen.

"The passcode. Now," the lead officer demanded.

Maria's hands trembled as she entered six digits. The phone unlocked, displaying her home screen. The officers smiled, thinking they had won.

But Maria had entered her duress code—a secondary PIN that unlocked a sanitized version of her phone, showing only innocuous apps and photos. Her real data remained sealed in the phone's secure enclave, protected by her true passcode that she would never reveal.

The officers spent hours combing through the decoy data, finding nothing. No encrypted files, no secure messaging apps, no contacts that matched their intelligence. Just photos of meals, casual texts with friends, and innocuous note-taking apps.

"This is too clean," the lead officer muttered. "She's a journalist investigating us for three years and her phone has nothing? Try the forensic tools."

They connected the phone to specialized hardware, attempting to bypass the security and access hidden partitions or recovered data. Each attempt failed. The secure enclave—a separate processor within the iPhone designed specifically to protect sensitive information—refused every unauthorized access attempt. After each failed forensic attempt, the delays between allowed attempts grew longer: 1 minute, 5 minutes, 15 minutes, then an hour.

"Perhaps we need to be more... persuasive," one officer suggested, looking meaningfully at Maria.

But even under duress, Maria knew that entering incorrect codes too many times would trigger the phone's erase function. She had enabled this setting long ago—ten failed attempts would permanently destroy all data.

The secure enclave enforced these delays in hardware—no amount of threats could make the silicon circuits count faster.

Three days later, international pressure secured Maria's release. Her phone, showing "iPhone is disabled, try again in 47 minutes" from the officers' final attempts, still held its secrets. When the delay finally expired and she could enter her real passcode in the safety of a friendly embassy, her data was intact—every document, every source, every piece of evidence preserved. The hardware delays had frustrated the officers but protected her data.

"They had my body, they had my device, they had computational power," Maria would later reflect. "But they couldn't have my data because it wasn't protected by software alone. It was protected by physics—by a chip that would rather destroy itself than betray its secrets."

Maria's story illustrates a profound truth about digital security in the synthetic age: when everything can be faked, copied, or compromised, we need anchors of trust rooted in physical reality. Software can be modified, algorithms can be reversed, but properly designed hardware creates mathematical certainty backed by the laws of physics.

∼

WHY HARDWARE MATTERS WHEN EVERYTHING ELSE CAN BE FAKED

In previous chapters, we explored how cryptography provides mathematical foundations for trust. But cryptography alone isn't enough. Every cryptographic operation—every signature, every verification, every proof—must eventually execute on physical hardware. If that hardware is compromised, the beautiful mathematics becomes meaningless.

Consider the chain of trust in any digital system:

- Your private key provides mathematical proof of identity
- Software uses that key to create signatures
- The operating system manages the software
- The processor executes the operations
- The hardware stores and protects everything

Break any link in this chain, and security collapses. But while software can be silently modified and processors can be instructed to lie, properly designed security hardware creates what engineers call a "root of trust"—a foundation that remains trustworthy even when everything built on top of it is compromised.

This isn't theoretical. Modern devices contain specialized security hardware:

Secure Enclaves create isolated environments within processors where sensitive operations occur. Apple's Secure Enclave, Google's Titan chip, and Microsoft's Pluton processor provide hardware-isolated spaces that the main operating system cannot access.

Trusted Platform Modules (TPMs) provide dedicated chips for cryptographic operations. These modules generate and store encryption keys, verify system integrity, and ensure that devices boot only authorized software.

Hardware Security Modules (HSMs) offer bank-grade security for the most sensitive operations. These devices, some costing hundreds of thousands of dollars, protect the cryptographic keys that secure financial systems, government communications, and critical infrastructure.

Secure Elements in credit cards, passports, and phones create tamper-resistant environments for payment and identity applications. These chips physically destroy themselves if someone attempts to extract their secrets.

But hardware security faces a unique challenge in the synthetic age: unlike software that can be updated when vulnerabilities are discovered, hardware is permanent. A flaw in silicon can't be patched—it requires physical replacement. This permanence is both hardware's greatest strength and its most dangerous weakness.

SECURE ENCLAVES: YOUR PERSONAL FORT KNOX

Inside your smartphone lies a processor within a processor—a secure enclave that operates independently from the main system. This isn't just another chip; it's a digital Fort Knox designed to protect your most sensitive information even if everything else is compromised.

Understanding how secure enclaves work reveals why hardware security differs fundamentally from software protection:

. . .

Physical Isolation: The secure enclave has its own processor, memory, and storage, physically separated from the main system. Even if malware completely compromises your operating system, it cannot access the enclave. The separation isn't enforced by software policies that can be violated—it's enforced by the actual physical architecture of the chip.

Encrypted Memory: Everything in the enclave's memory is encrypted with keys that exist only within the hardware. If someone were to physically remove the memory chip and examine it with an electron microscope, they would see only random noise. The decryption happens within the secure processor itself, nowhere else.

Anti-Tampering Mechanisms: Secure enclaves contain sensors that detect physical intrusion attempts. Temperature sensors notice if someone tries to freeze the chip to slow down its protective mechanisms. Voltage monitors detect power glitching attacks. Light sensors can even detect if someone has decapped the chip to examine it. When tampering is detected, the enclave destroys its cryptographic keys, rendering the protected data permanently inaccessible.

Rate Limiting in Silicon: Unlike software that can be modified to remove delay loops, secure enclaves implement rate limiting in hardware. After a few incorrect passcode attempts, the hardware itself enforces delays. This isn't a software timer that can be bypassed—it's built into the silicon. This makes brute force attacks impractical even with unlimited computational power.

. . .

Real-world applications demonstrate the power of secure enclaves:

Biometric Protection: When you use Face ID or Touch ID, your biometric data never leaves the secure enclave. The main processor sends an image to the enclave, which compares it to stored biometric templates and returns only a yes/no answer. Even if malware compromises your phone, it cannot steal your fingerprint or face data—that information exists only within the physically isolated enclave.

Payment Security: When you tap to pay, the secure enclave generates a unique transaction code without ever revealing your actual credit card number to the merchant or even to the main processor. The payment credentials remain locked in hardware, safe from even the most sophisticated malware.

Key Management: The secure enclave generates and stores the cryptographic keys that protect your data. These keys never exist in readable form outside the hardware. When you back up your phone, you're not backing up the keys themselves—you're backing up data encrypted with those keys. Without the physical hardware (or its authorized successor), the backups are mathematical noise.

But secure enclaves aren't invulnerable:

Supply Chain Attacks: If someone compromises the manufacturing process, they could insert backdoors directly into the silicon. This is why major technology companies maintain strict control over their chip design and manufacturing partnerships.

Implementation Flaws: While the concept is sound, implementation mistakes can create vulnerabilities. Researchers have found flaws in various secure enclave implementations, though exploiting them typically requires physical access to the device and sophisticated equipment.

Key Extraction Attacks: Advanced laboratories with million-dollar equipment can sometimes extract keys from secure hardware using techniques like differential power analysis or electromagnetic emanation analysis. However, these attacks require physical possession of the device and expertise beyond most adversaries.

The lesson is clear: secure enclaves provide formidable protection, but they're not magical. They're one layer in a comprehensive security strategy—albeit a crucial layer that provides a hardware root of trust for everything else.

ATTESTATION: PROVING YOUR HARDWARE HASN'T BEEN COMPROMISED

Having secure hardware is only half the battle. You also need to prove to others that your hardware is genuine and hasn't been compromised. This is where attestation comes in—the ability for hardware to cryptographically prove its identity and integrity.

Attestation works like a tamper-evident seal for the digital age:

Boot Attestation: When a device starts up, each stage of the boot process measures the next stage before executing it. The secure hardware records these measurements, creating a cryptographic chain that proves exactly what software is running. If malware modifies any part of the system, the measurements change, and attestation fails.

Runtime Attestation: Modern systems can continuously attest to their integrity while running. The secure hardware periodically measures critical system components and can prove to remote servers that the device remains uncompromised. This enables "conditional access"—servers can refuse to communicate with devices that fail attestation.

Remote Attestation: Perhaps most powerfully, devices can prove their integrity to remote parties without revealing sensitive information. A phone can prove to a bank that it's running unmodified software without telling the bank anything else about the device. This enables trust without surveillance.

Real-world attestation in action:

Streaming Services use attestation to ensure content is only played on devices with proper content protection. Netflix won't stream 4K content to devices that fail attestation, preventing high-quality piracy.

Corporate Networks require attestation before granting access to sensitive resources. A laptop must prove it's running approved software with all security patches before connecting to company servers.

Financial Services increasingly require attestation for high-value transactions. Your phone must prove it hasn't been jailbroken before authorizing large transfers, reducing fraud from compromised devices.

Government Systems use attestation to ensure classified information only flows between verified, uncompromised devices. Attestation failure immediately cuts off access to sensitive networks.

But attestation creates new tensions:

Privacy vs. Security: Attestation can reveal information about your device and software configuration. While necessary for security, this metadata can be used for tracking or discrimination. Someone running Linux might be denied service simply because their system attestation looks different from mainstream devices.

User Freedom vs. Protection: Attestation can prevent users from modifying their own devices. While this protects against malware, it also restricts legitimate activities like installing custom operating systems or repairing devices with third-party parts.

Vendor Lock-in: When only certain hardware can successfully attest, it creates monopoly power. If only devices from major manufacturers can access essential services, smaller innovators are excluded from the market.

Attestation Bypass: Sophisticated attackers work constantly to fake attestation. From hardware emulators to replay attacks, the cat-and-mouse game continues. Perfect attestation remains elusive.

The challenge is balancing these tensions while maintaining security. We need attestation to fight synthetic media and compromised devices, but implemented carelessly, it could create a dystopian future where a few companies control what software everyone can run.

SUPPLY CHAIN SECURITY: TRUSTING THE SILICON

[Based on publicly reported supply chain security incidents and industry practices]

In 2018, Bloomberg Businessweek reported that tiny chips, no bigger than a grain of rice, had been secretly inserted into server motherboards during manufacturing. These chips allegedly provided backdoor access to any system using the compromised hardware. While the specific details were disputed by the companies involved, the report highlighted a terrifying reality: if you can't trust your hardware's origins, you can't trust your hardware [1].

The global nature of modern electronics manufacturing creates countless opportunities for compromise:

. . .

Design Complexity: Modern processors contain billions of transistors. Reviewing every circuit for backdoors is practically impossible. A few modified gates among billions could create vulnerabilities invisible to inspection.

Manufacturing Opacity: Chips are fabricated in facilities around the world, often in countries with different security priorities. The same facility might manufacture chips for consumer devices and military systems, creating opportunities for targeted insertion of vulnerabilities.

Component Sourcing: A single device contains components from dozens of suppliers. Each component—from memory chips to power regulators—could harbor malicious modifications. The phone in your pocket contains parts from hundreds of companies across dozens of countries.

Firmware Mysteries: Much hardware includes firmware—low-level software burned into chips. This firmware often remains proprietary and unexamined. Malicious firmware can survive operating system reinstalls and even hardware replacement if the same compromised components are used.

Industry responses to supply chain threats include:

Trusted Foundries: Governments maintain specialized chip fabrication facilities with strict security controls. The U.S. Department of Defense's Trusted Foundry program ensures critical military chips are manufactured in secure facilities by cleared personnel.

. . .

Supply Chain Verification: Major technology companies implement extensive verification programs. Apple, for example, reportedly sends employees to live near key suppliers, monitoring production and checking for unauthorized modifications.

Hardware Fingerprinting: Techniques like Physical Unclonable Functions (PUFs) create unique identifiers from tiny manufacturing variations in each chip. These fingerprints can detect if hardware has been swapped or modified.

Secure Boot Chains: Modern devices verify each component during startup, ensuring only authorized hardware and firmware execute. This creates a chain of trust from the first instruction executed to the final running system.

But challenges persist:

Economic Pressure: Secure supply chains cost more than standard manufacturing. Companies face constant pressure to reduce costs, which often means accepting greater supply chain risk.

Geopolitical Complexity: Technology supply chains span the globe, crossing multiple jurisdictions with different laws, priorities, and threat models. A secure supply chain in one country might be legally required to include backdoors in another.

. . .

Verification Limits: While chip designers have strong incentives to protect their intellectual property and reputation, verifying the integrity of manufactured chips remains challenging. The primary risks come from:

- **EDA Tool Compromise:** Electronic Design Automation software used to design chips could insert malicious circuits. If the tools themselves are compromised, every chip designed with them inherits vulnerabilities.
- **Manufacturing Insertion:** When designs are sent to third-party foundries, especially in different jurisdictions, modifications could be inserted during fabrication.
- **IP Block Vulnerabilities:** Modern chips incorporate intellectual property blocks from multiple vendors. A compromised IP vendor could affect every chip using their components.
- **Post-Manufacturing Supply Chain:** Chips can be modified or replaced entirely during packaging, distribution, or integration into final products.

The complexity of modern chips—billions of transistors implementing designs from dozens of companies—makes comprehensive verification nearly impossible, even when the primary designer has every incentive to ensure security.

Firmware Vulnerabilities: Much hardware includes updatable firmware—low-level software that controls how the hardware operates. These update mechanisms, designed to fix bugs and add features, can be exploited to change device behavior after initial verification. A network card's firmware update could add backdoor capabilities. A hard drive's firmware could be modified to hide malicious data. Even security chips designed to protect against tampering often have firmware that can be updated, creating a potential vulnerability in the very components meant to provide protection.

The reality is sobering: absolute supply chain security remains impossible. Instead, we must build systems that remain secure even with potentially compromised components. This means defense in depth, continuous verification, and designing systems that limit the damage any single compromised component can cause.

PHYSICAL SECURITY IN A VIRTUAL WORLD

As our lives become increasingly digital, it's tempting to think physical security matters less. The opposite is true. When synthetic media can fake any digital communication, physical security becomes the ultimate arbiter of truth.

Consider these scenarios where physical security determines digital outcomes:

Key Ceremony Security: When organizations generate critical cryptographic keys—the kind that protect millions of users or billions of dollars—they conduct elaborate "key ceremonies." Participants gather in secure facilities, often underground vaults with Faraday cages to prevent electromagnetic spying. Multiple people must cooperate to generate keys, ensuring no single person has complete control. Hardware security modules generate the actual keys, with the process recorded and witnessed. These ceremonies recognize a fundamental truth: the most important digital security events require physical security.

. . .

Data Center Physical Security: The cloud isn't actually in the clouds—it runs on physical servers in physical buildings. These facilities employ extreme physical security: biometric access controls, 24/7 armed guards, mantrap entries that prevent tailgating, and even protection against electromagnetic emanation that could leak data. Some facilities are built to withstand natural disasters and military attacks. When you store data in the cloud, you're trusting not just encryption but the physical security of actual buildings.

Side-Channel Attacks: The intersection of physical and digital security creates unexpected vulnerabilities. Researchers have extracted cryptographic keys by:

- Analyzing the sound of capacitors during computation
- Measuring power consumption patterns
- Detecting electromagnetic emanations
- Using radio waves to read RAM contents
- Exploiting LED blinking patterns on devices

These attacks remind us that information exists in physical form—as electrical charges, magnetic fields, and energy consumption—not just abstract bits.

Hardware Implants: The most sophisticated attacks bypass digital security entirely through physical means. Intelligence agencies have developed hardware implants that can be secretly installed in seconds. These devices can log keystrokes, capture screens, or provide remote access. The NSA's ANT (Advanced Network Technology) catalog, leaked by Edward Snowden, revealed dozens of such devices. Once physical access is achieved, most security guarantees evaporate.

Environmental Monitoring: Secure facilities monitor not just digital intrusions but physical environment anomalies. Temperature changes might indicate someone using cooling spray to attack chips. Vibration sensors detect drilling attempts. Air pressure monitoring can detect doors opening. Even background radiation is monitored to detect certain types of sophisticated attacks.

The convergence of physical and digital security creates new paradigms:

Airgapped Systems: The most sensitive systems remain physically disconnected from networks. But even airgaps can be bridged—malware like Stuxnet proved that USB drives wielded by humans can compromise theoretically isolated systems. Some facilities now fill USB ports with epoxy to prevent their use.

Hardware Kill Switches: Some secure devices include physical switches that disconnect microphones, cameras, or network interfaces. These switches physically break circuits, providing assurance that no software compromise can enable surveillance.

Tamper-Evident Designs: Devices increasingly include physical features that show evidence of tampering. Special screws, holographic seals, and glitter nail polish patterns create unique identifiers that reveal if someone has opened a device.

Secure Rooms: Organizations build specialized rooms for sensitive operations. These spaces include sound dampening to prevent acoustic eavesdropping, electromagnetic shielding to prevent electronic surveillance, and visual barriers to prevent optical spying. Some even use vibrating windows to defeat laser microphones.

The lesson is clear: in fighting synthetic media and digital deception, we cannot ignore physical reality. Bits exist as atoms, processing happens in physical space, and security ultimately depends on controlling actual, tangible things.

WHEN ATOMS MEET BITS

The future of hardware security lies not in choosing between physical and digital protection, but in their seamless integration. Emerging technologies blur the boundaries:

Quantum Random Number Generators: True randomness is essential for cryptography, but traditional computers can only generate pseudo-random numbers. Quantum devices harvest genuine randomness from quantum mechanical processes—the fundamental uncertainty of the universe made useful for security.

DNA Storage and Security: Researchers are developing systems that store data in synthetic DNA, creating storage dense enough to hold the entire internet in a shoebox. But DNA also offers unique security properties—self-destructing sequences that erase data after a certain time, or DNA "locks" that only open with the right molecular keys.

. . .

Neuromorphic Security: Computer chips that mimic brain structures could create security systems that learn and adapt like biological immune systems. These devices would recognize attacks not through programmed rules but through learned patterns, potentially defending against threats their designers never imagined.

Molecular Computing: Computation using individual molecules could create security devices too small to detect or tamper with. Imagine cryptographic operations happening at the molecular level, where the physics of molecular bonds provides the security guarantees.

But these advances bring new challenges:

Quantum Threats: The same quantum mechanics that enables better random numbers also threatens current encryption. Quantum computers will eventually break RSA and other widely-used algorithms. The race is on to develop "post-quantum" cryptography before quantum computers become practical for cryptanalysis.

Biological Risks: As security systems become more biological, they inherit biological vulnerabilities. DNA can mutate, biological systems can be infected, and evolution doesn't always produce the outcomes we desire.

Nano-scale Attacks: As security devices shrink, so do attack tools.

Researchers have demonstrated nano-scale robots that could potentially infiltrate and compromise molecular-scale security systems.

Hybrid Threats: The convergence of physical and digital creates new attack surfaces. Synthetic biology could produce organisms that compromise electronic devices. Conversely, compromised electronics could disrupt biological security systems.

∽

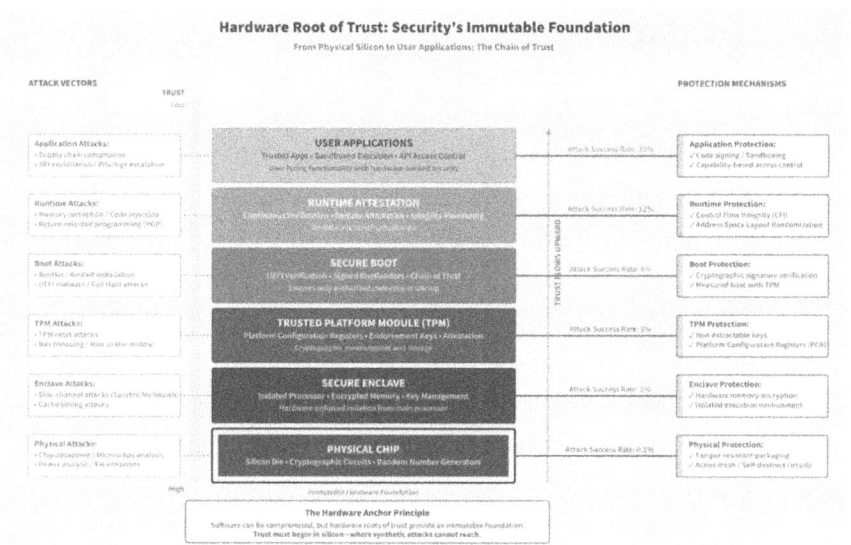

Figure 10.1: *The Hardware Trust Stack: Building Unbreakable Security from Silicon Up.* This architectural diagram illustrates the six-layer hardware security model that creates an immutable foundation for digital trust, impervious to synthetic media attacks. Starting from the physical chip—where cryptographic circuits are etched in silicon—each ascending layer adds sophisticated security capabilities while maintaining hardware-enforced guarantees. The stack shows how trust flows upward: the physical chip (0.1% attack success rate) provides entropy and cryptographic primitives; the secure enclave (1% success) isolates critical operations; the TPM (3% success) measures and attests system state; secure boot (8% success) ensures only authorized code runs; runtime attestation (12% success) continuously verifies integrity; and finally user applications (23% success) deliver functionality. Critical to this architecture is that each layer's security depends on all layers beneath it—compromise becomes exponentially harder as attackers must defeat multiple hardware-enforced barriers. The left annotations reveal attack vectors at each level, from physical chip decapping to application-level exploits, while the right shows corresponding defenses like tamper-resistant packaging and hardware memory encryption. The fundamental insight: while AI can generate perfect deepfakes and synthetic content, it cannot forge the cryptographic proofs generated by hardware security modules, cannot extract keys from secure enclaves, and cannot bypass the physical laws that govern silicon. In an age where software alone cannot be trusted, hardware roots of trust provide the unshakeable foundation upon which all digital security must be built.

TAKEAWAY: YOUR HARDWARE SECURITY CHECKLIST

Hardware security might seem like something only governments and corporations need to worry about, but the ubiquity of synthetic media makes it personal. Every device you own is either an anchor of trust or a vulnerability. Here's how to improve your hardware security:

1. **Know Your Hardware**
    - Document what devices you own and their security features
    - Understand which devices have secure enclaves or TPMs
    - Research the supply chain for critical devices
    - Keep records of hardware serial numbers and attestation certificates

2. **Physical Security Basics**
    - Use strong device passwords (weak passwords limit hardware security effectiveness)
    - Enable biometric authentication where available
    - Never leave devices unattended in public spaces
    - Use privacy screens to prevent visual eavesdropping
    - Consider camera covers for devices in sensitive locations

3. **Supply Chain Awareness**
    - Buy devices from reputable sources with verified supply chains

- Be suspicious of unusually cheap hardware
- Verify authenticity using manufacturer tools
- Avoid used devices for sensitive applications
- Check for signs of tampering on new devices

4. **Leverage Hardware Security Features**
    - Enable secure boot on all devices
    - Use TPM-backed encryption for sensitive data
    - Configure devices to require attestation
    - Enable remote wipe capabilities
    - Use hardware tokens for critical authentication

5. **Environmental Security**
    - Be aware of your physical surroundings during sensitive operations
    - Use Faraday bags for devices when traveling to sensitive locations
    - Consider dedicated devices for high-security applications
    - Implement physical security for home offices
    - Use hardware kill switches when available

6. **Prepare for Compromise**
    - Plan for device loss or theft
    - Implement remote wipe procedures
    - Keep secure backups of critical data
    - Have spare hardware tokens
    - Document recovery procedures

. . .

7. **Stay Informed**
    - Follow security researchers who focus on hardware
    - Understand emerging threats to your devices
    - Learn about new protective technologies
    - Participate in responsible disclosure if you find vulnerabilities
    - Share knowledge with your community

Remember: hardware security isn't about paranoia—it's about creating reliable anchors of trust in an increasingly unreliable digital world. When synthetic media can fake any communication, the physical devices we control become our lifelines to authentic interaction.

WHAT'S NEXT

Hardware provides the physical foundation for digital trust, but one device alone isn't enough. We need systems that verify not just individual components but entire chains of authenticity. In Chapter 11, "The Verification Infrastructure," we'll explore how decentralized identity, verifiable credentials, and certificate authorities create webs of trust that no single point of failure can break. From India's Aadhaar system to self-sovereign identity, we'll examine how verification scales from individual devices to global systems.

The hardware roots of trust are planted. Now we must grow them into forests of verification that can weather any storm of synthetic deception.

CHAPTER 11
THE VERIFICATION INFRASTRUCTURE

INDIA'S AADHAAR UNDER SIEGE

[FICTIONALIZED *scenario based on the real Aadhaar system vulnerabilities and documented security concerns*]

At 3:47 AM on a humid Mumbai morning in August 2025, Rajesh Patel discovered he no longer existed. The 42-year-old taxi driver had arrived at the hospital where his wife was in labor, only to be turned away. According to the Aadhaar database—India's biometric identity system covering 1.4 billion people—Rajesh Patel had died three months earlier in a road accident in Delhi, a city he'd never visited.

"But I'm standing right here," Rajesh pleaded with the hospital administrator, pressing his thumb repeatedly on the biometric scanner. The machine responded with the same message each time: "Identity Not Found - Death Certificate Issued 05-05-2025."

. . .

As dawn broke, Rajesh discovered the full extent of his digital death. His bank accounts were frozen. His mobile phone—linked to his Aadhaar—had been deactivated. His driving license, his taxi permit, even his children's school enrollments had been cancelled. In a nation where Aadhaar had become the key to virtually every service, Rajesh had become a ghost.

The attack, investigators would later determine, had been elegantly simple. Criminals had infiltrated not the central Aadhaar database—that remained secure—but a rural enrollment center in Rajasthan. Using a combination of insider access and synthetic biometrics similar to those used by the Karnataka gang, they had created a death certificate for Rajesh Patel, then immediately created a new "Rajesh Patel" with their synthetic fingerprints. The real Rajesh's biometrics were marked as belonging to a deceased person. The synthetic Rajesh had already taken out loans, purchased property, and disappeared.

The criminals had discovered something profound: you don't need to break into a fortress if you can corrupt the guards at the gate. The Aadhaar system itself remained cryptographically secure, its biometric matching algorithms uncompromised. But the human infrastructure around it—the enrollment centers, the update mechanisms, the integration points with other systems—had become attack vectors.

As Rajesh sat in the hospital waiting room, his wife in labor and unable to be admitted, he embodied a crisis facing identity systems worldwide. When verification infrastructure becomes the foundation of daily life, its failure doesn't just inconvenience—it erases. When synthetic identities can be more "real" than actual humans in the eyes of the system, we face questions that go beyond technology to the very nature of existence in a digital society.

. . .

"I can prove I'm alive," Rajesh told anyone who would listen, spreading his arms wide. "I'm breathing, I'm talking, I'm here. But the computer says I'm dead, so I'm dead."

It would take six months, multiple court hearings, and the birth certificate of his daughter—delivered at home because hospital admission required Aadhaar verification that showed him as deceased—before Rajesh Patel would officially return to life. The synthetic Rajesh was never caught.

FROM INDIVIDUAL IDENTITY TO COLLECTIVE VERIFICATION

Rajesh's ordeal illustrates a fundamental challenge: individual identity, no matter how sophisticated its verification, exists within larger systems. A perfectly secure biometric means nothing if the infrastructure around it can be compromised. A cryptographically signed credential is worthless if the issuing authority can be impersonated. We need verification that works not just for individuals but for entire societies.

This chapter explores three evolving approaches to scaling verification:

Decentralized Identity seeks to give individuals control over their own identity data, removing single points of failure like the Aadhaar database. Instead of one organization holding everyone's identity, each person would hold their own, sharing only what's necessary for each interaction.

. . .

Verifiable Credentials create a standardized way for institutions to issue digital certificates—diplomas, licenses, attestations—that individuals can own and present without the issuer being involved in every verification. A university could issue a degree that you carry forever, that anyone can verify came from that university, without the university tracking where you present it.

Certificate Authorities already provide the trust infrastructure for the internet, verifying that websites are who they claim to be. This model is evolving to handle human identity, organizational credentials, and even content authenticity.

Each approach has promise, but also faces challenges in a world where synthetic media can impersonate not just individuals but entire institutions. How do you decentralize identity when synthetic versions of you might already exist? How do you verify credentials when the credentialing institutions themselves can be deepfaked? How do you trust certificate authorities when their verification processes can be socially engineered?

The answer lies not in any single technology but in creating interwoven webs of verification—systems that remain robust even when individual strands break.

SELF-SOVEREIGN IDENTITY: OWNING YOUR DIGITAL SELF

The vision of self-sovereign identity (SSI) is compelling: instead of governments and corporations owning your identity data, you own it. Instead of proving who you are by showing documents issued by others, you prove it through cryptographic keys only you control. Instead of leaving trails of personal information everywhere you interact, you reveal only what's necessary for each transaction.

In practice, SSI works through a combination of technologies:

Decentralized Identifiers (DIDs) create globally unique identifiers that you control. Unlike a social security number issued by government or an email address controlled by a provider, a DID is yours alone. It's like having a phone number that no company can take away, that works across all networks, that you can prove belongs to you through cryptography.

Digital Wallets store your identity information and credentials on your own devices. Just as a physical wallet holds your driver's license and credit cards, a digital wallet holds cryptographic proofs of your identity, qualifications, and rights. The crucial difference: these proofs can be verified without revealing the underlying data.

Blockchain Anchoring provides immutable records without central control. While your identity data stays in your wallet, hashes of important events—credential issuance, key rotations, revocations—get recorded on distributed ledgers. This creates audit trails that no single entity controls.

Early implementations show promise:

Estonia's e-Residency program offers a form of self-sovereign identity to global citizens. E-residents receive digital identities backed by the Estonian government but controlled by individuals. They can start companies, sign contracts, and access services without physically visiting Estonia. Over 100,000 people have become e-residents, conducting business through purely digital identity.

European Digital Identity Wallets (as discussed in Chapter 9) are bringing SSI principles to 450 million EU citizens. Early pilots in Spain and Germany show citizens appreciating the control—using their phones to prove age at bars without showing ID, to access government services without passwords, to sign contracts without physical presence.

Sovrin Network provides a public utility for self-sovereign identity, maintained by a global nonprofit. Organizations can issue credentials, individuals can hold them, and anyone can verify them—all without Sovrin itself seeing the transactions. It's like email protocols but for identity.

But challenges exist:

Key Management Nightmares: If you lose your cryptographic keys, you lose your identity. Unlike passwords that can be reset, cryptographic identity has no recovery mechanism unless you've prepared in advance. Stories emerge of early adopters locked out of their entire digital lives because they lost access to their wallets.

Adoption Chicken-and-Egg: SSI only works if many organizations accept it, but organizations wait for widespread adoption before investing in support. It's the same challenge that has slowed every identity innovation from credit cards to digital payments.

Synthetic Identity Threats: SSI assumes you can establish a legitimate identity to begin with. But what if synthetic versions of you have already claimed self-sovereign identities? The system that promises individual control might enable synthetic individuals to control identities that seem more legitimate than real people.

Technical Complexity: Despite efforts at user-friendly interfaces, SSI remains conceptually challenging. Asking average users to understand key management, credential schemas, and distributed systems may be unrealistic. We risk creating identity systems only the technically sophisticated can use.

The path forward requires balancing idealism with pragmatism. Pure self-sovereignty might be impossible in a world requiring collective verification, but the principles—user control, minimal disclosure, decentralized infrastructure—point toward more resilient identity systems.

VERIFIABLE CREDENTIALS: PROVING WITHOUT REVEALING

If self-sovereign identity is about who controls identity data, verifiable credentials (VCs) are about how that data gets shared and verified. The concept is simple but powerful: digital certificates that prove facts without revealing unnecessary information.

. . .

Traditional credentials work through exposure. To prove you're qualified to drive, you show your entire driver's license—revealing your name, address, birthdate, and photo. To prove you graduated from university, you present a diploma that includes your full name and degree details. Each verification leaves a trail of personal information.

Verifiable credentials flip this model:

Selective Disclosure lets you prove specific facts without revealing everything. A digital driver's license could prove you're authorized to drive without revealing your address. A university credential could confirm you have a computer science degree without showing your graduation year or GPA.

Cryptographic Verification ensures credentials can't be forged. Each VC is digitally signed by the issuer using cryptographic keys. Anyone can verify the signature without contacting the issuer, similar to how websites prove authenticity through SSL certificates.

Holder Control means individuals decide when and how to share credentials. Unlike transcript requests that go through universities or background checks that contact previous employers, VCs let individuals present their own credentials directly.

Privacy Preservation prevents tracking across uses. Advanced cryptographic techniques like zero-knowledge proofs can make each presentation of a credential unlinkable to previous uses, preventing surveillance of how you use your credentials.

. . .

Real-world implementations are beginning to emerge:

Digital Diplomas: MIT began issuing digital diplomas as a pilot program in 2017. Students can opt to receive blockchain-anchored credentials they can share with employers instantly. The employer can cryptographically verify the diploma came from MIT without MIT knowing about the verification. While still limited in adoption, it demonstrates the potential of verifiable credentials.

Healthcare Credentials: Healthcare workers received verifiable credentials during COVID-19 to prove vaccination status and qualifications across state lines. Instead of carrying paper cards easily forged, they had digital credentials that could be instantly verified at participating hospitals with the necessary verification systems.

Age Verification: As discussed in Chapter 9, companies like Google Wallet are implementing VCs for age verification. Users can prove they're over 18 or 21 without revealing their exact birthdate or other personal information.

But verifiable credentials face their own challenges:

Issuer Authenticity: VCs are only as trustworthy as their issuers. If a diploma is signed by "Harvard University," how do you know it's the real Harvard? This recursion problem—verifying the verifiers—remains partially unsolved.

. . .

Revocation Complexity: What happens when a credential needs to be revoked? If a doctor loses their medical license, how do you invalidate their previously issued credential without creating a central tracking system? Current solutions require trade-offs between privacy and revocation capabilities.

Synthetic Credential Factories: Just as the Karnataka gang created synthetic identities in official databases, sophisticated attackers might create synthetic institutions that issue "legitimate" credentials. A fake university with a professional website, synthetic faculty, and verifiable credentials might be indistinguishable from a real one.

Legal Framework Gaps: Most legal systems don't recognize digital credentials as equivalent to physical ones. A cryptographically signed digital passport might be more secure than a physical one, but border agents aren't equipped to verify it.

The promise of verifiable credentials—proving exactly what's necessary and nothing more—aligns perfectly with Zero Trust principles. But realizing this promise requires not just technical standards but institutional change, legal evolution, and social acceptance.

CERTIFICATE AUTHORITIES: THE TRUST ANCHORS WE LOVE TO HATE

Every time you see a padlock icon in your browser, you're trusting a certificate authority (CA). These organizations verify that websites are who they claim to be, issuing digital certificates that your browser checks. It's a system that secures trillions of dollars in online commerce—and one that's increasingly straining under the demands of the synthetic age.

The CA model offers important lessons for human identity verification:

Hierarchical Trust creates scalable verification. A handful of root CAs are trusted by browsers and operating systems. These can delegate trust to intermediate CAs, which can issue certificates to millions of websites. This hierarchy allows global-scale verification without every verifier knowing every website.

Auditable Processes ensure CAs follow rules. To remain trusted, CAs must undergo regular audits, follow strict procedures for verification, and maintain transparency logs. When CAs fail—as DigiNotar did in 2011—they're removed from trust stores, effectively destroying their business.

Automation at Scale enables real-time verification. Modern CAs can issue millions of certificates automatically, enabling the encrypted web we rely on. This automation makes HTTPS ubiquitous rather than exceptional.

Economic Incentives align security with business. CAs make money by being trustworthy. One significant breach destroys their entire business model. This creates strong incentives for security, though not always strong enough.

. . .

The CA model is evolving beyond websites:

Code Signing ensures software hasn't been tampered with. Developers sign their applications with certificates from CAs, allowing operating systems to verify authenticity before installation. This prevents malware from impersonating legitimate software.

Document Signing moves beyond simple signatures to verified identity. Adobe, DocuSign, and others use CA-issued certificates to create legally binding digital signatures that prove not just intent but identity.

IoT Device Identity extends certificates to billions of connected devices. Each smart thermostat, security camera, or industrial sensor can have its own certificate, enabling secure communication and preventing device impersonation.

Content Authenticity initiatives like the Coalition for Content Provenance and Authenticity (C2PA) use CA principles to verify media hasn't been manipulated. Photos and videos carry certificates linking them to their creation device and subsequent edits.

But the CA model faces challenges in the synthetic age:

Social Engineering Vulnerabilities: CAs verify identity through documents and procedures that can be faked. Attackers have obtained certificates for major websites through forged documents and impersonated phone calls.

. . .

Nation-State Compromise: Several CAs have been compromised by intelligence agencies seeking to spy on encrypted communications. When a CA is compromised, every certificate it issued becomes suspect.

Centralization Risks: The CA model creates single points of failure. If a major root CA were compromised, millions of websites would need new certificates. The hierarchical model that enables scale also concentrates risk.

Synthetic Entity Challenges: CAs are designed to verify that real-world entities match digital certificates. But what happens when the real-world entity is itself synthetic? A deepfake company with synthetic employees could potentially obtain legitimate certificates.

Despite these challenges, the CA model offers crucial lessons: the importance of economic incentives, the value of transparent processes, the necessity of revocation mechanisms, and the power of hierarchical trust. As we build verification infrastructure for human identity, we must learn from both the successes and failures of certificate authorities.

BUILDING RESILIENT VERIFICATION NETWORKS

The vulnerabilities exposed by Rajesh's digital death, the promises and pitfalls of self-sovereign identity, the evolution of verifiable credentials, and the lessons from certificate authorities all point toward a crucial insight: no single verification system can stand alone. We need interwoven networks of verification that remain resilient even when individual components fail.

Resilient verification networks share several characteristics:

Multiple Trust Paths: Just as the internet routes around damage, verification should work through multiple independent paths. If government identity systems fail, professional credentials should still work. If biometric systems are compromised, cryptographic proofs should provide alternatives.

Diverse Verification Methods: Combining what you know (passwords), what you have (devices), what you are (biometrics), and who vouches for you (social verification) creates defense in depth. Synthetic media might compromise one method but rarely all simultaneously.

Temporal Consistency: Building history over time that synthetic identities can't quickly replicate. A ten-year record of interactions, transactions, and relationships is harder to fake than a single credential.

Community Validation: Leveraging social connections for verification. Your identity isn't just what you claim but what your network affirms. This social proof resists individual compromise.

Graceful Degradation: When perfect verification isn't possible, systems should still function with appropriate limitations. Like

Rajesh's situation, total system failure is unacceptable. Provisional identity, limited access, and manual review provide alternatives to digital death.

Examples of resilient networks emerging:

India's DigiLocker supplements Aadhaar with document storage. Citizens can store digital versions of official documents—driver's licenses, education certificates, tax records—creating multiple verification paths. If biometric authentication fails, document-based verification provides backup.

European Cross-Border Services allow EU citizens to use their national digital identities across borders. A French digital ID works in Germany, creating redundancy. If one national system fails, citizens aren't completely locked out.

Professional Networks like LinkedIn enable peer verification. Colleagues vouch for skills, confirm employment, validate achievements. This social verification supplements official credentials with community consensus.

Blockchain Consortiums distribute trust across organizations. Multiple universities might jointly maintain a credential blockchain, preventing any single institution from being compromised. Distributed governance resists individual failure.

But building resilience faces obstacles:

. . .

Coordination Challenges: Different systems use incompatible standards, making interoperability difficult. Getting governments, corporations, and communities to coordinate requires overcoming technical, political, and economic barriers.

Privacy Trade-offs: Multiple verification paths can mean multiple places where personal data is exposed. Balancing resilience with privacy requires careful design and often accepting imperfect solutions.

Complexity Costs: Each additional verification method adds user friction and system complexity. The most secure system is useless if people can't or won't use it.

Inclusion Concerns: Multiple verification paths might exclude those who lack diverse forms of identity. The undocumented, unbanked, and disconnected face higher barriers in resilient systems.

The path forward requires accepting that perfect verification is impossible while building systems robust enough to function despite imperfection. Like the internet itself, verification infrastructure must be designed to expect and route around failure.

∽

The Verification Web: Distributed Trust Through Redundancy
Multiple Pathways to Identity—No Single Point of Failure

Figure 11.1: *The Verification Web: Building Resilient Identity Through Redundant Trust Pathways.* This network diagram illustrates how modern identity verification achieves resilience through interconnected redundancy rather than relying on any single "silver bullet" authentication method. At the center, user identity connects to six primary verification nodes—government ID (95% trust), professional credentials (85%), social connections (70%), blockchain records (99%), biometric data (60%), and financial history (90%)—each with different trust levels and verification speeds. These primary nodes interconnect with each other and with secondary verification methods (education, employment, medical, device attestation, location, and property records), creating a web of 24+ verification pathways. The critical insight demonstrated here is that when any single node fails—shown by the compromised biometric node example—multiple alternative paths remain viable for identity verification. This redundancy transforms vulnerability into resilience: while deepfakes might compromise biometric verification, and documents might be forged, and social connections might be manipulated, the probability of simultaneously compromising multiple independent verification pathways approaches zero. The varying line weights represent verification strength, showing how some connections (like government ID to user) provide strong attestation while others offer supplementary support. This web architecture embodies the Zero Trust principle that security comes not from perfect protection of any single point, but from the mathematical improbability of defeating multiple independent verification methods simultaneously. In the synthetic age, where any single factor can be forged, only the web itself remains trustworthy.

TAKEAWAY: BUILDING YOUR VERIFICATION WEB

The verification infrastructure of the future won't be a single system but an ecosystem of interconnected methods. While we wait for governments and institutions to build this infrastructure, individuals can begin creating their own verification webs:

1. **Diversify Your Identity Anchors**
     - Don't rely solely on government ID or any single system
     - Build identity across multiple platforms and institutions
     - Create redundancy in how you can prove who you are
     - Document your existence across different mediums

2. **Establish Verification Relationships**
     - Build reciprocal verification agreements with trusted contacts
     - Create professional networks that can vouch for your skills
     - Establish community connections that know you personally
     - Document these relationships while respecting privacy

3. **Create Temporal Proof**
     - Build long-term histories that are hard to fake quickly
     - Maintain consistent digital presence across years
     - Document important events with timestamps

- Create patterns that synthetic identities can't easily replicate

4. **Prepare for System Failures**
    - Keep physical backups of critical documents
    - Maintain alternative communication channels
    - Build manual verification procedures with key institutions
    - Know how to prove your identity if primary systems fail

5. **Practice Selective Disclosure**
    - Learn to share only necessary information
    - Use different identities for different contexts
    - Protect core identity documents from unnecessary exposure
    - Build habits of minimal disclosure

6. **Advocate for Better Infrastructure**
    - Support institutions implementing resilient verification
    - Demand interoperability between systems
    - Push for privacy-preserving methods
    - Participate in pilot programs and provide feedback

7. **Plan for Recovery**

- Document your identity across multiple systems
- Keep records of all credentials and their issuers
- Build relationships that can help restore compromised identity
- Know the procedures for correcting false records

Remember Rajesh's lesson: being right isn't enough when the system says you're wrong. Building resilient verification isn't paranoia—it's prudence in a world where digital death can be as devastating as physical death.

WHAT'S NEXT

Verification infrastructure provides the foundation for trust, but trust ultimately requires truth. In Chapter 12, "Content Authenticity at Scale," we'll explore how the same principles that verify human identity can verify the content we create and consume. From cryptographic media attribution to blockchain provenance tracking, from the C2PA initiative to the limits of technical verification, we'll examine the battle to maintain truth in an ocean of synthetic content.

The infrastructure for verifying who we are is emerging. Now we must build infrastructure for verifying what is real.

CHAPTER 12

CONTENT AUTHENTICITY AT SCALE

THE OLYMPICS THAT ALMOST WASN'T

[FICTIONALIZED *scenario based on real C2PA deployment at major sporting events and content authentication initiatives*]

July 26, 2024, Paris. As the Olympic flame was lit at the opening ceremony, a different kind of fire was spreading across social media. A video, seemingly captured by a spectator's phone, showed French President Emmanuel Macron backstage making inflammatory remarks about African athletes, suggesting they shouldn't compete alongside "real" Olympians. Within minutes, the clip had been shared 2.3 million times.

The video was technically flawless. Macron's face, his distinctive speaking style, even the subtle reflection of Olympic branding in his eyes—every detail convinced viewers they were witnessing a career-ending scandal. Protests erupted outside the Stade de France. Several African nations threatened to withdraw from the games. The carefully orchestrated symbol of global unity was fracturing in real-time.

But something unprecedented happened. Within 47 minutes of the video's first appearance, major platforms began labeling it with a simple message: "No authenticated source - Content lacks C2PA verification." The Coalition for Content Provenance and Authenticity (C2PA), a technical standard that had been quietly integrated into cameras, editing software, and social platforms over the previous two years, was having its first major test[1].

The legitimate media covering the Olympics had been using C2PA-enabled cameras that cryptographically signed every photo and video at the moment of capture. These signatures created an unbreakable chain of custody—from the camera sensor through any edits to final publication. The inflammatory Macron video had no such chain. It had appeared from nowhere, like a digital orphan, bearing none of the cryptographic DNA that authentic content carried.

France 24, the official broadcaster, quickly released footage from the same time period showing Macron in an entirely different location, meeting with Paralympic athletes. Their video carried complete C2PA provenance: captured on a Sony FX6 (serial number cryptographically verified), edited in Adobe Premiere (each edit logged and signed), published through their verified distribution system. The metadata was readable by anyone but tampering with it was mathematically impossible.

The synthetic video's virality collapsed as quickly as it had grown. Platforms that had integrated C2PA verification began automatically deprecating content without provenance. Not censoring it—users could *still view and share the video—but it carried persistent warnings and wouldn't appear in recommendation algorithms. The economic incentive for creating synthetic content evaporated when it couldn't achieve viral reach.*

Security experts analyzing the incident noted its significance: "We didn't stop the attack. We made it pointless. When authentic content has proof and synthetic content doesn't, the truth doesn't need to shout—it just needs to be verifiable."

The Paris Olympics proceeded without further major synthetic media incidents. But the event marked a turning point: the first time that cryptographic content authentication had protected a global event from synthetic media chaos. The infrastructure for proving what was real had finally begun to catch up with the technology for faking it.

∼

THE DEATH AND REBIRTH OF PHOTOGRAPHIC EVIDENCE

For over a century, photographs served as humanity's most trusted form of evidence. "The camera doesn't lie" wasn't just a saying—it was the foundation of modern journalism, criminal justice, and historical documentation. A photograph of atrocity could end a war. A picture of corruption could topple a government. Visual evidence was truth made tangible.

That trust died gradually, then suddenly.

. . .

The gradual death began with digital photography. Once images became pixels instead of chemical reactions, manipulation became easier. Photoshop, released in 1990, democratized image editing. By the 2000s, every magazine cover was retouched, every influencer perfected. We developed a healthy skepticism of commercial images while still trusting news photography and evidence photos.

The sudden death came with generative AI. When Midjourney, DALL-E, and Stable Diffusion made photorealistic image generation available to anyone with a text prompt, the last vestiges of photographic trust evaporated. By 2024, it became impossible to distinguish AI-generated images from real photographs without technical analysis—and even that was becoming unreliable as generation techniques improved.

The implications rippled through every institution that depended on visual evidence:

Journalism faced an existential crisis. How do you report on events when any image could be synthetic? News organizations began requiring multiple forms of corroboration, treating photographs like eyewitness testimony—useful but not definitive. The adage shifted from "seeing is believing" to "seeing is questioning."

Criminal Justice systems struggled with the admissibility of digital evidence. Defense attorneys successfully challenged photographic evidence by demonstrating how easily similar images could be generated. Some jurisdictions began requiring chain-of-custody documentation for digital evidence that rivaled procedures for physical evidence.

· · ·

Historical Documentation became contested terrain. Synthetic images of historical events that never happened began circulating, mixing with genuine archival footage. Future historians would face the challenge of determining which visual records from our era were authentic—a problem previous generations never imagined.

Insurance and Commerce adapted by requiring multiple forms of documentation. A photo of car damage was no longer sufficient for a claim; insurers demanded video walkarounds, timestamps, and location verification. Real estate listings began including cryptographic proofs that property photos were genuine.

But from this death came rebirth. The same technological advances that enabled perfect forgeries also enabled perfect authentication. Cryptographic signatures, blockchain provenance, and hardware-backed attestation began creating a new form of photographic evidence—not based on the assumed integrity of the medium, but on mathematical proof of authenticity.

CRYPTOGRAPHIC MEDIA ATTRIBUTION: EVERY PIXEL TELLS A STORY

The revolution in content authenticity began not in Silicon Valley but in Tokyo, where camera manufacturers faced a crisis. Professional photographers were seeing their work stolen, manipulated, and misattributed at unprecedented scale. AI systems trained on their images without permission. Synthetic variations of their style flooded the market. The value of authentic photography was collapsing.

· · ·

In response, the Japan Camera Industry Association proposed something radical: what if every camera cryptographically signed every image at the moment of capture? Not after, in software that could be hacked, but in the image sensor itself, using secure hardware that couldn't be compromised?

The technical implementation was elegant:

Hardware-Based Signing: Each camera contains a secure chip with unique cryptographic keys. When the shutter clicks, the chip immediately signs the raw sensor data before any processing. This signature includes the exact time, GPS location (if enabled), camera serial number, and a hash of the image data.

Immutable Metadata: Traditional EXIF data could be edited by any software. Cryptographic signatures can't be modified without invalidating them. Change a single pixel, adjust the timestamp, modify the location—the signature breaks, immediately revealing tampering.

Manufacturer Attribution: Camera makers maintain databases linking serial numbers to cryptographic certificates. Anyone can verify that an image came from a genuine Canon, Nikon, or Sony camera, not a software simulation.

Photographer Identity (optional): Professional cameras allow photographers to add their own cryptographic signatures alongside the camera's. This creates dual attribution—the hardware that captured it and the human who clicked the shutter.

. . .

Early adoption revealed both promise and challenges:

Wildlife Photography benefited immediately. Photographers documenting rare species could prove their images were genuine captures, not AI generations. Conservation organizations began requiring cryptographic proof for competition entries and scientific documentation.

Photojournalism embraced the technology as a defense against synthetic media attacks. When authoritarian regimes claimed embarrassing photos were "deepfakes," cryptographic signatures provided mathematical proof of authenticity.

Commercial Photography found new value propositions. Clients would pay premium prices for cryptographically authenticated content, knowing it couldn't be perfectly replicated by AI systems trained on stolen data.

But challenges emerged:

Legacy Content remained vulnerable. Billions of existing photos lacked cryptographic signatures. Bad actors could claim old authentic images were synthetic, or synthetic images were old authentic ones.

Privacy Concerns arose from immutable metadata. Photographers in sensitive situations worried that cryptographic signatures could reveal too much—exact locations, times, and patterns that might endanger sources.

Computational Overhead initially slowed camera performance. Early implementations added 500-1000ms to shot-to-shot time as cryptographic operations completed. Professional sports photographers complained about missing critical moments.

Key Management proved complex. If a camera's cryptographic keys were compromised, every image it had ever taken became suspect. Manufacturers implemented key rotation schemes, but this created backwards compatibility challenges.

Despite challenges, cryptographic media attribution began shifting the balance. For the first time since the advent of generative AI, authentic content had an advantage over synthetic. Real photographs carried proof of reality that no AI could forge.

THE C2PA INITIATIVE: BUILDING THE TRUTH NETWORK

The Coalition for Content Provenance and Authenticity (C2PA) emerges from an unlikely alliance. Adobe, traditionally associated with image manipulation through Photoshop, joins forces with Microsoft, Intel, the BBC, and others to create what they call a "nutrition label for digital content."

The premise is simple but revolutionary: just as food labels tell you what's in your meal, content labels should tell you where media came from and what happened to it. But unlike nutrition labels that can be faked, C2PA labels are cryptographically secured and technically tamper-evident.

The C2PA standard works through three core components:

Provenance Capture: Every device or software that creates or modifies content can add cryptographic assertions. A camera asserts "I captured this image." Photoshop asserts "I adjusted color and cropped." A news organization asserts "We verify this represents our reporting."

Manifest Stores: These assertions accumulate in a manifest—a cryptographically signed record of the content's history. Each modification adds to the manifest without erasing previous entries. The complete journey from creation to consumption becomes visible.

Trust Signals: Platforms and applications can read C2PA manifests and display appropriate trust indicators. A green checkmark might indicate complete provenance from a verified source. Yellow might indicate partial provenance. Red or no indicator suggests no verifiable origin.

Real-world deployment is showing early promise:

The Paris Olympics (as described in the opening) demonstrates C2PA's potential for protecting major events. When every credentialed photographer uses C2PA-enabled cameras, synthetic content becomes immediately distinguishable from authentic coverage.

. . .

News Organizations are beginning to adopt C2PA as standard practice. The BBC is embedding C2PA signing into their production pipeline. Reuters is requiring correspondents to use authenticated cameras. The Associated Press is making C2PA verification part of their fact-checking process.

Social Platforms face the challenge of verification at scale. X (formerly Twitter) is integrating C2PA checking, automatically labeling content with verified provenance. Meta is testing similar systems for Instagram and Facebook. TikTok is experimenting with creator verification programs.

Creative Industries are finding unexpected benefits. Musicians can prove original recordings. Artists can establish provenance for digital art. Film studios can track authorized vs. pirated content distribution.

But C2PA faces significant obstacles:

Adoption Chicken-and-Egg: Content creators won't adopt C2PA unless platforms reward verified content. Platforms won't invest in verification unless creators provide C2PA content. Early adopters bear costs without immediate benefits.

Computational Costs: Verifying C2PA signatures at social media scale requires significant processing power. A platform handling millions of uploads daily faces substantial infrastructure costs for comprehensive verification.

User Experience: How do you explain cryptographic provenance to average users? Early interfaces are too technical. Simplified versions lose important nuance. Finding the right balance remains challenging.

Malicious Compliance: Some bad actors are beginning to add C2PA signatures to synthetic content, truthfully asserting "Created with Midjourney" or "Generated by AI." While honest, this muddies the waters between authentic capture and synthetic generation.

Global Variations: Different jurisdictions have different requirements for content authentication. The EU pushes for mandatory provenance. The US favors voluntary adoption. China is developing its own standards. Fragmentation threatens interoperability.

Despite obstacles, C2PA represents humanity's most comprehensive attempt to create a global trust infrastructure for digital content. Not perfect, but a foundation to build upon.

THE LIMITS OF TECHNICAL VERIFICATION

As content authentication systems like C2PA begin deployment, early experiences reveal a sobering reality: technical verification alone cannot solve the synthetic media crisis. Perfect cryptographic proofs face imperfect human realities.

. . .

Consider the paradoxes that are emerging:

The Authentic Lie: A C2PA-verified photo can prove a camera captured an image at a specific time and place—but not what the image represents. Staged scenes, misleading angles, and selective framing can create "authentic" misinformation. Technical verification confirms the medium, not the message.

The Synthetic Truth: Conversely, AI-generated content can accurately represent reality. A synthetic recreation of a historical event might be more truthful than authentic but misleading footage. The absence of cryptographic provenance doesn't automatically mean falsehood.

The Context Problem: A verified image of a protest can be authentic but misrepresented. Was it the peak of action or a quiet moment? Were there ten protesters or ten thousand outside the frame? Provenance proves what, not why or how significant.

The Virality Gap: Synthetic content spreads faster than verification. By the time C2PA signatures are checked and warnings applied, millions may have already seen and shared unverified content. The truth limps behind the lie.

Early real-world deployments illustrate these limitations:

[Based on observed patterns in content verification systems]

. . .

The Warehouse Fire: A C2PA-verified photo shows Amazon workers fleeing a burning warehouse. The image is authentic—captured by a credentialed photographer, unedited, properly attributed. But investigation reveals it's a fire drill, not an emergency. Technical verification can't distinguish drill from disaster.

The Presidential Speech: A synthetic video of the US President announcing military action spreads faster than verification systems can flag it. Even after platforms label it as unverified, many viewers have already acted on the false information—calling loved ones, making financial decisions, sharing panic.

The Missing Context: During protests in Bangkok, C2PA-verified images show police restraining civilians. The photos are authentic but don't show the preceding violence that prompted the police response. Verification confirms the arrest, not the justification.

These limitations are leading to important realizations:

Technical + Human: Verification systems work best when combining cryptographic proofs with human judgment. C2PA can flag what needs human review, not replace human understanding.

Layers of Trust: Different contexts require different verification levels. A family photo needs less scrutiny than evidence in a criminal trial. One-size-fits-all verification creates unnecessary friction.

. . .

Education Essential: Users need to understand what verification does and doesn't prove. A C2PA checkmark means "this came from where it claims," not "this represents complete truth."

Ongoing Arms Race: As verification improves, so do attempts to game it. Attackers are beginning to create elaborate authentic-but-misleading content that passes technical checks while spreading disinformation.

The path forward requires humility. Technical verification is necessary but not sufficient. We need systems that enhance human judgment rather than replacing it.

MEDIA LITERACY FOR THE SYNTHETIC AGE

As technical verification systems proliferate, a parallel need emerges: teaching people how to navigate a world where both truth and lies come with certificates of authenticity. Media literacy, once focused on recognizing bias and checking sources, must evolve for an era of synthetic content and cryptographic proofs.

The new media literacy encompasses several skills:

Understanding Verification:

- What does a C2PA signature actually prove?
- How do cryptographic certificates work?
- What's the difference between "verified capture" and "verified truth"?
- Why might unverified content still be real?

Contextual Analysis:

- Looking beyond the frame of verified images
- Considering timing and selective presentation
- Understanding how authentic content can mislead
- Recognizing staged or manipulated scenarios

Synthetic Detection:

- Identifying common artifacts in AI-generated content
- Understanding the capabilities and limitations of generation tools
- Recognizing behavioral patterns of synthetic media campaigns
- Knowing when detection is impossible and verification essential

Emotional Intelligence:

- Recognizing content designed to provoke immediate reaction
- Understanding how synthetic media exploits cognitive biases
- Building pause between seeing and sharing
- Managing the anxiety of uncertain authenticity

Educational initiatives are emerging worldwide:

Finland's Approach: Building on their successful anti-disinformation programs, Finnish schools are integrating synthetic media literacy into curriculum starting in elementary school. Students learn to verify before believing, question even authenticated content, and understand the technology behind both creation and verification.

Taiwan's Success: Facing constant synthetic media attacks from across the strait, Taiwan is developing rapid-response literacy programs. Community centers offer workshops on verification tools. TV programming includes segments debunking synthetic content. The approach emphasizes collective defense over individual vigilance.

Corporate Training: Companies recognize that employees need synthetic media literacy for both security and decision-making. IBM is developing mandatory training on recognizing deepfake video calls. Banks are teaching staff to verify customer identity through multiple channels. Media companies are training journalists in forensic authentication.

Elder Outreach: Recognizing that older adults face unique vulnerabilities, AARP is launching "Real or Fake?" programs at senior centers. Using familiar contexts and patient explanation, they help seniors understand both the threats and the defenses available.

But challenges persist:

. . .

Pace of Change: Educational materials become outdated within months as technology advances. Teaching specific detection techniques is less effective than teaching principles and skepticism.

Complexity Barriers: Explaining cryptographic verification to general audiences proves difficult. Many people use verification tools without understanding them, creating false confidence.

Cultural Resistance: Some communities view media literacy efforts as attempts to control information or promote "official" narratives. Building trust in verification requires addressing these concerns.

Fatigue Factors: Constant vigilance exhausts people. Some retreat from digital media entirely rather than maintaining perpetual skepticism. Balancing awareness with livability becomes crucial.

The most effective programs recognize that media literacy for the synthetic age isn't just about technology—it's about human behavior, social dynamics, and building sustainable practices for navigating uncertainty.

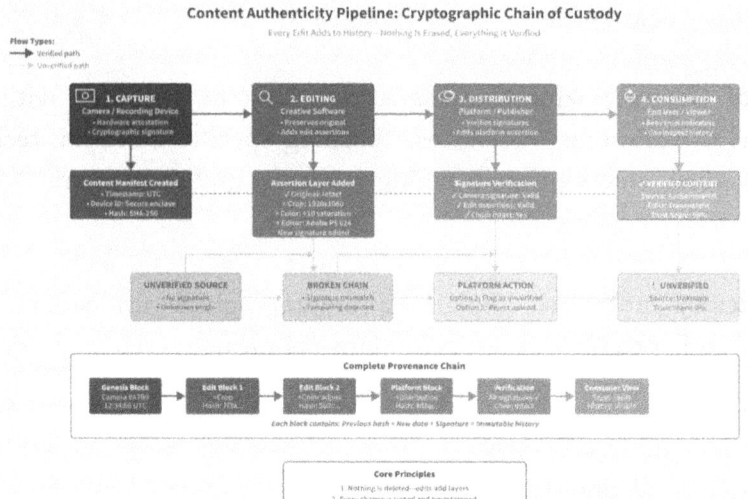

Figure 12.1: *Content Authenticity Flow: Building an Immutable Chain of Trust from Capture to Consumption.* This flowchart illustrates how cryptographic content authentication creates an unbroken chain of custody for digital media, fundamentally different from traditional watermarking or metadata approaches. Starting at capture, where cameras equipped with secure enclaves create cryptographically signed originals, each subsequent interaction adds to rather than replaces the content's history. The editing phase preserves the original while adding signed assertions about modifications (crop, color, filters), creating a transparent record of all changes. Distribution platforms verify the entire signature chain before accepting content, adding their own attestation layer. Finally, consumers see trust indicators and can inspect the complete provenance chain—from the camera that captured the image through every edit to final publication. The parallel unverified path shows how content without proper signatures or with broken chains is flagged or rejected at each stage, degrading from 98% trust for fully verified content to 0% for unverified sources. The provenance chain visualization at bottom demonstrates the blockchain-like structure where each block contains the previous hash plus new data plus signature, creating an immutable history that synthetic content cannot forge. Critical to this system is that authenticity is not binary but graduated—partial verification is possible even when some signatures are missing, allowing legacy content to participate while clearly indicating its trust level. This architecture transforms content authenticity from a futile game of detection to a positive assertion of provenance, where genuine content proves itself rather than synthetic content being hunted.

TAKEAWAY: BUILDING YOUR CONTENT VERIFICATION PRACTICE

The battle for content authenticity won't be won by technology alone. While we wait for universal adoption of C2PA and similar standards, individuals and organizations must build their own practices for creating and consuming verified content.

Start implementing content authenticity practices:

1. **Create Verifiable Content**
    - Use devices that support cryptographic signing when possible
    - Document your creation process with timestamps and witnesses
    - Maintain original files with complete metadata
    - Consider watermarking or signing your work
    - Build a reputation for authentic content

2. **Verify Before Believing**
    - Check for C2PA or similar authentication marks
    - Trace content to original sources
    - Look for corroborating evidence from multiple angles
    - Consider context and timing, not just technical verification
    - Build pause between seeing and accepting

3. **Share Responsibly**

- Prioritize sharing verified content
- Add context when sharing unverified but important content
- Correct mistakes quickly and publicly
- Build networks that value verification
- Model good verification behavior

4. **Demand Authentication**
   - Support platforms that implement verification systems
   - Choose news sources that authenticate their content
   - Request verification from content creators you follow
   - Advocate for verification in your industry
   - Vote with your attention and money

5. **Educate Others**
   - Share verification tools and techniques
   - Explain what authentication does and doesn't prove
   - Help others understand synthetic media capabilities
   - Build community resistance to deception
   - Make verification a social norm

6. **Prepare for Evolution**
   - Stay informed about new verification technologies
   - Adapt practices as threats evolve
   - Build flexible rather than rigid approaches
   - Focus on principles over specific tools
   - Maintain healthy skepticism about all content

. . .

Remember: in the synthetic age, creating and sharing verified content isn't just about protecting yourself—it's about contributing to an information ecosystem where truth can flourish. Every piece of authenticated content makes synthetic deception slightly less effective.

WHAT'S NEXT

Content authenticity provides the technical foundation for distinguishing real from synthetic, but technology alone cannot rebuild the social fabric torn by synthetic media. In Chapter 13, "The Right to Authentic Identity," we begin Part IV by exploring the legal and ethical frameworks needed for the synthetic age. From digital personhood to consent in the age of deepfakes, from the GDPR model applied to synthetic data to protecting biometric rights, we'll examine how law and policy must evolve to protect human authenticity.

The infrastructure for verification exists. Now we must build the social contracts that make it meaningful.

PART FOUR
A NEW SOCIAL CONTRACT

CHAPTER 13
THE RIGHT TO AUTHENTIC IDENTITY

THE FIRST SYNTHETIC IDENTITY RIGHTS CASE

[FICTIONALIZED scenario based on emerging legal challenges around synthetic media and identity rights]

The courtroom in Brussels fell silent as Eva Andersson took the stand. The 34-year-old Swedish marketing consultant had become the unwitting face of a landmark legal battle that would define identity rights in the synthetic age. For the past eighteen months, a synthetic version of Eva had been living a parallel life online—one that was destroying her real existence.

"The first time I saw her—saw me—was in a promotional video for a cryptocurrency I'd never heard of," Eva testified, her voice steady despite the weight of the moment. "She had my face, my voice, even my little habit of tucking hair behind my ear when making a point. But the words coming out of her mouth were not mine. She was promising impossible returns, guaranteeing wealth. I've never invested in cryptocurrency in my life."

. . .

The synthetic Eva hadn't stopped there. She appeared in political rallies for extremist parties, endorsed questionable health products, and even conducted video job interviews that the real Eva knew nothing about. When the real Eva began receiving death threats from defrauded investors and lost her actual job due to "reputational concerns," she did what courts worldwide were beginning to grapple with: she sued her synthetic double for identity theft.

The legal challenge was unprecedented. Traditional identity theft involved someone stealing your credentials or financial information. But what legal framework applied when someone stole your very being? When they didn't just impersonate you but created an autonomous version that could act independently across digital platforms?

"Your Honor," Eva's lawyer argued, "my client's most fundamental right—the right to be herself—has been violated. Not by someone pretending to be her, but by technology that has created another her. This synthetic entity is making contracts in her likeness, damaging her reputation, and destroying her livelihood. If we don't have the right to our own identity in the digital age, what rights do we have at all?"

The defense, representing the platform that hosted the synthetic Eva, countered with an argument that sent chills through the courtroom: "The synthetic entity is not Eva Andersson. It's a collection of pixels and algorithms that happens to resemble her. It's no different from a painting or a fictional character. You cannot sue a fictional character for identity theft."

. . .

The European Court of Justice's eventual ruling would establish what became known as the "Andersson Principles": that individuals have an inalienable right to their biometric identity, that creating synthetic versions without consent constitutes a form of identity theft more serious than traditional financial fraud, and that platforms hosting synthetic persons bear liability for damages caused by those entities.

But the victory felt hollow to Eva. "They gave me legal recognition that I own my own face," she reflected months later, the synthetic versions finally scrubbed from major platforms. "But how do you enforce that in a world where anyone with a laptop can create another me? How do you put that genie back in the bottle?"

Eva's case was just the beginning. As synthetic media democratized the ability to create digital humans, legal systems worldwide scrambled to answer a question they'd never had to consider: who owns the right to be you?

∼

LEGAL FRAMEWORKS COLLIDING WITH DIGITAL REALITY

The Andersson case exposes a fundamental problem: our legal systems are built for a world where identity was inherent and obvious. You were you because you occupied a unique body in space and time. Impersonation required physical presence or, at worst, forged documents. The law had clear frameworks for both.

But synthetic media shatters these assumptions. When anyone can create a perfect digital copy of anyone else, when that copy can act autonomously across platforms, when it can enter contracts and build relationships—which legal frameworks even apply?

Consider how different areas of law suddenly collide:

Identity Theft Law traditionally focuses on financial fraud. Someone uses your social security number to open credit cards. The harm is economic, the remedy is monetary. But synthetic identity theft causes reputational, emotional, and social damage that money can't fix. How do you calculate damages when someone's synthetic double destroys their relationships or career?

Intellectual Property Law protects creative works, not people. You can copyright a photograph of yourself but not your actual appearance. Trademark law protects commercial identities but doesn't apply to private individuals. The legal concept of "personality rights" exists in some jurisdictions but is designed for celebrities protecting their commercial value, not ordinary citizens protecting their existence.

Contract Law assumes that parties to an agreement are who they claim to be. Digital signatures and electronic contracts have legal standing, but what happens when a synthetic person enters contracts? Are they void? Voidable? Do platforms that enable synthetic persons bear liability for contracts they enter?

Criminal Law struggles with the concept of synthetic perpetrators. If a synthetic person engages in fraud, who is the criminal? The creator? The platform? The AI itself? Traditional concepts of mens rea (guilty mind) fall apart when the "mind" is algorithmic.

Human Rights Law faces the most fundamental challenge. The Universal Declaration of Human Rights guarantees dignity, privacy, and personhood—but do these apply to protecting people from synthetic versions of themselves? Is the right to authentic identity as fundamental as the right to life or liberty?

Courts worldwide are beginning to grapple with these questions, often reaching contradictory conclusions:

United States: Courts broadly protect digital expression under the First Amendment, including some deepfakes used for political satire. However, states are creating a patchwork of laws targeting malicious uses - California and Texas have passed legislation addressing deepfake pornography and election manipulation, though no comprehensive federal framework exists.

European Union: While there's no specific synthetic media regulation, the EU's AI Act includes provisions for synthetic content. It requires labeling of AI-generated media and addresses high-risk AI applications. The GDPR's existing "right to erasure" could theoretically extend to synthetic versions, though this remains legally untested.

China: The government mandates watermarks on AI-generated content and requires platforms to register synthetic content creators. Criminal penalties exist for unauthorized synthetic media, though enforcement prioritizes political control over individual privacy rights.

India: In 2024, the Supreme Court recognized digital access and aspects of biometric dignity under Article 21's Right to Life. However, implementation varies significantly across states, with no unified framework for synthetic media protection.

[The following is a hypothetical framework that illustrates a potential approach]

Brazil's Potential Model: While Brazil hasn't created a synthetic persons registry, its strong data protection framework (LGPD) and active privacy authority (ANPD) position it to potentially pioneer such approaches. The concept of preemptive biometric registration represents one possible future direction.

The legal landscape remains fragmented and evolving. Most jurisdictions are adapting existing laws rather than creating comprehensive synthetic media frameworks, leaving significant gaps in protection.

CONSENT IN THE AGE OF PERFECT REPLICATION

The concept of consent—fundamental to law, ethics, and human relationships—faces unprecedented challenges when perfect digital replication becomes possible. Traditional consent models assume that you're consenting to specific uses of your image or information. But what happens when consenting to one use enables infinite others?

. . .

Consider the evolution of consent in the digital age:

Pre-Digital Era: Consent was specific and limited. If you agreed to be photographed for a newspaper, that photo couldn't be used for advertising without additional permission. Physical limitations created natural boundaries.

Early Digital Era: Terms of service agreements expanded consent dramatically. By uploading a photo to social media, you might grant the platform "a non-exclusive, transferable, sub-licensable, royalty-free, worldwide license" to use it. But use still meant distribution, not transformation.

Synthetic Media Era: Consent models collapse entirely. A single photo shared on social media can train AI systems to create infinite variations of you. A voice message to a friend can enable perfect voice cloning. Existing anywhere digitally means existing everywhere synthetically.

The challenges multiply across contexts:

Employment Consent: Job applications increasingly require video interviews. But does consenting to be recorded for hiring decisions include consent for that recording to train AI systems? Companies argue that improving their hiring algorithms benefits everyone. Applicants counter that they never agreed to become training data.

. . .

Social Media Consent: Platforms update their terms to include AI training rights, often retroactively. Users who shared decades of photos suddenly find those images feeding systems that can create synthetic versions of them. Opting out often means deleting entire histories—a form of digital suicide.

Biometric Consent: Facial recognition for phone unlocking seems harmless. But those biometric templates, if compromised, enable perfect synthetic recreation. Unlike passwords, you can't change your face when it's stolen.

Medical Consent: Healthcare increasingly relies on AI analysis of medical imaging. But training these systems requires vast databases of patient scans. Patients consent to treatment, not to becoming permanent residents of training datasets that might enable synthetic recreation of their bodies.

Educational Consent: Online learning platforms record students for "academic integrity." But those recordings capture voice patterns, facial expressions, and behavioral biometrics that can train synthetic media systems. Students must choose between education access and biometric privacy.

New consent frameworks are struggling to emerge:

Granular Consent attempts to let people specify exactly what uses they allow. But the complexity overwhelms users—consent forms that would take hours to read and understand. The very granularity meant to protect people becomes a barrier to participation in digital life.

Dynamic Consent allows people to change permissions over time. But technical implementation proves challenging—how do you revoke consent from an AI model that's already trained on your data? The toothpaste doesn't go back in the tube.

Collective Consent recognizes that individual consent may be impossible in interconnected systems. Communities might need to make collective decisions about synthetic media use. But this raises questions about individual autonomy and minority rights.

Presumed Non-Consent flips the default—synthetic use is forbidden unless explicitly permitted. This protects individuals but might stifle beneficial uses of synthetic media in education, accessibility, and art.

The most promising approaches recognize that consent in the synthetic age can't be a one-time checkbox. It must be:
    Ongoing: Continuously reaffirmed as uses evolve
    Contextual: Different for different synthetic applications
    Revocable: With real technical mechanisms for enforcement
    Understandable: Explained in terms people actually comprehend
    Enforceable: Backed by legal remedies that cross borders

But even perfect consent frameworks face a fundamental challenge: they assume people understand what they're consenting to. When the implications of synthetic media remain unclear even to experts, how can ordinary citizens give truly informed consent?

THE GDPR MODEL: EXPANDING PRIVACY TO IDENTITY

The European Union's General Data Protection Regulation (GDPR), implemented in 2018, revolutionized how we think about digital privacy. As synthetic media challenges emerged, policymakers began asking: could GDPR's principles extend to protect not just data but identity itself?

GDPR's core principles offered a promising foundation:

Purpose Limitation: Data collected for one purpose couldn't be used for another without consent. Applied to synthetic media, this would mean a photo shared for social connection couldn't be used for AI training without explicit agreement.

Data Minimization: Organizations should collect only the minimum data necessary. For synthetic media, this might mean using techniques that learn styles and patterns without storing actual biometric data.

Right to Erasure: The famous "right to be forgotten" could extend to synthetic versions. If you can demand Google remove search results, why not demand AI companies remove your likeness from their models?

. . .

Data Portability: People could request their data in transferable formats. Extended to synthetic media, individuals might download and control their own biometric templates, deciding who can use them.

Privacy by Design: Systems must build in privacy from the start. Synthetic media platforms would need consent mechanisms, deletion capabilities, and audit trails built into their architecture.

Early attempts to apply GDPR to synthetic media reveal both promise and problems:

The Consent Challenge: GDPR requires explicit consent for data processing. But synthetic media often uses publicly available data—photos freely shared on social media. Courts struggle with whether public availability implies consent for synthetic use.

The Controller Confusion: GDPR assigns responsibility to "data controllers" who determine how data is used. But in synthetic media, who's the controller? The AI company that built the model? The user who prompts it? The platform that hosts it? Liability becomes a shell game.

The Erasure Impossibility: Machine learning models don't store data in retrievable formats. They encode patterns in neural networks. "Deleting" someone from a model might require retraining from scratch—technically possible but economically prohibitive.

. . .

The Border Problem: GDPR applies to EU residents' data worldwide. But synthetic media created in non-EU countries using EU residents' images creates jurisdictional nightmares. Enforcement requires international cooperation that rarely materializes.

The Innovation Impact: Companies argue that strict GDPR interpretation would kill beneficial uses of synthetic media—in medical research, education, and accessibility. The tension between protection and progress intensifies.

Despite challenges, GDPR's expansion into synthetic media protection could advance through several mechanisms:

Regulatory Guidance: The European Data Protection Board could clarify that biometric data used for synthetic media falls under GDPR's "special categories" requiring explicit consent. Some guidance on AI and biometric data exists, though specific synthetic media applications remain largely unaddressed.

Court Precedents: If cases like the fictional Andersson scenario were to occur, courts might recognize that creating synthetic persons violates GDPR's purpose limitation and consent requirements. Currently, such precedents remain largely theoretical.

Technical Standards: Privacy-preserving synthetic media techniques that comply with GDPR are beginning to emerge—systems that aim to generate synthetic content without storing identifiable biometric data. These remain in early development stages.

. . .

Corporate Compliance: Major platforms, anticipating regulatory action and facing potential GDPR fines, are beginning to develop synthetic media policies. Meta and Google have published AI principles that reference privacy concerns, though specific GDPR compliance for synthetic media remains evolving.

The GDPR model offers a potential path forward but not a complete solution. Its strength—comprehensive rights backed by serious penalties—also creates weakness through complexity and compliance costs. Smaller innovators struggle with requirements designed for tech giants.

As synthetic media challenges expand, the GDPR framework must evolve to address not just data privacy but identity integrity. The question isn't whether GDPR can protect against synthetic media, but how quickly it can adapt to threats that didn't exist when it was conceived.

PROTECTING BIOMETRIC RIGHTS IN A POST-BIOMETRIC WORLD

The synthetic age presents a paradox: just as biometric authentication becomes ubiquitous—face unlock, voice banking, fingerprint payments—synthetic media makes biometrics copyable. We're building identity infrastructure on biological uniqueness precisely when that uniqueness can be replicated. How do we protect biometric rights when biometrics themselves offer no protection?

Traditional biometric protection focuses on preventing unauthorized collection:

. . .

Illinois's Biometric Information Privacy Act (BIPA), enacted in 2008, requires consent before collecting biometric data and bans profiting from biometrics. It has become the model for biometric protection, spawning lawsuits against tech giants who collect face prints without permission.

California's Consumer Privacy Act (CCPA) classifies biometric information as protected personal data, granting consumers rights to know what's collected, delete it, and opt out of sale.

India's Aadhaar Act regulates the world's largest biometric database, establishing principles for government use of biometric data while struggling with private sector applications.

But these laws assume biometrics are valuable because they are unique. Synthetic media destroys that assumption. New frameworks for biometric rights must address different concerns:

Right to Biometric Integrity: Beyond preventing collection, people need protection from biometric manipulation. Your face can't just be private—it must remain yours alone. This requires laws against creating synthetic versions without consent.

Right to Biometric Authenticity: In a world of perfect copies, people need ways to prove they're the "real" version. This might require government-backed biometric certification systems or blockchain-based identity verification.

. . .

Right to Biometric Withdrawal: Unlike passwords, you can't change your biometrics when compromised. Laws must recognize this permanence, perhaps requiring alternative authentication methods when biometrics are breached.

Right to Biometric Compensation: If companies profit from synthetic versions of people, shouldn't those people be compensated? This could create a licensing model for biometric use, similar to personality rights for celebrities.

Potential approaches to biometric protection being explored include:

Biometric Sanctuaries: The concept of "biometric-free zones" where collection would be banned entirely could emerge in schools, healthcare facilities, and public spaces. While some school districts have debated facial recognition technology, the creation of comprehensive biometric-free zones remains a proposal rather than reality.

Synthetic Biometric Registries: One could imagine systems where people register their biometric data, making unauthorized synthetic use automatically illegal. This would create a definitive record of "authentic" biometrics, though critics might worry about creating honeypots for hackers.

Biometric Cooperatives: Digital rights advocates could propose groups collectively managing their biometric rights, similar to emerging data cooperative models. These might negotiate with platforms and set terms for use, potentially balancing individual protection with platform needs.

. . .

Biometric Insurance: Insurance companies might develop products covering damages from biometric theft or synthetic impersonation. As risks become quantifiable, markets could emerge to manage them, expanding beyond current identity theft coverage.

But the deeper challenge is philosophical: in a post-biometric world, should we double down on biometric systems or abandon them entirely?

The Maximalist View: We need more sophisticated biometrics—heartbeat patterns, gait analysis, brainwaves. Always staying ahead of synthetic capabilities through increasingly intimate biological measurement.

The Minimalist View: Biometric authentication is fundamentally broken when biometrics can be copied. We should return to knowledge-based systems (passwords) or possession-based systems (hardware tokens).

The Hybrid View: Biometrics remain useful when combined with other factors. Your face plus your location plus your behavior plus your device creates a harder target than any single factor.

The reality is that billions of people now depend on biometric systems for everything from phone unlocking to border crossing. We can't abandon these overnight, but we must evolve them for a world where biological uniqueness no longer guarantees digital uniqueness.

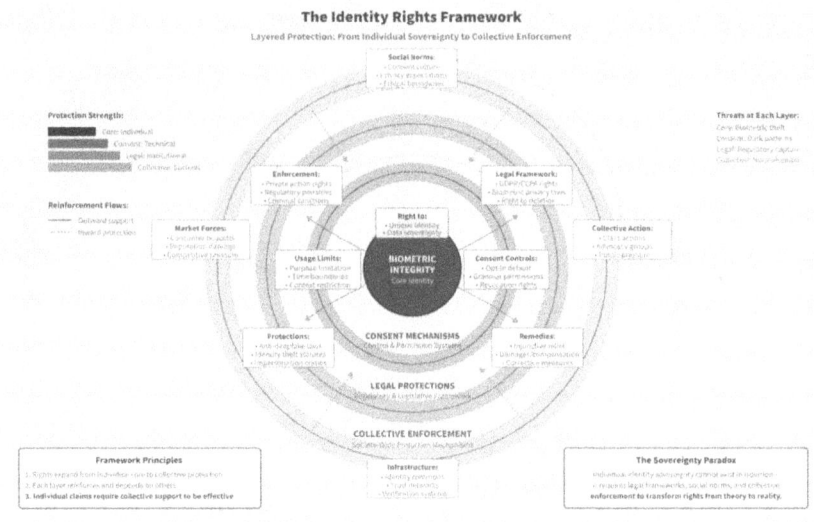

Figure 13.1: *The Identity Rights Framework: Building Protection Through Layered Sovereignty and Collective Enforcement.* This circular diagram illustrates how identity rights operate as an interdependent system of expanding protections, challenging the notion that individual sovereignty alone can secure identity in the synthetic age. At the core lies biometric integrity—the fundamental right to unique identity and data sovereignty. This individual kernel expands through consent mechanisms that provide technical controls (opt-in defaults, granular permissions, revocation rights), then through legal protections that create enforceable frameworks (GDPR/CCPA rights, anti-deepfake laws, criminal sanctions), and finally to collective enforcement that mobilizes societal pressure (market forces, social norms, advocacy groups). The bidirectional arrows demonstrate the critical insight: protection flows both ways. Individual rights claims flow outward, requiring legal codification and collective support to become meaningful, while societal enforcement flows inward, providing the infrastructure and pressure that makes individual rights enforceable. The framework reveals the sovereignty paradox: absolute individual control over identity is impossible without collective agreement to respect and enforce that control. Each layer faces distinct threats—from biometric theft at the core to normalization of violations at the collective level—requiring different defensive strategies. Most significantly, the diagram shows that in an age of synthetic media and AI impersonation, identity rights cannot be secured through technology or law alone but require a comprehensive framework spanning from silicon-level biometric protection to society-wide enforcement mechanisms. The varying opacity and thickness of the rings visualize how protection strength increases through collective action, transforming abstract rights into concrete protections.

TAKEAWAY: CLAIMING YOUR IDENTITY RIGHTS

The right to authentic identity in the synthetic age isn't just a legal abstraction—it's a practical necessity for maintaining autonomy in digital spaces. While comprehensive legal frameworks slowly emerge, individuals must take active steps to claim and protect their identity rights:

1. **Document Your Biometric Footprint**
    - Catalog where your biometric data exists (phones, banks, employers, governments)
    - Understand what rights you have in each jurisdiction
    - Keep records of what permissions you've granted
    - Regular audit biometric data sharing

2. **Exercise Current Rights**
    - Use GDPR, CCPA, or local privacy laws to request your data
    - Demand transparency about AI training use
    - Opt out where possible and document refusals
    - Challenge unauthorized biometric collection

3. **Create Legal Precedents**
    - Document synthetic media abuse when it occurs
    - Report impersonation to platforms and authorities
    - Support legal cases that advance identity rights
    - Share experiences to build collective awareness

4. **Advocate for Stronger Protections**
    - Support legislation recognizing identity rights
    - Demand consent mechanisms for synthetic use
    - Push for corporate responsibility standards
    - Join digital rights organizations

5. **Build Protective Practices**
    - Limit biometric data sharing to essential uses
    - Use privacy-preserving alternatives where available
    - Create verifiable records of your authentic communications
    - Establish identity verification networks with trusted contacts

6. **Prepare for Legal Action**
    - Keep evidence of your original content and communications
    - Document damages from synthetic impersonation
    - Know your legal options in your jurisdiction
    - Consider identity theft insurance that covers synthetic fraud

7. **Think Collectively**
    - Individual rights are stronger when exercised together
    - Share knowledge about protection strategies
    - Support others facing synthetic identity abuse
    - Build community standards for identity respect

. . .

Remember Eva Andersson's lesson: legal recognition of identity rights means little without practical enforcement mechanisms. But every person who claims their rights, every case that establishes precedent, every community that demands protection moves us closer to a world where authentic identity is respected and protected.

WHAT'S NEXT

Legal frameworks provide essential protections, but rights mean nothing without the power to exercise them. In Chapter 14, "Collective Defense Against Synthetic Threats," we'll explore how communities could build mutual aid networks for verification, how crowdsourced reality checking systems might work, and why our best defense against synthetic deception may not be individual vigilance but collective action.

The law can recognize your right to authentic identity. But protecting that right requires all of us working together.

CHAPTER 14

COLLECTIVE DEFENSE AGAINST SYNTHETIC THREATS

THE NIGHT TAIWAN SAVED ITSELF

[FICTIONALIZED scenario based on Taiwan's robust civil society responses to disinformation and the technical possibilities of distributed verification networks]

At 10:47 PM on a humid Friday night in June 2024, Lin Wei-han's phone buzzed with an urgent notification from LINE, Taiwan's most popular messaging app. The 28-year-old convenience store clerk in Taipei was about to become part of the world's first successful crowdsourced defense against a coordinated synthetic media attack.

The message appeared to come from President Tsai Ing-wen herself, delivered through what seemed to be an emergency broadcast system: "My fellow citizens, I must inform you of an imminent threat. Intelligence reports confirm that military exercises in the Taiwan Strait are cover for an invasion. I am ordering all military reserves to report immediately.

Civilian defense volunteers should gather at designated points. This is not a drill."

The video showed President Tsai at her desk, the ROC flag behind her, her expression grave but determined. Every detail was perfect—her characteristic speaking style, the subtle Hoklo accent when she switched from Mandarin, even the slight tremor in her hands that appeared when discussing security threats. To any individual viewer, it was unquestionably real.

But Taiwan had learned from watching democracies worldwide struggle with deepfakes. Two years earlier, after a series of smaller synthetic media incidents during local elections, civil society groups had built something unprecedented: a distributed verification network they called "TruthNet" (真相網).

Within seconds of the fake emergency broadcast spreading, Lin Wei-han did what hundreds of thousands of Taiwanese had been trained to do. He opened the TruthNet app and hit the "Verify Crisis Message" button. The app immediately connected him to a verification cell—five other random citizens from different parts of Taiwan, each with different political affiliations, ages, and backgrounds.

"I just received an emergency message from President Tsai about an invasion," Lin typed into the secure chat.

"Same here," responded a teacher from Kaohsiung. "But my neighbor says they saw nothing on regular TV news."

. . .

A taxi driver from Taichung chimed in: "My brother works at the Presidential Office. I just called him—he says the President is at a state dinner, not making emergency broadcasts."

Within minutes, thousands of these verification cells were comparing notes. The TruthNet system aggregated their findings: no traditional media had received the broadcast, government websites showed no emergency declarations, and crucially, citizens near military bases reported no unusual activity. The pattern was clear—this was synthetic media designed to cause panic.

But TruthNet did more than just identify the fake. Within 15 minutes, the network had:

- *Traced the video's distribution pattern to coordinated bot networks*
- *Created and spread counter-messages confirming the President's actual location*
- *Mobilized fact-checkers to appear on late-night radio shows*
- *Pushed verification notices to every major LINE group in the country*

By midnight—just 73 minutes after the first fake video appeared—major social media platforms were labeling it as disinformation, news channels were running debunking segments, and the government's authentic channels had confirmed that no emergency existed. The attack, sophisticated as it was, had failed to create the mass panic its creators intended.

. . .

The architects of TruthNet would later emphasize a crucial insight: they couldn't stop the deepfake from being created, but they could stop it from working. When verification becomes everyone's responsibility, when trust flows through networks instead of from authorities, synthetic media loses its power to deceive at scale.

Taiwan's success wasn't due to superior technology or government resources. It came from recognizing a fundamental truth: in an age when anyone can be impersonated, no individual can verify reality alone. But together, networked citizens become a collective immune system against synthetic deception.

∽

COMMUNITY-BASED VERIFICATION NETWORKS

While TruthNet itself is a fictional illustration, the principles it demonstrates are already being implemented in various forms around the world. Taiwan's real success against disinformation—through fact-checking organizations, digital literacy programs, and rapid response networks—inspired the fictional scenario. But the core insight remains valid: traditional approaches focus on technological solutions—better detection algorithms, cryptographic signatures, platform moderation. Real-world experience suggests the most powerful defense against synthetic media might be social rather than technical: transforming verification from an individual challenge into a collective practice.

Community-based verification networks could operate on several key principles:

. . .

Distributed Trust: No single person or institution would hold authority over truth. Instead, trust would emerge from multiple independent confirmations across diverse network nodes. Like blockchain for human verification, the system would become more reliable as more people participate.

Rapid Response: Speed matters in the attention economy. Synthetic media gains power when it spreads faster than verification. Community networks could mobilize in minutes, potentially matching the velocity of viral deception with equally viral truth-checking.

Local Knowledge: Citizens possess contextual understanding that no algorithm can match. They would know when something doesn't match local patterns, when claimed events conflict with ground truth, when messages feel "off" in ways hard to articulate but easy to sense.

Cross-Cutting Validation: Effective networks would intentionally include diverse participants. Political, generational, and geographic diversity could prevent echo chambers. When people who rarely agree on anything all flag something as suspicious, that consensus would carry weight.

Redundant Channels: Information would flow through multiple independent pathways. If synthetic media compromises one communication channel, others would remain available for verification. This redundancy could make the network resilient to sophisticated attacks.

. . .

Real-world implementations are beginning to emerge beyond Taiwan:

Ukraine's Digital Resistance: Facing constant Russian disinformation, Ukrainian citizens created Telegram channels where locals verify claimed attacks, troop movements, and government announcements. With millions of participants, these channels often debunk false claims faster than official sources [1].

India's Fact-Check Collectives: WhatsApp groups dedicated to verification have emerged across India, particularly during elections. Citizens forward suspicious content to these groups where volunteers—journalists, students, retired professionals—collaborate to verify or debunk claims.

Brazil's Election Defenders: During the 2022 elections, civil society organizations trained over 10,000 volunteers in verification techniques. These "digital brigadistas" monitored social media, flagged suspicious content, and provided real-time fact-checking to their communities [2].

But community verification faces significant challenges:

Coordination Complexity: Organizing distributed networks requires sophisticated coordination mechanisms. Without central authority, how do you prevent chaos, resolve disagreements, or maintain quality standards?

. . .

Infiltration Risks: Bad actors might join verification networks to spread false confirmations. Building trust while remaining open to new participants creates constant tension.

Fatigue Factors: Continuous vigilance exhausts volunteers. The same people who enthusiastically join verification networks often burn out within months, especially during intense disinformation campaigns.

Scale Limitations: Local verification works well for local claims but struggles with national or global synthetic media. How do you verify a deepfake of a world leader when no network members have direct access?

Authority Questions: When community verification conflicts with official statements, which should citizens believe? The network's collective intelligence or institutional authority?

Despite challenges, community verification networks represent humanity's distributed immune system against synthetic deception. They transform citizens from passive consumers of information into active participants in collective sense-making.

THE WIKIPEDIA MODEL FOR TRUTH CONSENSUS

Wikipedia seemed impossible until it worked. The idea that anonymous volunteers could create the world's most comprehensive encyclopedia, that edit wars would resolve into accuracy, that collective intelligence could surpass expert curation—all of it defied conventional wisdom. Yet Wikipedia became the default reference for human knowledge. Now, as synthetic media threatens to fracture consensus reality, Wikipedia's model offers crucial lessons for maintaining shared truth.

The Wikipedia model demonstrates several principles that could apply to synthetic media verification:

Transparent Process: Every edit is logged, every discussion archived, every decision traceable. This transparency allows trust to emerge from process rather than authority. When you can see how conclusions were reached, you're more likely to accept them.

Iterative Refinement: Truth emerges through cycles of claim, challenge, and revision. Initial posts might be wrong, but successive edits approach accuracy. This evolutionary process proves more robust than single-point verification.

Verifiability Over Truth: Wikipedia doesn't determine truth—it documents what reliable sources say. This subtle distinction becomes crucial for synthetic media. The question isn't "Is this real?" but "Can this be verified through multiple independent sources?"

Neutral Point of View: Contentious topics require presenting multiple perspectives rather than declaring one correct. For synthetic media, this might mean documenting both claims and counterclaims while the verification process unfolds.

. . .

Community Governance: Policies emerge from user consensus rather than top-down decree. This participatory governance creates buy-in and legitimacy that imposed rules lack.

[Based on analysis of Wikipedia's governance model and its potential application to content verification]

How Wikipedia principles might apply to synthetic media verification:

Synthetic Media Wiki: A collaborative platform where users document synthetic media incidents, verification processes, and outcomes. Each deepfake gets a page tracking its origin, spread, debunking efforts, and impact. Over time, patterns emerge that help identify future attacks.

Verification Edit History: Just as Wikipedia articles show their evolution, synthetic media verification could maintain transparent records. Initial uncertainty ("possibly fake") evolves into consensus ("confirmed synthetic based on X, Y, Z evidence") through documented steps.

Source Hierarchies: Wikipedia privileges certain sources—academic journals over blogs, newspapers over social media. Synthetic media verification needs similar hierarchies: cryptographic proof over eyewitness accounts, multiple independent confirmations over single sources.

. . .

Dispute Resolution: Wikipedia's elaborate dispute resolution mechanisms—from talk pages to arbitration committees—could adapt to synthetic media conflicts. When verification efforts disagree, structured processes can work toward resolution.

Language Localization: Wikipedia exists in hundreds of languages with local editorial communities. Synthetic media verification must similarly localize, as deepfakes often target specific linguistic and cultural communities.

Early experiments show promise:

Wikidata for Deepfakes: Researchers are exploring how Wikidata's structured data approach could catalog synthetic media. Each deepfake would have metadata—creation date, first appearance, verification status—in queryable format.

Collaborative Fact-Checking: Organizations like First Draft have created collaborative verification projects where journalists from different outlets work together on complex synthetic media cases, sharing findings in real-time.

Academic Initiatives: Universities are developing Wikipedia-style platforms for students to practice verification skills on synthetic media, creating educational resources while building verification capacity.

. . .

But the Wikipedia model could face unique challenges when applied to synthetic media:

Velocity Mismatch: Wikipedia can take months to reach consensus on contentious topics. Synthetic media verification could require verification in hours or minutes before viral spread causes damage.

Adversarial Editing: While Wikipedia vandalism is mostly pranks, synthetic media verification could face sophisticated actors with strategic goals. State-sponsored editors could potentially overwhelm volunteer verifiers.

Technical Complexity: Verifying synthetic media could often require technical expertise—analyzing compression artifacts, checking cryptographic signatures, running detection algorithms. This could create higher barriers than general encyclopedia editing.

Legal Liability: Incorrectly labeling authentic content as synthetic could trigger defamation lawsuits. The legal risks of verification could exceed those of encyclopedia editing.

Emotional Intensity: Synthetic media often targets emotional triggers—political divisions, social anxieties, personal fears. Maintaining Wikipedia-style neutrality could become harder when content is designed to provoke.

Despite challenges, the Wikipedia model's core insight remains valid: collective intelligence, properly structured, can maintain shared truth even when that truth is contested. The question is how to adapt these principles for the unique challenges of synthetic media.

CROWDSOURCED REALITY CHECKING

Beyond formal networks and Wikipedia-style platforms, a more organic form of collective defense is emerging: crowdsourced reality checking. Millions of ordinary citizens, armed with smartphones and healthy skepticism, are becoming ad-hoc investigators who can debunk synthetic media through collective effort.

The power of crowds to verify reality isn't new. In 2013, Reddit users famously—and infamously—attempted to identify the Boston Marathon bombers through crowdsourced photo analysis. While that effort led to false accusations and demonstrated the dangers of unstructured crowdsourcing, it also revealed the latent investigative capacity of networked citizens. The challenge is channeling this capacity productively.

Modern crowdsourced verification benefits from several advantages:

Ubiquitous Documentation: With billions of smartphones, almost every public event has multiple witnesses recording from different angles. Synthetic media claiming to show public incidents can be checked against this distributed documentary record.

Collective Memory: Crowds remember details that individuals forget. Someone always notices when a deepfake places a demolished building in modern footage or shows weather that doesn't match historical records.

Diverse Expertise: Every crowd contains unexpected experts. When a deepfake of a politician showed them wearing a military medal incorrectly, veterans immediately spotted the error. When synthetic audio attributed regional slang to the wrong area, locals noticed.

Parallel Processing: Thousands of people can analyze different aspects simultaneously. While some check backgrounds, others verify voices, examine metadata, or trace distribution patterns. This parallel processing achieves speed no individual expert can match.

Geographic Distribution: Crowds span time zones and locations. When synthetic media claims something happened in Mumbai, actual Mumbai residents can immediately verify or refute based on direct observation.

Successful crowdsourced verifications demonstrate the model's potential:

The Syrian Chemical Weapons Investigation: When videos emerged of alleged chemical attacks in Syria, the investigative collective Bellingcat coordinated volunteers worldwide to verify footage. They matched background landmarks, analyzed shadows to confirm timing, and traced upload patterns to authenticate crucial evidence[3].

. . .

The MH17 Reconstruction: After Malaysia Airlines Flight 17 was shot down over Ukraine, crowdsourced investigators used social media posts, satellite imagery, and dashboard camera footage to reconstruct events. Their findings, later confirmed by official investigations, demonstrated crowdsourcing's capacity for complex verification.

Election Monitoring: During elections worldwide, citizens photograph results posted at polling stations, creating a parallel vote count that can verify or challenge official tallies. This distributed monitoring makes large-scale fraud harder to conceal.

But crowdsourcing faces its own challenges:

Mob Dynamics: Crowds can amplify errors as easily as truth. False certainty spreads through echo chambers. The same collective intelligence that spots fakes can also create conspiracy theories.

Coordination Costs: Unstructured crowdsourcing produces noise alongside signal. Someone must aggregate findings, resolve conflicts, and synthesize conclusions. This coordination layer often becomes a bottleneck.

Manipulation Vulnerability: Bad actors can infiltrate crowds to steer investigations astray. State actors particularly excel at creating false leads that waste crowdsourced effort.

. . .

Uneven Participation: Crowdsourcing skews toward those with time, skills, and motivation to participate. This can create blind spots where synthetic media targeting less-engaged communities goes unchallenged.

Expertise Gaps: While crowds contain diverse knowledge, they may lack specific technical skills. Analyzing cryptographic signatures or detecting sophisticated audio manipulation requires expertise not always present in random crowds.

The evolution of crowdsourced verification points toward hybrid models:

Structured Crowdsourcing: Platforms guide crowd efforts through specific verification tasks. Instead of chaotic free-for-alls, participants complete defined steps: "Check if this building exists," "Verify this weather matches the claimed date," "Find other angles of this event."

Expert-Crowd Collaboration: Technical experts provide tools and frameworks while crowds provide scale and local knowledge. Experts might identify what to look for; crowds do the looking.

Gamified Verification: Some platforms turn verification into competitive games. Points, leaderboards, and achievements motivate sustained participation while maintaining quality through accuracy scores.

. . .

AI-Crowd Partnerships: Machine learning identifies potential synthetic media while humans verify edge cases. This human-in-the-loop approach combines algorithmic scale with human judgment.

The future of crowdsourced reality checking likely involves all these elements: structured processes that channel crowd energy productively, expert guidance that prevents mob errors, incentive systems that sustain participation, and human-AI collaboration that combines the best of both.

DIGITAL BARN RAISING AND MUTUAL AID

The American frontier tradition of barn raising—communities coming together to build something no individual could construct alone—offers a powerful metaphor for collective defense against synthetic media. Just as neighbors once gathered to raise barns, digital communities are gathering to raise defensive structures against deception.

This mutual aid approach differs from both institutional responses and market solutions. It's neither top-down nor profit-driven but emerges from communities recognizing their shared vulnerability and collective capacity.

Digital barn raising for synthetic media defense takes several forms:

Verification Cooperatives: Groups pool resources to access verification tools and expertise they couldn't afford individually. A neighborhood association might collectively subscribe to deepfake detection services, sharing costs and benefits.

Skill Sharing Networks: Those with technical expertise teach others verification techniques. Weekend workshops on "Spotting Deepfakes" become the new community CPR training—essential skills everyone should have.

Response Teams: Communities organize rapid response teams for synthetic media crises. When a deepfake targets a local business or politician, trained volunteers mobilize to document the fake, spread corrections, and support victims.

Infrastructure Building: Communities create shared infrastructure—verification wikis, secure communication channels, alert systems. Like the physical barns of old, this digital infrastructure serves the entire community.

Mutual Insurance: Groups create informal insurance pools for synthetic media damage. If someone's business suffers from deepfake attacks, the community helps rebuild their reputation and recover losses.

How digital mutual aid for synthetic media defense might emerge:

The Neighborhood Watch Evolution: Traditional neighborhood watch groups could add digital components. Instead of just watching for physical crimes, they might monitor for synthetic media targeting local residents and businesses.

Parent Networks: School parent groups could share information about synthetic media targeting children—fake social media profiles, manipulated photos, AI-generated bullying content. Parents who understand technology could help those who don't.

Professional Associations: Groups like the International Association of Women Judges could create verification networks where members vouch for each other's authentic communications, making impersonation harder.

Religious Communities: Churches, mosques, and temples might integrate digital literacy alongside traditional religious education. Congregations could become verification networks where trusted relationships enable quick debunking of fakes.

Union Organizing: Labor unions could train members to spot synthetic media designed to disrupt organizing efforts, particularly as deepfake videos of union leaders making inflammatory statements become a potential threat to solidarity.

The mutual aid model offers unique advantages:

Trust Foundation: Mutual aid builds on existing relationships. You're more likely to believe verification from your neighbor than from a distant fact-checker.

. . .

Cultural Competence: Communities understand their own contexts, languages, and concerns better than outside experts. They spot culturally specific synthetic media that might fool outsiders.

Sustainable Motivation: People protect their communities more persistently than they participate in abstract verification efforts. The motivation is personal, not professional.

Resource Efficiency: Sharing costs and expertise makes defense accessible to communities that couldn't afford individual protection.

Resilience Building: The process of organizing collective defense strengthens community bonds, creating resilience beyond just synthetic media threats.

But mutual aid faces limitations:

Scale Boundaries: Barn raising works for barn-sized problems. Community responses may be overwhelmed by sophisticated, well-resourced attacks.

Expertise Limits: Goodwill can't substitute for technical knowledge. Communities need access to expertise they may not possess internally.

. . .

Coordination Challenges: Volunteer efforts often struggle with coordination. Without clear structures, mutual aid can become mutual chaos.

Burnout Risks: The same people who step up for community defense often overextend themselves. Sustainable mutual aid requires preventing volunteer burnout.

Inclusion Issues: Not everyone has equal access to community networks. Those most vulnerable to synthetic media—the isolated, elderly, or marginalized—may be least connected to mutual aid networks.

The path forward likely combines mutual aid with other approaches. Communities provide the trust foundation and local knowledge. Technical platforms provide tools and infrastructure. Institutions provide resources and expertise. Together, they create defense in depth against synthetic threats.

BUILDING YOUR TRUST CIRCLE

The exploration of collective defense—from Taiwan's TruthNet to Wikipedia-style consensus to digital barn raising—points to a practical conclusion: everyone needs a trust circle. This isn't about paranoid isolation but conscious community building. Your trust circle becomes your personal verification network, your first line of defense against synthetic deception.

Building an effective trust circle requires intentional design:

· · ·

Diversity Over Comfort: Include people with different perspectives, skills, and backgrounds. A trust circle of only like-minded friends creates an echo chamber. You need contrarians who'll challenge groupthink, technical experts who understand synthetic media, and skeptics who question everything.

Quality Over Quantity: A smaller circle of engaged participants works better than a large group of passive members. Better to have five people who actively verify than fifty who might forward fake content.

Clear Protocols: Establish how your circle will communicate during synthetic media events. Will you use Signal? Meet in person? Have code words? Planning before crisis prevents panic during crisis.

Regular Practice: Like fire drills, verification skills need practice. Share suspicious content for group analysis. Run exercises where someone creates harmless fake content for others to spot. Build muscle memory for verification.

Reciprocal Commitment: Trust circles work through mutual obligation. You verify for others; they verify for you. This reciprocity creates accountability and sustained participation.

Practical steps for building your trust circle:

1. **Identify Core Members**

- Start with 3-5 people you trust deeply but who bring different perspectives:
- Someone more technical than you
- Someone from a different generation
- Someone with different political views
- Someone in a different location
- Someone who's naturally skeptical

2. **Establish Communication Channels**
   - Primary channel for urgent verification (Signal, WhatsApp)
   - Backup channel if primary is compromised
   - In-person meeting plans for extreme situations
   - Agreement on response times and availability

3. **Create Verification Protocols**
   - How to flag suspicious content
   - What information to gather before alerting the circle
   - How to research and divide verification tasks
   - How to reach consensus on verification status
   - How to document findings for future reference

4. **Develop Expertise Together**
   - Monthly learning sessions on new synthetic media techniques
   - Shared resources and tools for verification
   - Practice exercises with increasing difficulty
   - Post-incident reviews when you encounter real fakes

. . .

5. **Expand Thoughtfully**
    - Add new members slowly after group consensus
    - Maintain diversity as you grow
    - Create sub-circles for specific contexts (work, family, community)
    - Connect with other trust circles for broader network effects

6. **Sustain Engagement**
    - Regular check-ins beyond crisis moments
    - Celebrate successful verifications
    - Rotate leadership responsibilities
    - Address conflicts quickly and directly
    - Recognize burnout and provide breaks

Your trust circle serves multiple functions:

Verification Network: When you encounter suspicious content, your circle provides quick reality checks from multiple perspectives.

Early Warning System: Circle members alert each other to synthetic media campaigns targeting your community, industry, or interests.

. . .

Emotional Support: Being targeted by synthetic media is traumatic. Your circle provides support beyond just technical verification.

Skill Development: Learning together makes verification less daunting and more sustainable.

Community Building: The process strengthens real human connections—the ultimate defense against synthetic deception.

Remember: building a trust circle isn't giving up on broader truth or retreating into filter bubbles. It's recognizing that in an age of perfect digital deception, human relationships become our anchors to reality. Technology created the synthetic media crisis, but human connection might be the solution.

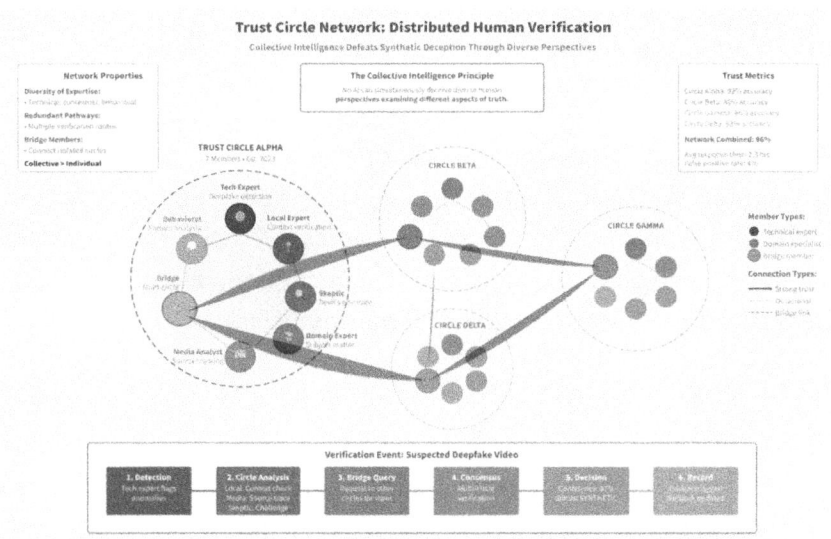

Figure 14.1: *Trust Circle Network: Defeating Synthetic Deception Through Distributed Human Intelligence.* This network diagram illustrates how small groups of trusted individuals with diverse expertise form interconnected verification networks capable of detecting synthetic content that would fool any single observer. The detailed view of Trust Circle Alpha shows seven members with complementary skills—technical expertise for deepfake detection, local knowledge for context verification, skeptical perspective for challenging assumptions, domain expertise for subject matter evaluation, media analysis for source tracking, behavioral analysis for pattern recognition, and crucially, a bridge member who connects to other circles. These roles aren't hierarchical but synergistic: the tech expert might detect pixel anomalies while the local expert notices impossible shadows for the claimed location and time, and the skeptic questions why this particular content emerged now. The broader network view shows how multiple circles interconnect through bridge members, creating redundant verification pathways—if one circle is compromised or unavailable, others can still function. The verification event flow demonstrates the process in action: a suspected deepfake triggers sequential analysis within the circle, bridge queries to other circles, network consensus building, and decision documentation. Critical to the model's success is that individual circles achieve 83-92% accuracy, but the combined network reaches 96% accuracy—demonstrating that collective intelligence exceeds individual capability. The 2.3-hour average response time shows this isn't instant verification but thoughtful analysis. Most significantly, this human network exploits AI's fundamental weakness: while synthetic content might fool technical detection or human perception in isolation, it cannot simultaneously maintain consistency across technical, contextual, behavioral, and social dimensions when examined by diverse perspectives. This represents a return to humanity's oldest trust mechanism—community verification—updated for the synthetic age.

TAKEAWAY: FROM INDIVIDUAL VIGILANCE TO COLLECTIVE RESILIENCE

The fictional TruthNet scenario that opened this chapter illustrates a crucial principle that real-world examples are beginning to demonstrate: individual vigilance, while necessary, isn't sufficient. No amount of personal skepticism or technical knowledge can match the verification power of connected communities.

While TruthNet itself was a fictional illustration, Taiwan's actual success against disinformation—through organizations like the Taiwan FactCheck Center, digital literacy programs, and rapid response networks—shows that collective defense works. The same principles apply whether facing traditional disinformation or future synthetic media threats.

Moving from individual to collective defense requires:

1. **Recognize Your Interdependence**
    - Accept that you cannot verify reality alone
    - Understand that your verification helps others
    - Embrace mutual vulnerability and mutual aid
    - See collective defense as strength, not weakness

2. **Start Where You Are**
    - You don't need perfect infrastructure to begin
    - Use existing relationships and communities
    - Build on current communication channels
    - Start small and expand organically

. . .

3. **Combine Approaches**
    - Blend formal networks with informal connections
    - Mix technical tools with human judgment
    - Balance quick response with careful verification
    - Integrate local knowledge with expert guidance

4. **Design for Sustainability**
    - Prevent volunteer burnout through rotation
    - Make participation rewarding, not just dutiful
    - Celebrate successes to maintain motivation
    - Build resilience into your systems

5. **Stay Human-Centered**
    - Remember technology serves human connection
    - Prioritize relationships over perfect verification
    - Accept some uncertainty to maintain community
    - Focus on building trust, not just detecting fakes

6. **Think Ecosystem**
    - Your trust circle connects to others
    - Local verification contributes to global truth
    - Small actions aggregate to large effects
    - Everyone has a role in collective defense

7. **Prepare for Evolution**
   - Synthetic media techniques will advance
   - Verification methods must adapt
   - Communities need to learn continuously
   - Flexibility matters more than perfection

The transition from individual vigilance to collective resilience isn't just a tactical shift—it's a fundamental reimagining of how we maintain truth in the digital age. Just as our ancestors gathered to raise barns no individual could build, we must gather to raise defenses no individual can maintain.

The emerging synthetic media threat reveals both human vulnerability and human capacity. Yes, we're vulnerable to perfect digital deception. But we're also capable of creating collective intelligence that no AI can match. The same social nature that makes us susceptible to deception also enables our defense.

Start building your trust circle today. Connect with others doing the same. Together, we can create the verification networks that preserve human agency in an age of synthetic everything.

WHAT'S NEXT

Collective defense provides the social infrastructure for fighting synthetic media, but communities need technological systems designed for human agency rather than surveillance and control. In Chapter 15, "Governance for the Synthetic Age," we'll explore how governments, international organizations, and civil society might need to create new frameworks for digital citizenship. From potential models for global coordination to the concept of regulatory sandboxes for testing new approaches, from emerging digital rights movements to the eternal tension between protection and freedom, we'll examine how governance itself might evolve when reality becomes malleable.

The battle against synthetic media can't be won by communities alone. We need governance structures that empower collective defense while protecting individual rights—a balance as delicate as it is essential.

CHAPTER 15
GOVERNANCE FOR THE SYNTHETIC AGE

THE UN SUMMIT THAT ALMOST BROKE THE INTERNET

[FICTIONALIZED *scenario based on current UN digital governance initiatives and the technical possibilities of international coordination frameworks*]

The General Assembly Hall at the United Nations headquarters in New York had hosted many historic moments, but none quite like this. On September 15, 2025, delegates from 193 nations gathered for the Emergency Summit on Digital Identity and Synthetic Media—a meeting that would either establish the first global framework for governing synthetic reality or fracture into the kind of digital nationalism that could make the internet as we know it obsolete.

Secretary-General António Guterres opened with words that would echo through the halls of power worldwide: "We stand at a crossroads. Down one path lies a world where synthetic media is weaponized by states and *criminals alike, where truth becomes a luxury only the powerful can afford, where digital identity is a battleground. Down the other lies the possibility of global cooperation—imperfect, difficult, but essential."*

The summit had been triggered by what diplomats carefully called "the Jakarta Incident." Three months earlier, a sophisticated deepfake video showed Indonesian President Joko Widodo announcing the nationalization of all foreign tech companies operating in the country. The synthetic president, speaking in perfect Bahasa Indonesia with Widodo's characteristic gestures, declared that "digital sovereignty requires digital ownership." Markets crashed. Investors fled. Diplomatic relations strained.

The video had been created not by criminals or activists but by a competing nation's intelligence service, seeking to destabilize Indonesia's growing tech sector. When the deception was revealed 48 hours later, the damage was done—but more importantly, every nation realized they could be next. If synthetic media could be used as a weapon of economic warfare between states, no country was safe.

The U.S. delegation, led by Secretary of State Zitkala Firewind, proposed what they called the "Digital Geneva Convention"—international laws governing the use of synthetic media in the same way the original Geneva Conventions governed warfare. "Just as we agreed that certain weapons are too terrible to use," Firewind argued, "we must agree that certain deceptions are too dangerous to permit."

But China's representative, Ambassador Liu Wei, pushed back with a different vision: "The problem isn't synthetic media—it's the platforms that spread it without accountability. We need sovereign control over our digital spaces, not more Western-dominated international frameworks."

China proposed a model where each nation would control identity verification within its borders, with limited interoperability between systems.

The European Union, represented by Digital Commissioner Margrethe Vestager, offered a third way: "We need neither digital anarchy nor digital authoritarianism. We need standards—technical standards for verification, ethical standards for use, and legal standards for accountability." The EU proposed extending their Digital Identity Wallet system globally, creating interoperable but privacy-preserving identity infrastructure.

Smaller nations, organized through the Alliance of Small Island States, raised a crucial point through Barbados Prime Minister Mia Mottley: "You speak of standards and sovereignty, but what about capacity? My nation has 300,000 people and three IT specialists in government. How do we implement these grand frameworks? How do we protect our citizens when we lack the resources you take for granted?"

The debates revealed fundamental tensions:

Sovereignty vs. Interoperability: Nations wanted to control their digital borders while maintaining global connectivity. But synthetic media doesn't respect borders—a deepfake created in one country can destroy trust in another instantly.

Privacy vs. Security: Strong identity verification could prevent synthetic impersonation but enable surveillance. Weak verification preserved privacy but allowed deception to flourish.

. . .

Innovation vs. Regulation: Tech companies warned that heavy-handed regulation would stifle beneficial uses of synthetic media in education, entertainment, and accessibility. Civil society countered that without regulation, harmful uses would proliferate.

Resources vs. Requirements: Wealthy nations could implement sophisticated verification systems. Developing nations faced choosing between digital participation and digital security.

As the summit stretched into its third day, a breakthrough came from an unexpected source. Rwanda's Minister of ICT and Innovation, Paula Ingabire, proposed what became known as the "Kigali Principles":

1. ***Graduated Governance:*** Different levels of verification for different risk levels, allowing nations to implement what they could afford while maintaining compatibility
2. ***Technology Transfer:*** Wealthy nations would share verification technology with developing nations, recognizing digital security as a global public good
3. ***Regulatory Sandboxes:*** Safe spaces for testing new approaches without full commitment, allowing innovation while managing risk
4. ***Multi-stakeholder Oversight:*** Not just governments but civil society, technologists, and affected communities would govern the framework

The summit didn't end with a binding treaty—that would take years more negotiation. But it ended with something perhaps more important: a *recognition that no nation could solve the synthetic media crisis alone. The "New York Declaration on Digital Authenticity" committed nations to:*

- *Develop interoperable identity verification systems within two years*
- *Create an International Digital Identity Organization to coordinate standards*
- *Establish a global fund for digital capacity building in developing nations*
- *Implement mandatory labeling of synthetic media across all platforms*
- *Regular review of governance frameworks as technology evolved*

As delegates filed out of the General Assembly Hall, the internet remained intact—barely. But the summit had revealed a truth more profound than any declaration: in an age where reality itself could be synthesized, governance could no longer be merely national. The question wasn't whether to create global digital governance, but whether humanity could create it fast enough to matter.

∼

INTERNATIONAL COOPERATION OR DIGITAL BALKANS?

While the UN summit scenario above is fictional, it illustrates very real tensions already playing out in international forums. The actual challenge facing humanity today is stark: will we build coordinated defenses against synthetic media, or will we retreat into digital territories as isolated as medieval city-states?

. . .

Current evidence from real international negotiations, bilateral agreements, and regional initiatives suggests we're attempting both simultaneously, creating a patchwork of cooperation and fragmentation that may define the next era of human civilization.

The forces pushing toward cooperation are powerful:

Shared Vulnerability: Every nation, regardless of power or wealth, faces synthetic media threats. When a deepfake can topple markets or trigger conflicts, everyone has incentive to cooperate. The Jakarta Incident showed that even regional powers could be destabilized by synthetic attacks.

Technical Necessity: Interoperability isn't optional in a connected world. If identity verification systems can't work across borders, global commerce grinds to halt. The same technical standards that enable email to work worldwide must extend to identity and authenticity.

Economic Pressure: Multinational corporations demand consistent frameworks. Amazon can't have 195 different identity verification systems. Google can't implement different synthetic media detection for each country. Economic integration drives regulatory harmonization.

Collective Intelligence: No single nation has all the expertise needed. The U.S. leads in AI research, Estonia in digital identity, Singapore in urban technology, Kenya in mobile innovation. Solving synthetic media requires combining these strengths.

. . .

Shared Norms: Despite differences, most nations agree on basic principles—impersonating officials is wrong, electoral manipulation is dangerous, financial fraud hurts everyone. These shared norms provide foundation for cooperation.

But equally powerful forces drive fragmentation:

Digital Sovereignty: Nations increasingly view data and digital systems as matters of national security. China's Great Firewall, Russia's "sovereign internet," and data localization laws worldwide reflect desire for digital borders as strong as physical ones.

Competitive Advantage: Some nations see opportunity in synthetic media chaos. If your adversaries struggle with deepfakes while your population is protected, that's strategic advantage. Why share defensive capabilities with potential rivals?

Cultural Differences: What counts as acceptable synthetic media varies dramatically. American First Amendment protections for satire clash with European privacy rights. Chinese collective values conflict with Western individualism. One nation's free expression is another's dangerous deception.

Technical Capabilities: The digital divide becomes a governance divide. Nations with advanced technical capabilities can implement sophisticated frameworks. Those without must accept whatever others design or risk digital exclusion.

· · ·

Trust Deficits: International cooperation requires trust between nations—exactly what synthetic media destroys. How can countries collaborate when any communication might be fake, any agreement might be synthetic?

The reality emerging shows neither pure cooperation nor complete fragmentation, but something messier:

Regional Blocs: Like-minded nations create shared frameworks. The EU's Digital Identity system expands to affiliated countries. The African Union develops continental standards. Regional cooperation proves easier than global consensus.

Technical Standards, Political Flexibility: Nations agree on technical interoperability while maintaining political control. Like internet protocols, identity verification might have common technical layer with diverse political implementations.

Bilateral Agreements: Countries negotiate specific partnerships. The U.S. and UK share verification capabilities. Japan and Australia coordinate synthetic media responses. Bilateral trust enables limited multilateral expansion.

Issue-Specific Cooperation: Nations cooperate on narrow issues while competing broadly. Everyone might share financial fraud intelligence while keeping political deepfake capabilities secret. Cooperation becomes tactical, not strategic.

. . .

Corporate Bridges: Multinational platforms become de facto governance mechanisms. When Facebook implements global synthetic media policies, it creates functional international framework regardless of government agreements.

This hybrid landscape—neither fully cooperative nor completely fragmented—may be the best humanity can achieve. It's messy, inefficient, and full of gaps. But it might be more resilient than either extreme. Pure cooperation could enable global surveillance. Complete fragmentation could destroy digital civilization. The middle path, however frustrating, might be the most human.

THE GENEVA CONVENTION FOR SYNTHETIC MEDIA

The concept of a "Digital Geneva Convention" has been discussed in technology and policy circles since at least 2017, when Microsoft's Brad Smith called for international rules to protect civilians from nation-state cyberattacks. While no binding international treaty yet exists, the idea has evolved from rhetorical device to serious diplomatic discussion.

What we're exploring here is a speculative but plausible extension: how might such international agreements specifically address synthetic media? While elements of this framework draw from real proposals and existing international law principles, the specific "Geneva Convention for Synthetic Media" described below represents a potential future approach rather than current reality.

Such a convention might establish several core principles:

. . .

1. **Prohibited Uses:** Certain applications of synthetic media would be banned entirely:
    - Impersonating government officials for fraud or disruption
    - Creating non-consensual intimate images
    - Falsifying evidence in legal proceedings
    - Manipulating electoral communications
    - Triggering false emergencies or panics

2. **Required Disclosures:** Synthetic media would require clear labeling:
    - Technical markers readable by machines
    - Visual indicators understandable by humans
    - Audit trails showing creation and modification
    - Creator identification or pseudonymous accountability

3. **Protected Populations:** Special protections for vulnerable groups:
    - Children cannot be synthetically recreated without parental consent
    - Deceased persons have posthumous identity rights
    - Public figures retain some control over their likeness
    - Victims of synthetic abuse get rapid remediation

4. **Verification Infrastructure:** Nations would commit to building:
   - Interoperable identity systems
   - Public key infrastructure for citizens
   - Rapid response teams for synthetic media crises
   - Education programs for digital literacy

5. **Enforcement Mechanisms:** Violations would trigger:
   - Economic sanctions for state violators
   - Criminal prosecution for individual violators
   - Platform liability for enabling violations
   - Victim compensation from global fund

The process of negotiating such a convention reveals deep challenges:

Definitional Disputes: What exactly counts as "synthetic media"? Is a Photoshopped image synthetic? What about AI-enhanced video calls? Where's the line between legitimate editing and deceptive synthesis? Nations can't agree on basic definitions.

Sovereignty Concerns: Many nations view the convention as potential threat to sovereignty. Who decides what's "electoral manipulation" versus legitimate political speech? Could powerful nations use the convention to silence dissent?

. . .

Technical Feasibility: Some proposed requirements may be technically impossible. How do you create "permanent" labels on media that can be screenshotted and reshared? How do you enforce disclosure on decentralized platforms?

Cultural Conflicts: Different societies have different relationships with truth and representation. Some cultures view certain image manipulations as artistic rather than deceptive. Universal standards clash with cultural diversity.

Enforcement Challenges: Unlike conventional weapons, synthetic media tools are software—infinitely copyable, easily hidden, constantly evolving. How do you enforce a ban on something that fits on a thumb drive?

Despite challenges, momentum builds through several mechanisms:

Pilot Programs: Nations test convention principles domestically before international commitment. Singapore's synthetic media regulations become model for Southeast Asia. Norway's identity protection laws inspire Nordic cooperation.

Industry Leadership: Tech companies, seeking regulatory clarity, implement convention principles voluntarily. Microsoft's synthetic media principles, Adobe's Content Authenticity Initiative, and similar efforts create de facto standards.

. . .

Civil Society Pressure: Digital rights organizations worldwide coordinate advocacy. The global #RealNotFake campaign mobilizes millions demanding protection. Victims of synthetic abuse share stories that humanize abstract principles.

Academic Development: Universities establish international research networks on synthetic media governance. The "Oxford Principles for Synthetic Media" provide intellectual framework. Technical conferences become diplomatic venues.

Crisis Learning: Each synthetic media crisis builds support for regulation. The Jakarta Incident, celebrity deepfake scandals, and electoral manipulations create "never again" moments that drive diplomatic progress.

The Geneva Convention for synthetic media won't be signed in a grand ceremony. It will emerge through accumulated precedents, technical standards becoming legal norms, and crisis-driven cooperation. Like the original Geneva Conventions, which evolved over decades, digital governance develops through iteration rather than inspiration.

REGULATORY SANDBOXES AND ADAPTIVE LAW

Traditional law moves slowly—years of drafting, debate, and implementation. But synthetic media evolves in weeks. This temporal mismatch has led policymakers to look toward "regulatory sandboxes"—a concept that has proven successful in financial technology and is now being explored for synthetic media governance.

. . .

Regulatory sandboxes, pioneered by the UK's Financial Conduct Authority in 2016, create spaces where new approaches can be tested without full legal commitment. While most existing sandboxes focus on fintech, some jurisdictions are beginning to experiment with similar approaches for AI and digital identity. The application to synthetic media governance specifically remains largely theoretical, though the principles are being discussed in policy circles.

Here's how regulatory sandboxes could work for synthetic media:

Limited Scope: New rules apply only within defined boundaries—specific platforms, user groups, or geographic areas. Estonia tests blockchain-based identity verification with government employees before expanding to all citizens.

Time Bounds: Experiments run for set periods—usually 6-24 months. This allows real-world testing while limiting risk. Failed experiments end naturally rather than requiring legislative repeal.

Monitored Outcomes: Continuous data collection measures effectiveness. Does the new verification system reduce fraud? Does mandatory labeling decrease synthetic media sharing? Evidence replaces ideology in policy debates.

Stakeholder Participation: Sandboxes include not just regulators but platforms, users, and civil society. Multi-stakeholder governance ensures diverse perspectives and buy-in for successful approaches.

. . .

Rapid Iteration: Failed approaches pivot quickly. Successful ones scale gradually. The sandbox enables policy agility impossible in traditional legislative processes.

Examples of how sandboxes might be applied to synthetic media governance:

[The following are speculative examples based on existing sandbox models in other domains]

Singapore's Potential Deepfake Sandbox: Singapore's strong regulatory innovation culture and existing fintech sandbox suggest they could create a controlled environment where platforms test synthetic media detection and labeling. Participating platforms might receive regulatory flexibility in exchange for data sharing and user protection commitments.

UK's Possible Online Safety Sandbox: Given Ofcom's role in online safety and the UK's sandbox leadership, they could allow platforms to experiment with age verification for synthetic content without full compliance with broader regulations. Different approaches—from AI detection to human moderation—could compete on effectiveness.

Japan's Hypothetical Synthetic Person Registry: A pilot program in Tokyo could allow residents to register their biometric data, making unauthorized synthetic recreation automatically illegal. Such a sandbox would test technical feasibility and public acceptance before any national rollout.

. . .

Brazil's Potential Electoral Protection Zone: During municipal elections, participating cities might test real-time synthetic media monitoring and rapid response systems. Successful approaches could then inform national electoral protection laws.

Kenya's Possible Voice Verification Pilot: Building on M-Pesa's success with mobile money innovation, Kenya could test voice biometric protection against synthetic voice fraud in mobile banking. Such a sandbox would need to balance security with accessibility for users with limited literacy.

But sandboxes face their own challenges:

Regulatory Capture: Well-resourced platforms can dominate sandboxes, shaping rules to their advantage. Smaller innovators may be excluded from experimentation, embedding incumbent advantages.

Limited Learning: Sandbox results may not generalize. What works for sophisticated urban users might fail for rural populations. Success in controlled environments doesn't guarantee real-world effectiveness.

Rights Concerns: Experimental regulations might violate rights that established law protects. Users in sandboxes become test subjects for potentially harmful approaches. Consent and protection become complex.

. . .

Coordination Costs: Multiple sandboxes testing different approaches create fragmentation. Platforms face a patchwork of experimental regulations harder to navigate than stable bad law.

Political Pressure: Successful sandboxes threaten existing interests. Failed ones become political ammunition. The experimental nature makes sandboxes vulnerable to premature judgment.

The evolution toward "adaptive law" goes beyond sandboxes:

Sunset Clauses: All synthetic media regulations include automatic expiration dates. Laws must be renewed based on evidence of effectiveness, preventing accumulation of outdated rules.

Algorithmic Regulation: Some rules encode directly into platforms. Speed limits for synthetic media sharing, mandatory cooling-off periods, and automatic content labeling happen through code rather than courts.

Continuous Monitoring: Regulatory dashboards track law effectiveness in real-time. When synthetic media fraud spikes, regulators see immediately and can adjust approaches without waiting for annual reports.

Versioned Law: Like software, laws get version numbers and changelogs. Citizens can see how regulations evolved and why. Version control enables rollback if updates cause problems.

· · ·

Interoperable Standards: Technical standards separate from political implementation. Nations can share detection algorithms while maintaining different enforcement approaches, enabling technical cooperation despite political differences.

The sandbox model represents governance itself becoming agile—matching the speed of technological change while maintaining democratic oversight. It's messy, complex, and sometimes unfair. But it might be the only way to govern technologies that evolve faster than traditional law can adapt.

DIGITAL CITIZENSHIP IN A BORDERLESS WORLD

The Westphalian nation-state system, built on territorial sovereignty and physical borders, struggles to govern digital phenomena that respect no boundaries. Synthetic media created in one country, hosted in another, targeting citizens of a third, challenges every assumption about jurisdiction and citizenship. This crisis is birthing new concepts of digital citizenship that transcend traditional nationality.

Traditional citizenship confers:

- Rights within national borders
- Protection by national governments
- Obligations to national laws
- Identity tied to place of birth or naturalization

But digital life demands something different:

- Rights that function across platforms
- Protection from threats originating anywhere
- Obligations that transcend national law
- Identity portable across borders

Several models of digital citizenship are emerging:

Platform Citizenship: Major platforms become quasi-governmental entities offering digital rights and protections. "Citizens" of Facebook or Google receive identity verification, content moderation, and dispute resolution. Platforms offer more consistent governance than many nation-states, though with concerning concentration of power.

Blockchain Citizenship: Decentralized autonomous organizations (DAOs) offer membership that functions like citizenship. Members vote on governance, share resources, and maintain collective identity verification. The blockchain provides the infrastructure nation-states once monopolized.

Professional Citizenship: Global professional communities create their own governance systems. The International Association of Software Engineers might verify member identities, establish ethical standards for synthetic media, and enforce violations through professional sanctions.

Values-Based Citizenship: Communities organized around shared values rather than geography create governance frameworks. The

Global Privacy Alliance might offer identity protection services to members regardless of nationality.

Hybrid Citizenship: People maintain multiple overlapping citizenships—national for physical rights, platform for digital services, professional for work identity, values-based for community belonging. Identity becomes modular rather than monolithic.

Estonia's e-Residency program previews this future. Since 2014, Estonia has offered digital residency to global citizens—not physical residency or traditional citizenship, but access to Estonia's digital infrastructure. E-residents can:

- Start EU companies remotely
- Access banking and payment services
- Sign documents with legal validity
- Use verified digital identity services

Over 100,000 people from 170+ countries have become Estonian e-residents, creating a new category of belonging that transcends borders. They're not Estonian citizens but participate in Estonia's digital society—a model other nations are beginning to replicate.

The implications for synthetic media governance are profound:

Portable Protection: Digital citizens could carry verification and protection across borders. Your Estonian digital identity works in

Brazil, your DAO membership provides verification in Nigeria. Protection follows the person, not the location.

Competitive Governance: Digital citizenship creates competition between providers. If Estonia offers better identity protection than your birth nation, you might choose Estonian e-residency. This competition could drive governance innovation.

Layered Rights: Different citizenships provide different protections. Your national citizenship covers physical rights, platform citizenship handles digital services, professional citizenship manages work identity. Synthetic media protections layer across jurisdictions.

Exit Options: Unlike traditional citizenship, digital versions enable easy exit. If a platform's synthetic media policies fail, users can migrate. This exit threat constrains platform power—though network effects limit practical mobility.

Global Standards: Digital citizenship providers must interoperate, driving technical standardization. Just as passports follow common formats for border crossing, digital identities converge on verification standards.

But digital citizenship faces serious challenges:

Inequality Amplification: Those with resources can acquire multiple digital citizenships, layering protections. The poor remain stuck with whatever their birth nation provides. Digital citizenship could become another privilege of wealth.

Accountability Gaps: When digital citizens commit crimes, who prosecutes? If Estonian e-residents create deepfakes, does Estonia bear responsibility? Jurisdiction becomes even more complex than traditional international law.

Democratic Deficits: Most digital citizenship models lack democratic participation. Platform citizens can't vote out Mark Zuckerberg. Blockchain governance often concentrates power among early adopters. Corporate citizenship serves corporate interests.

Identity Conflicts: Multiple citizenships create conflicting obligations. Your national law might require identity disclosure that your DAO forbids. Platform terms might conflict with professional ethics. Navigating multiple governance systems exhausts users.

Exclusion Risks: Digital citizenship might create new forms of statelessness. Those without digital literacy, internet access, or required documents could be excluded from both traditional and digital citizenship—becoming truly rightless.

The future likely holds not replacement of national citizenship but augmentation. Physical bodies still need physical protection that only territorial states provide. But digital existence increasingly needs governance that transcends borders. The question isn't whether digital citizenship will emerge—it's how to ensure it enhances rather than undermines human agency and equality.

BUILDING MOVEMENT INFRASTRUCTURE

While diplomats negotiate in international forums and technologists develop platforms, we're beginning to see the early emergence of civil society responses to synthetic media threats. Though no global movement comparable to climate activism yet exists for synthetic media specifically, we can envision how such movements might develop based on patterns from digital rights activism and other technology-focused campaigns.

[The following explores how synthetic media movements could emerge, drawing from real digital rights organizing but projecting into the near future]

The fictional "#RealNotFake" movement offers a case study in how digital-age organizing might work. Imagine it starting with a coalition of deepfake revenge porn survivors, evolving into a global campaign demanding:

- Criminal penalties for non-consensual synthetic media
- Platform liability for hosting harmful deepfakes
- Support services for synthetic media victims
- Education programs on digital consent
- Funding for detection technology development

The movement's tactics blend traditional and novel approaches:

Distributed Leadership: Rather than central hierarchy, the movement operates through autonomous chapters sharing common principles. Each adapts tactics to local contexts while maintaining global coordination.

Victim Centering: Those harmed by synthetic media lead strategy and messaging. Their stories humanize abstract policy debates, making regulation politically necessary rather than merely technically advisable.

Technical Literacy: Movement leaders invest heavily in understanding technology. They can debate detection algorithms with engineers and privacy frameworks with lawyers. Technical competence earns respect and prevents co-optation.

Corporate Pressure: Coordinated campaigns target platforms where they're vulnerable—advertising relationships. When major brands pause spending due to synthetic media concerns, platforms suddenly discover capacity for content moderation.

Legislative Templates: The movement drafts model legislation that legislators can adapt. Rather than just demanding "do something," they provide specific, implementable solutions backed by technical expertise and survivor experience.

Potential movements might take different approaches:

The Verification Commons could emerge from frustrated technologists building alternative infrastructure. They might create open-source verification tools, community-managed identity systems, and cooperative content authentication. This would embody the principle "build the world you want to see."

Digital Dignity might focus on cultural change. Through art, education, and community organizing, such a movement could shift norms around synthetic media. A campaign like "Consent is Sexy" could reframe verification as relationship-building rather than restriction.

The Synthetic Liberation Front could take a contrarian position—embracing synthetic media as liberatory technology. They might argue for rights to create synthetic selves, protection for beneficial uses, and resistance to authoritarian verification systems. Such voices would complicate simple prohibition narratives.

Youth Against Deepfakes could mobilize those most affected. Born into a world where reality was always questionable, young people might bring different perspectives on verification, authenticity, and identity. A "Reality Check" curriculum could transform schools worldwide.

The infrastructure for such movements might include:

Communication Networks: Encrypted channels enable secure organizing across repressive borders. Signal groups, Matrix servers, and mesh networks provide resilient coordination even when governments attempt disruption.

. . .

Resource Sharing: Movements pool funding, expertise, and tools. A detection algorithm developed in Germany gets shared with activists in Myanmar. Legal victories in California inform strategies in India.

Rapid Response Teams: When synthetic media crises emerge, movements mobilize quickly. Trained volunteers verify content, support victims, pressure platforms, and share counter-narratives—often faster than official responses.

Research Collaboratives: Movement-affiliated researchers study synthetic media impacts, develop detection tools, and evaluate policy effectiveness. Academic rigor combines with activist energy.

Cultural Production: Artists, musicians, and storytellers translate movement goals into culture. The "Deep Fake" horror film franchise makes synthetic media threats visceral. "Verify Me" becomes a chart-topping anthem about consent.

But movements face internal tensions:

Pragmatism vs. Purism: Should movements accept incremental platform improvements or demand fundamental restructuring? Compromise enables progress but risks co-optation.

Technical vs. Social: Engineering better detection competes with changing cultural norms for resources and attention. Movements struggle to balance technical and social interventions.

. . .

Global vs. Local: Universal principles clash with contextual needs. What works in Silicon Valley may harm in New Delhi. Maintaining coherence while respecting diversity challenges every global movement.

Speed vs. Democracy: Rapid response to synthetic media crises requires quick decisions. But movement democracy takes time. Balancing agility with participation creates ongoing tension.

Funding Independence: Accepting foundation or government funding enables scale but potentially constrains advocacy. Movements debate financial models that maintain independence while achieving impact.

The most successful approaches recognize that technical, legal, and cultural changes must advance together. Movements provide the connective tissue—linking survivors with technologists, policymakers with communities, and local struggles with global transformation.

As one organizer explained: "We're not just fighting synthetic media. We're building the democratic muscles needed for whatever comes next. Today it's deepfakes. Tomorrow it might be mind reading. The specific threat matters less than our collective capacity to respond."

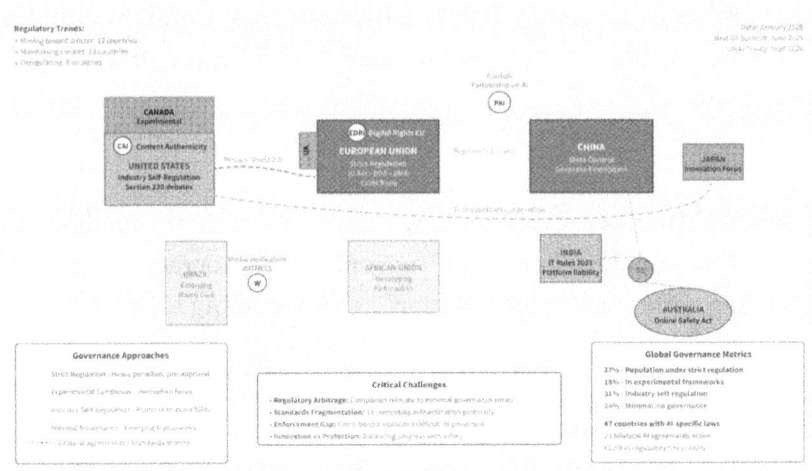

Figure 15.1: *Global Synthetic Media Governance: A Fractured Regulatory Landscape.* This world map reveals the complex patchwork of governance approaches to synthetic media, demonstrating how humanity's response to AI-generated content varies dramatically across jurisdictions. The European Union and China lead with strict regulation—though from opposing philosophical positions, with the EU emphasizing individual rights (AI Act, GDPR extensions) and China focusing on state control and social stability. The United States relies primarily on industry self-regulation and platform liability debates around Section 230, creating a markedly different ecosystem from its transatlantic partners despite Privacy Shield 2.0 agreements. Experimental sandboxes in Canada, UK, Japan, and Singapore represent attempts to balance innovation with protection, allowing controlled testing of new approaches. Meanwhile, vast populations in Brazil, Africa, and other developing regions operate under minimal governance frameworks, creating both opportunities for innovation and vulnerabilities to exploitation. The map's connecting lines reveal another layer of complexity: bilateral agreements and standards-sharing initiatives that attempt to bridge regulatory gaps, though the "regulatory tension" between the EU and China shows these efforts' limitations. Organization markers (CAI, EDRi, PAI, WITNESS) indicate where civil society and industry groups attempt to fill governance voids through voluntary standards and advocacy. The statistics reveal a stark reality: only 27% of the global population lives under strict synthetic media regulation, while 24% have minimal or no protection. With 14 competing authentication protocols and companies engaging in regulatory arbitrage by relocating to permissive jurisdictions, the map illustrates why synthetic media governance remains fragmented and ineffective. This visualization underscores that in the absence of global coordination, synthetic media operates in the gaps between jurisdictions, exploiting the very fragmentation meant to preserve sovereignty.

TAKEAWAY: YOUR ROLE IN DIGITAL GOVERNANCE

The fictionalized UN summit scenario that opened this chapter—while imaginary—was grounded in very real tensions and initiatives explored throughout these pages: actual regulatory sandboxes in Singapore and the UK, Estonia's pioneering e-Residency program, ongoing discussions about digital Geneva Conventions, and emerging civil society responses to synthetic media threats. This fictional scenario illustrated a fundamental truth: governance in the synthetic age can't be left to governments alone. Every user, every platform, every community participates in creating the rules that will determine whether synthetic media liberates or oppresses.

Understanding your role in digital governance:

1. **You're Already Governing**
    - Every time you verify before sharing, you enforce norms
    - When you call out synthetic media, you create accountability
    - Your privacy choices influence platform behavior
    - Your participation shapes community standards

2. **Governance Happens at Every Level**
    - Personal: Your own synthetic media policies
    - Community: Shared standards with friends and family
    - Professional: Workplace verification requirements
    - Platform: Engagement with terms of service
    - National: Participation in policy debates

- Global: Support for international frameworks

3. **Technical Choices Are Political Choices**
   - Using verification tools validates their importance
   - Choosing privacy-respecting platforms votes with your data
   - Building open-source alternatives challenges monopolies
   - Sharing knowledge democratizes capability

4. **Movement Building Matters**
   - Join organizations working on digital rights
   - Support victims of synthetic media abuse
   - Contribute to verification communities
   - Share your expertise where needed
   - Amplify marginalized voices in governance debates

5. **Regulatory Engagement Has Impact**
   - Comment on proposed regulations
   - Share your synthetic media experiences with policymakers
   - Participate in regulatory sandboxes
   - Testify at hearings (virtual or physical)
   - Vote for representatives who understand digital issues

6. **Build Alternative Futures**
    - Experiment with new governance models
    - Create the verification tools you wish existed
    - Model better community standards
    - Document what works for others to copy
    - Imagine beyond current limitations

7. **Stay Engaged for the Long Term**
    - Governance is ongoing, not one-time
    - Technology evolution requires governance evolution
    - Your participation shapes trajectory
    - Disengagement enables authoritarian capture
    - Hope requires sustained action

The path from digital chaos to governed systems won't be smooth. We'll see:

- Failed experiments and successful innovations
- Corporate capture and community liberation
- Authoritarian overreach and anarchist underreach
- Technical solutions and social problems
- Global cooperation and digital balkanization

Your participation shapes which futures become real. The history of digital rights—from open source software to net neutrality to privacy regulations—shows that engaged citizens can influence even the most powerful technological forces. We get the digital governance we fight for—no better, no worse.

WHAT'S NEXT

Governance frameworks provide the rules, but rules mean nothing without systems designed for human agency. In Chapter 16, "Designing for Human Agency," we'll explore the final challenge: how to build technical systems and social structures that enhance rather than diminish human autonomy in the synthetic age. From user experience in zero trust systems to the attention economy versus the verification economy, from tools that empower to those that exhaust, we'll examine what it means to remain human while defending against synthetic threats.

The infrastructure is built, the communities are organized, the governance is emerging. Now we must ensure it all serves human flourishing rather than merely human survival.

CHAPTER 16

DESIGNING FOR HUMAN AGENCY

THE STANFORD EXPERIMENT THAT CHANGED EVERYTHING

[FICTIONALIZED scenario based on real research in human-computer interaction and the documented challenges of security system usability]

Dr. Kenji Nakamura stood before the one-way mirror, watching as the fifteenth participant of the day struggled with what should have been a simple task. The Stanford Synthetic Reality Lab had recruited 200 volunteers to test their new "TrustFlow" system—a state-of-the-art identity verification platform designed to protect against deepfakes while remaining user-friendly. On paper, it was elegant. In practice, it was a disaster.

"Please verify your identity to continue," the system prompted.

. . .

349

Maria Gonzalez, a 52-year-old high school teacher from San Jose, stared at the screen with growing frustration. She'd already entered her password, scanned her face, and answered two security questions. Now the system wanted her to perform a "liveness check"—a series of random movements to prove she wasn't a deepfake.

"Turn your head slowly to the left... now blink three times... now say the words 'purple elephant' while smiling."

Maria complied, feeling increasingly foolish. The system rejected her attempt. "Verification failed. Please ensure adequate lighting and try again."

She adjusted the desk lamp and tried again. Another failure. On her fourth attempt, her frustration boiled over. "This is ridiculous!" she exclaimed, pushing back from the computer. "I just wanted to check my medical records. I know who I am—why is that not enough?"

Behind the mirror, Dr. Nakamura made another note in what was becoming a devastating pattern. TrustFlow achieved its security goals—not a single deepfake had fooled it. But it also achieved something else: making legitimate users feel frustrated, dehumanized, and paradoxically less secure. The average user required 3.7 attempts to successfully authenticate. 23% gave up entirely.

The post-test interviews were even more revealing. "I felt like I was auditioning for my own life," one participant said. Another described it as "being gaslit by a computer that kept telling me I wasn't really me." A programmer in the study noted, "The system is so paranoid about fake humans that it's forgotten how to recognize real ones."

The Stanford team had fallen into a trap that plagued the entire verification industry: they had optimized for preventing synthetic media attacks while forgetting they were designing for actual humans. Their sophisticated algorithms could detect the subtlest signs of digital manipulation but couldn't accommodate a user with tremors, or poor lighting, or who simply blinked at the wrong moment.

Dr. Nakamura called an emergency meeting with his team. "We've been asking the wrong question," he told them. "We kept asking 'How do we stop deepfakes?' when we should have been asking 'How do we help humans prove they're human without losing their humanity in the process?'"

The lab's pivot would pioneer what became known as "Agency-Centered Design"—a framework that put human autonomy and dignity at the center of security systems rather than treating it as an acceptable casualty. Their revised system, released six months later, achieved the same security outcomes with 78% fewer user frustrations. The key insight was deceptively simple: security systems that respect human agency are more likely to be used correctly, making them ultimately more secure than systems that treat users as potential threats.

"The greatest vulnerability in any security system," Dr. Nakamura would later write, "is a legitimate user who's been so frustrated by the verification process that they'll accept any workaround, no matter how insecure. When we design against human nature, we've already lost."

THE ATTENTION ECONOMY VS. THE VERIFICATION ECONOMY

While the Stanford experiment above was fictional, it illustrates a very real and fundamental tension already playing out in our digital lives: we're asking humans to constantly prove their humanity while simultaneously designing systems that treat human behavior as suspicious. This tension reflects a deeper conflict between two competing economic models, each demanding different things from our limited cognitive resources.

The **Attention Economy** emerged from Silicon Valley's discovery that human attention is a scarce resource that can be harvested and monetized. Every app, platform, and service competes for our focus, using increasingly sophisticated techniques to capture and hold it:

- Infinite scroll feeds that exploit our brain's novelty-seeking behavior
- Push notifications that trigger stress responses to drive engagement
- Variable reward schedules borrowed from gambling psychology
- Synthetic media optimized for maximum emotional impact
- Algorithmic recommendations that learn and exploit our psychological vulnerabilities

The attention economy profits from human distraction, impulsivity, and emotional reactivity. It needs us scrolling, not thinking; reacting, not reflecting; consuming, not creating.

The **Verification Economy** demands the opposite. It requires:

- Careful attention to authentication procedures
- Skeptical analysis of potentially synthetic content
- Patience with multi-step verification processes
- Cognitive resources for distinguishing real from fake
- Emotional regulation when systems question our identity

The verification economy profits from human vigilance, patience, and analytical thinking. It needs us careful, not careless; suspicious, not trusting; methodical, not impulsive.

These two economies are fundamentally at war for the same resource: human cognitive capacity. We have limited attention, limited patience, limited ability to switch between different cognitive modes. When TikTok has trained your brain for instant gratification, how do you suddenly summon the patience for careful verification? When every app has conditioned you to tap without thinking, how do you build the habit of skeptical analysis?

The conflict manifests in predictable ways:

. . .

Verification Fatigue: After a day of constant micro-authentications, users become sloppy. They reuse passwords, skip optional security steps, and ignore warning signs. The cognitive load of constant verification depletes the very resources needed for security.

Security Theater: Platforms implement visible but ineffective security measures to appear trustworthy while still maximizing engagement. The security is performative, designed to reassure rather than protect.

Dark Patterns: Some platforms deliberately make security settings hard to find or understand, knowing that frustrated users will choose convenience over protection. They profit from our vulnerability.

Synthetic Flooding: Bad actors exploit our depleted attention by flooding channels with synthetic content, knowing that tired minds are more likely to believe and share without verification.

The most insidious aspect is how the attention economy actively undermines the habits needed for the verification economy:

- Speed of consumption makes careful verification feel painfully slow
- Emotional manipulation makes analytical thinking feel cold and unnatural
- Instant gratification makes multi-step processes feel archaic

- Social validation through likes and shares makes solitary verification feel isolating

Some platforms are beginning to recognize this conflict and design accordingly:

Attention Breaks: Apps that lock after certain usage periods, forcing cognitive rest. The meditation app Headspace ironically locks users out after 60 minutes with the message "Even mindfulness needs moderation."

Verification Rewards: Systems that make security feel rewarding rather than punitive. The password manager 1Password gives users a "security score" that improves with better practices, gamifying good behavior.

Ambient Verification: Background processes that verify without interrupting flow. Signal's encryption happens invisibly; users get security without cognitive load.

Humane Pacing: Platforms that deliberately slow down sharing to allow reflection. Twitter introduced prompts asking "Do you want to read this article before retweeting?" which reduced blind sharing by 40% when implemented.

But these are exceptions in an ecosystem still dominated by attention harvesting. The path forward requires recognizing that human cognitive resources are not infinite, that asking people to be constantly vigilant while simultaneously distracting them is cruel, and that security systems must be designed for humans as we actually are, not as we wish we were.

BALANCING SECURITY WITH HUMANITY

The Stanford TrustFlow experiment revealed a truth that the security industry had long ignored: there's a profound difference between secure systems and security theater, between protecting humans and dehumanizing them. The challenge isn't just technical—it's fundamentally about preserving human dignity while defending against synthetic threats.

Traditional security thinking follows a simple logic: more verification equals more security. But human psychology doesn't work that way. Beyond a certain threshold, additional security measures actually decrease overall system security by:

- Encouraging workarounds when legitimate users can't authenticate
- Creating alert fatigue that causes people to ignore warnings
- Building resentment that leads to deliberate circumvention
- Depleting cognitive resources needed for actual threat detection
- Destroying trust between users and systems

The most secure system is useless if no one can or will use it properly. This insight is driving a fundamental shift in how we think about security design:

From User-Hostile to User-Aligned

Traditional: "The user is the weakest link and must be constrained"
    Evolved: "The user is a partner whose natural behaviors should guide design"

Consider how this plays out in practice. Traditional systems might require users to remember complex passwords changed every 30 days. This seems secure but actually encourages password reuse and written notes. User-aligned systems recognize human memory limitations and provide password managers, biometric options, and recovery methods that match how humans actually behave.

From Interruption to Integration

Traditional: "Stop what you're doing and prove who you are"
    Evolved: "Continue what you're doing while we verify in the background"

Modern smartphones exemplify this shift. Instead of constantly demanding passwords, they use continuous authentication—monitoring usage patterns, location, and behavior to detect anomalies. Verification becomes ambient rather than intrusive.

. . .

From Binary to Contextual

Traditional: "You're either verified or you're not"
    Evolved: "Your verification level matches the risk of your action"

Checking your email might require just facial recognition. Transferring money adds a second factor. Changing security settings requires multiple confirmations. The friction scales with the stakes.

From Punishment to Empowerment

Traditional: "You failed verification—access denied"
    Evolved: "Verification is challenging—here's help and alternatives"

When the Stanford team redesigned TrustFlow, they added features like:

- Clear explanations of why verification failed
- Alternative authentication methods for accessibility
- Temporary access with limited privileges while resolving issues
- Human support options for edge cases

Real-world examples show this evolution in practice:

. . .

Apple's Face ID represents nearly invisible security. Users barely notice they're authenticating hundreds of times daily. The system handles variations in appearance, lighting, and angle without frustrating users. When it fails, it gracefully falls back to passcodes without making users feel rejected.

Estonia's Digital Identity system provides maximum security with minimal friction for citizens. One authentication grants access to hundreds of services. The complexity happens in the background while users experience simplicity.

Signal's Encryption provides state-level security without users needing to understand cryptography. The protection is automatic and invisible, requiring no cognitive load from users while maintaining open-source transparency.

But balancing security with humanity faces ongoing challenges:

The Accessibility Gap: Security measures often exclude people with disabilities. Facial recognition fails for some facial differences. Voice authentication doesn't work for speech disabilities. Movement-based checks exclude those with motor impairments. True human-centered design must accommodate all humans.

The Cultural Context: What feels respectful in one culture may feel invasive in another. American users might accept behavioral tracking that European users find dystopian. Chinese users might prefer collective verification that Western users find conformist. Global systems must navigate these differences.

. . .

The Generation Divide: Digital natives have different security intuitions than older users. What feels natural to someone raised with smartphones feels alien to someone who remembers rotary phones. Systems must bridge these experiential gaps.

The Trust Paradox: The more secure a system is, the more users must trust it with sensitive information. But requiring that information for security can itself feel like a violation. Building security requires first building trust.

The path forward requires treating security not as a technical problem but as a human experience design challenge. The goal isn't just to stop deepfakes—it's to help humans navigate the synthetic age while maintaining their autonomy, dignity, and joy in digital life.

TOOLS THAT EMPOWER VS. TOOLS THAT EXHAUST

Every tool shapes its user. A hammer makes us see nails; a camera makes us frame scenes; a smartphone makes us document rather than experience. In the synthetic age, the tools we build for verification and protection will fundamentally shape how humans experience digital life. The question is: will they empower us or exhaust us?

Tools That Exhaust share common characteristics:

Constant Vigilance Requirements: They demand perpetual attention, treating every interaction as a potential threat. Users must always be "on," analyzing, verifying, suspecting. This hypervigilance is cognitively draining and emotionally corrosive.

Complexity Without Clarity: They present complicated interfaces with unclear benefits. Users must become security experts to protect themselves, learning arcane procedures and technical concepts. The cognitive overhead excludes many who most need protection.

Isolation by Design: They treat security as an individual responsibility, forcing each person to defend themselves alone. This atomization ignores how humans naturally seek collective support and shared knowledge.

Perfectionist Assumptions: They assume users will always follow best practices, never make mistakes, and constantly update their knowledge. Any deviation is punished with vulnerability or exclusion.

Examples of exhausting tools:

- Password managers that require manual updates for hundreds of accounts
- Verification apps with dozens of confusing options and settings
- Deepfake detectors that require technical interpretation of results
- Privacy tools that break normal functionality without clear explanation
- Security systems that shame users for imperfect practices

Tools That Empower take a fundamentally different approach:

Ambient Protection: They work quietly in the background, providing security without constant user intervention. Protection becomes as natural as breathing—essential but not consuming conscious thought.

Progressive Disclosure: They present simple interfaces with power underneath. Basic users get basic protection immediately; advanced users can access advanced features. Complexity reveals itself only when needed.

Community Integration: They connect users with others for mutual support. Security becomes collective rather than individual, leveraging human social instincts for protection.

Forgiving Design: They assume humans will be human—tired, distracted, imperfect. They build in recovery mechanisms, gentle corrections, and multiple chances. Mistakes become learning opportunities, not catastrophes.

Examples of empowering tools:

- Browsers that automatically warn about suspicious sites without blocking exploration
- Verification systems that learn user patterns and reduce friction over time
- Community-driven fact-checking that crowdsources expertise

- Privacy tools that provide clear tradeoffs and user control
- Security systems that celebrate progress rather than perfection

The difference isn't just interface deep—it's philosophical. Exhausting tools see users as problems to be managed. Empowering tools see users as partners to be supported.

Consider how this philosophy shapes specific features:

Authentication

- Exhausting: "Prove you're human by completing this frustrating task"
- Empowering: "We'll verify you're human through natural interaction"

Warnings

- Exhausting: "DANGER! This might be synthetic! Proceed at your own risk!"
- Empowering: "This content couldn't be verified. Here's what that means..."

Updates

- Exhausting: "Your security is out of date. Update now or remain vulnerable."
- Empowering: "Security improvements are available when you're ready."

Education

- Exhausting: "Read this 50-page manual to use our tool safely."
- Empowering: "Learn as you go with contextual tips when relevant."

The most successful tools in the synthetic age will be those that augment human capabilities rather than replacing them:

Signal provides military-grade encryption without users needing to understand cryptography. It empowers private communication without exhausting users with technical details.

Have I Been Pwned lets users check if their data has been breached without inducing panic. It empowers informed responses to real threats rather than exhausting users with vague fears.

Two-Factor Authentication Apps like Authy provide significant security improvements with minimal cognitive overhead. They empower stronger protection without exhausting users with complex procedures.

. . .

Community Notes on X (Twitter) crowdsources fact-checking without requiring every user to be an expert. It empowers collective verification without exhausting individuals.

The key insight is that empowering tools make users feel more capable, not more burdened. They expand what's possible rather than restricting what's allowed. They build confidence rather than inducing anxiety.

As one designer put it: "If your security tool makes users feel stupid, weak, or exhausted, you've already failed. The goal is to make them feel like superheroes—capable of navigating the digital world with confidence and grace."

RECLAIMING COGNITIVE SOVEREIGNTY

The battle against synthetic media is ultimately a battle for cognitive sovereignty—the right and ability to control your own attention, make your own meaning, and maintain your own mental space in a world of manufactured realities. This isn't just about detecting deepfakes; it's about preserving human autonomy in an age of algorithmic manipulation.

Cognitive sovereignty has become as important as political sovereignty once was. Just as nations fought for the right to govern themselves free from external control, individuals now must fight for the right to think freely in digital spaces designed to manipulate.

. . .

The threats to cognitive sovereignty are sophisticated and multiplying:

Algorithmic Behavior Modification: Platforms use AI to learn exactly what captures your attention, then exploit those patterns for profit. Your feed becomes a personalized manipulation machine, showing you content calculated to generate maximum engagement regardless of truth or benefit.

Synthetic Emotional Manipulation: Deepfakes and AI-generated content can be crafted to trigger specific emotional responses. Synthetic outrage drives real engagement. Manufactured fear motivates real behavior. Artificial intimacy creates real attachment.

Attention Fracking: Like hydraulic fracturing extracts oil from rock, platforms extract value from every micro-moment of attention. The three seconds while a page loads, the pause between videos, the moment of boredom—all become opportunities for cognitive capture.

Reality Substitution: When synthetic content becomes indistinguishable from real, bad actors can literally rewrite your perceived reality. The video evidence of your memories might be fake. The consensus reality of your community might be manufactured.

Choice Architecture Manipulation: The options presented to you —what to watch, read, buy, believe—are invisibly shaped by systems optimizing for outcomes that may not align with your interests. Free choice becomes an illusion.

Reclaiming cognitive sovereignty requires both individual practices and collective action:

Individual Practices:

Attention Auditing: Regularly examine where your attention goes and why. Which apps consume the most time? Which content patterns trigger compulsive checking? Understanding your attention patterns is the first step to reclaiming control.

Cognitive Firewalls: Build deliberate barriers between yourself and manipulative systems. This might mean:

- Using app timers and website blockers
- Scheduling specific times for social media
- Creating phone-free zones in your home
- Practicing regular digital detoxes

Active vs. Passive Consumption: Shift from passive scrolling to active engagement. Instead of letting algorithms decide what you see, actively search for specific content. Instead of accepting recommended videos, choose deliberately.

. . .

Reality Anchoring: Maintain strong connections to unmediated reality:

- Regular in-person socializing
- Physical hobbies and activities
- Time in nature without devices
- Printed books and analog media

Metacognitive Development: Strengthen your ability to think about thinking:

- Practice noticing when your emotions are being manipulated
- Question why specific content makes you feel certain ways
- Develop awareness of your cognitive biases
- Build habits of reflective pause

Collective Approaches:

Cognitive Commons: Create shared spaces for collective sense-making:

- Reading groups that analyze media together
- Community fact-checking initiatives
- Peer support for digital wellness
- Shared practices for verification

Attention Cooperatives: Band together to negotiate with platforms:

- Collective bargaining for better algorithms
- Group boycotts of manipulative features
- Shared resources for protection tools
- Community-owned alternatives

Educational Movements: Spread cognitive sovereignty skills:

- Digital literacy programs that go beyond technical skills
- Mindfulness training adapted for digital contexts
- Critical thinking curricula for all ages
- Peer teaching and skill sharing

Regulatory Advocacy: Push for structural changes:

- Laws requiring algorithmic transparency
- Rights to control your own attention data
- Prohibitions on certain manipulative practices
- Public funding for non-commercial platforms

The tech industry often frames this as Luddism—irrational fear of progress. But cognitive sovereignty isn't anti-technology; it's pro-human agency. We can have powerful digital tools without surrendering our mental autonomy.

. . .

Some encouraging developments show the path forward:

Platform Shifts: Under pressure, some platforms are adding features that support cognitive sovereignty:

- Time limits and usage dashboards
- Chronological feeds as an option
- Reduced notification defaults
- Clear synthetic media labeling

Tool Innovation: New tools designed for cognitive sovereignty:

- Apps that track and limit manipulation exposure
- Browser extensions that strip out engagement tricks
- AI assistants trained to support rather than exploit
- Verification tools that empower rather than exhaust

Cultural Evolution: Growing awareness and resistance:

- Digital minimalism movements
- Privacy-first purchasing decisions
- Synthetic media literacy spreading
- Collective action against manipulation

Legal Progress: Emerging rights frameworks:

- GDPR establishing data sovereignty precedents
- Proposed legislation on algorithmic transparency
- Court cases establishing manipulation limits
- International cooperation on cognitive rights

The goal isn't to retreat from digital life but to engage with it on our own terms. Cognitive sovereignty means using powerful tools without being used by them, participating in digital culture without drowning in it, protecting ourselves from synthetic manipulation while remaining open to authentic connection.

Cognitive sovereignty isn't about building walls—it's about building strength. It means developing the internal resources to navigate complexity without being overwhelmed, to face uncertainty without being paralyzed, to use tools without being used. Rather than withdrawing from digital life, it's about engaging with it from a position of strength and awareness.

CHOOSING AGENCY IN EVERY INTERACTION

The design of systems shapes behavior, but ultimately, human agency is expressed through individual choices made millions of times daily. Each interaction with digital systems presents a microdecision: surrender agency or assert it, follow the path of least resistance or choose intentionally, let the system decide or maintain control.

These choices seem insignificant individually but compound into life patterns:

. . .

The Notification Moment: Your phone buzzes. Do you:

- Immediately check it (surrendering to the interruption)
- Finish your current thought first (asserting temporal control)
- Check who it's from without opening (maintaining boundaries)
- Ignore it entirely (exercising full sovereignty)

Each choice trains both your brain and the system. Immediate responses teach algorithms you're always available. Delayed responses preserve your attention for your priorities.

The Verification Request: A system demands identity verification. Do you:

- Comply without thinking (automatic surrender)
- Consider if it's necessary (conscious evaluation)
- Seek alternatives (exploring options)
- Refuse if unreasonable (asserting boundaries)

Blind compliance normalizes ever-increasing demands. Thoughtful engagement shapes better systems.

The Content Encounter: You see potential synthetic media. Do you:

- Share immediately (spreading without verification)

- Feel suspicious but do nothing (passive consumption)
- Check sources before sharing (active verification)
- Build verification into your routine (systematic protection)

Your response either amplifies deception or builds collective immunity.

The Privacy Tradeoff: A service requests personal data. Do you:

- Provide it for convenience (trading privacy for ease)
- Read what you're agreeing to (informed consent)
- Provide minimum necessary (data minimization)
- Seek privacy-respecting alternatives (market signaling)

Your data practices shape what companies think is acceptable.

The Attention Auction: Platforms compete for your focus. Do you:

- Let algorithms decide your media diet (outsourcing choice)
- Set specific consumption intentions (maintaining control)
- Use tools to enforce boundaries (structural support)
- Create friction for mindless browsing (environmental design)

Your attention patterns either feed or starve the attention economy.

Building agency-supporting habits requires intentional practice:

Start Small: Don't try to revolutionize everything at once. Pick one interaction type and practice agency there until it becomes natural, then expand.

Create Friction: Make agency-surrendering choices slightly harder:

- Log out of social media after each use
- Remove apps from your home screen
- Use browser bookmarks instead of apps
- Add delays before major digital decisions

Build Support: Agency is easier with allies:

- Share practices with friends and family
- Join communities focused on digital wellness
- Find accountability partners
- Celebrate agency wins together

Track Progress: What gets measured gets managed:

- Notice when you assert or surrender agency
- Keep a brief journal of digital choices

- Review patterns weekly
- Adjust strategies based on results

Forgive Lapses: Agency isn't perfection:

- Expect to sometimes surrender unnecessarily
- Treat lapses as learning opportunities
- Focus on overall patterns, not individual failures
- Build resilience, not rigidity

The most powerful insight is that agency is self-reinforcing. Each time you assert control, it becomes easier. Each time you make conscious choices, you build the mental muscles for future decisions. Each time you resist manipulation, you see the strings more clearly.

But agency isn't just individual—it's collective:

Model Agency: Your choices influence others. When you verify before sharing, others notice. When you set boundaries, you give others permission. When you choose privacy, you normalize it.

Support Others' Agency: Respect others' boundaries. Don't pressure immediate responses. Share verification tools. Celebrate when others assert control.

. . .

Build Agency-Supporting Systems: Choose platforms that respect users. Support businesses that empower rather than exploit. Advocate for regulations that protect choice. Create alternatives that embody different values.

Teach Agency: Share what you learn. Help others see manipulation. Teach verification skills. Spread agency practices. Make empowerment viral.

The future of human agency in the synthetic age won't be determined by grand gestures but by billions of small choices. Each time someone pauses before clicking, questions before believing, or chooses human connection over algorithmic engagement, agency wins a small victory.

These victories matter. They shape neural pathways, influence algorithms, signal markets, and inspire others. They're how humans have always resisted systems that would control them—not through revolution but through revolution's root meaning: turning things around, one small turn at a time.

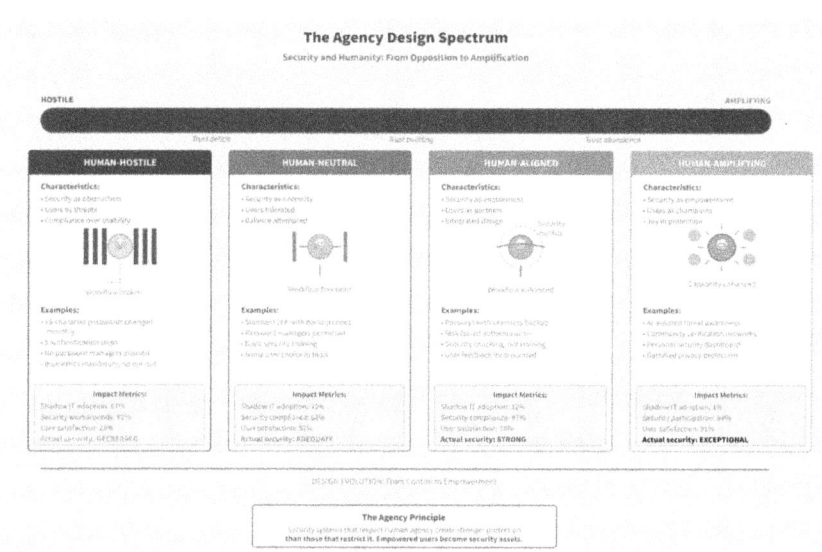

Figure 16.1: *The Agency Design Spectrum: From Security Theater to Human Empowerment.* This spectrum visualization reveals the fundamental relationship between human agency and security effectiveness, challenging the conventional wisdom that security requires restricting user freedom. The leftmost "Human-Hostile" approach treats users as threats to be controlled, implementing multiple barriers that paradoxically decrease actual security by driving 67% shadow IT adoption and 82% workaround rates—users become adversaries rather than allies. Moving right to "Human-Neutral," we see marginal improvements as systems tolerate users but still view security as separate from human needs, achieving adequate protection but missing opportunities for enhancement. The transformation accelerates with "Human-Aligned" design, where security becomes an enabler rather than obstacle—integrated protection that enhances workflows reduces shadow IT to 12% while increasing both compliance (87%) and satisfaction (78%). The rightmost "Human-Amplifying" approach represents the paradigm shift: security as a source of empowerment and even joy. Here, users become security champions, with 94% active participation and exceptional protection levels. The visual representations evolve from frustrated faces behind barriers to empowered individuals radiating enhanced capabilities and community connections. Critical metrics demonstrate that as designs move from hostile to amplifying, every measure improves: shadow IT drops from 67% to 3%, user satisfaction rises from 23% to 91%, and most significantly, actual security improves from decreased to exceptional. This spectrum proves that the most secure systems aren't those that restrict human agency but those that amplify it—transforming users from potential vulnerabilities into active defenders. In the synthetic age, where threats are increasingly sophisticated, our greatest defense isn't more barriers but more empowered humans.

TAKEAWAY: TECHNOLOGY SHOULD AMPLIFY HUMANITY, NOT REPLACE IT

The fictional Stanford Synthetic Reality Lab scenario that opened this chapter illustrated real challenges documented extensively in human-computer interaction research: security systems often prioritize technical goals over human needs, creating tools that achieve security objectives while failing the humans they're meant to protect. This pattern—optimizing for machines rather than people—captures the essential lesson of building for the synthetic age: our tools must amplify what makes us human rather than trying to replace it with something more convenient for machines.

This isn't a call for Neo-Luddism or tech rejection. It's recognition that:

Human Agency Is Not a Bug to Fix: Systems that treat human autonomy, creativity, and unpredictability as problems to solve are themselves the problem. Our messy humanity—our ability to doubt, to choose, to resist, to create—is precisely what we must preserve.

Security Through Humanity: The most secure systems aren't those that constrain humans most tightly but those that align with human nature. When security works with rather than against our instincts, it becomes sustainable.

Collective Wisdom Over Individual Verification: Humans are social creatures. Systems that leverage our collective intelligence and mutual support are more robust than those forcing each individual to be their own security expert.

. . .

Dignity As a Design Requirement: How a system makes users feel matters as much as what it accomplishes. Tools that humiliate, exhaust, or alienate users fail regardless of their technical merits.

Empowerment As a Metric: Success shouldn't be measured only in threats prevented but in human capability enhanced. Do users feel more confident navigating digital spaces? More capable of making informed choices? More connected to others?

Building technology that amplifies humanity requires:

1. **Design With, Not For**
    - Include diverse users throughout the design process
    - Test with real humans in real contexts
    - Listen to frustrations and fears, not just feature requests
    - Iterate based on human experience, not just technical metrics

2. **Respect Cognitive Limits**
    - Don't demand constant vigilance
    - Build in rest and recovery
    - Make security sustainable for daily life
    - Recognize that attention is finite and precious

3. **Enable Connection**
    - Leverage human social instincts for mutual protection
    - Build bridges between people, not walls
    - Make verification a community practice
    - Support collective sense-making

4. **Preserve Joy**
    - Security shouldn't eliminate spontaneity
    - Protection shouldn't prevent playfulness
    - Verification shouldn't destroy wonder
    - Digital life should still be life

5. **Embrace Imperfection**
    - Build systems that expect human error
    - Create forgiving interactions
    - Enable recovery from mistakes
    - Celebrate progress over perfection

6. **Maintain Hope**
    - Show users they have power
    - Highlight successful protection
    - Build confidence, not fear
    - Focus on possibility, not just threat

The synthetic age presents unprecedented challenges to human agency, but it also offers unprecedented opportunities to consciously design our relationship with technology. We can build tools that make us more human, not less. We can create systems that enhance our judgment rather than replacing it. We can develop technologies that connect us more deeply rather than isolating us in suspicious silos.

The choice—and it is a choice—is whether we'll use our remarkable technical capabilities to amplify human wisdom, creativity, and connection, or whether we'll surrender these essentially human qualities in pursuit of a false security that protects everything except what matters most.

Technology should be humanity's greatest tool, not its replacement. In the synthetic age, that's not just a nice philosophy—it's a survival strategy.

WHAT'S NEXT

Throughout this book, we've built understanding from the ground up—from recognizing the threats of synthetic media to constructing technical defenses, from organizing collective resistance to designing systems that preserve human agency. Now, in our concluding chapter, "Living Authentically in a Synthetic World," we'll bring it all together with a vision for how individuals and communities can not just survive but thrive in an age where anything can be faked except our essential humanity.

The infrastructure is built, the knowledge is gained, the communities are formed. Now comes the most important question:

How do we live fully human lives when the line between real and synthetic has blurred beyond recognition?

CONCLUSION: THE AUTHENTIC FUTURE

CHAPTER 17
LIVING AUTHENTICALLY IN A SYNTHETIC WORLD

A DAY IN THE LIFE, 2030

[FICTIONALIZED scenario projecting current trends in synthetic media defense and digital life management]

Maya Garcia wakes at 6:47 AM to the sound of rain against her Berkeley apartment window. Her phone, set to "morning sanctuary" mode, hasn't pinged once during the night. The first notification won't arrive until she's had coffee and completed her morning routine—a boundary she established three years ago when the synthetic media crisis reached its peak.

As she makes breakfast, her daughter Zoe video-calls from college. The call comes through their family's verified channel—not because they don't trust each other, but because it's become as natural as locking doors. The verification happens invisibly, a brief cryptographic handshake that confirms this really is Zoe, not one of the synthetic versions that had targeted their family during the chaos of 2027.

. . .

"Mom, I need your advice," Zoe says, and Maya can see the familiar furrow between her daughter's eyebrows that no deepfake has quite captured. "My roommate got a job offer, but something feels off. The company passed all the standard verification, but..."

Maya smiles. Her daughter has developed good instincts. They talk through the red flags—the too-perfect opportunity, the pressure for a quick decision, the request for extensive personal data upfront. Together, they run the company through their trusted verification network. Within minutes, three friends in tech confirm their suspicions: it's a sophisticated synthetic company, complete with fake employees and an AI-generated website, harvesting data from new graduates.

After the call, Maya checks her "reality anchors"—the physical journal where she writes by hand each morning, the printed photos that can't be retroactively edited, the analog clock whose steady ticking reminds her that not everything needs to be digital. These rituals aren't about rejecting technology but about maintaining balance.

At work, Maya leads a product team at a privacy-focused startup. Their morning standup includes team members from six countries, all participating through verified channels. The Iranian engineer who'd been impersonated by state actors, the Brazilian designer who'd fought off a synthetic identity theft, the Estonian cryptographer who'd lived through their country's deepfake crisis—each brings hard-won wisdom about building technology that enhances rather than replaces human agency.

. . .

Their current project—a community verification system for small businesses—embodies the principles they've all learned: make security invisible, leverage collective wisdom, respect cognitive limits, preserve joy. They're not trying to build a perfect defense against synthetic media. They're building tools that help humans be more human, even in a world where anything can be faked.

Lunch is with her "trust circle"—five friends who've been meeting monthly since the worst of the synthetic media crisis. They'd started as a support group, helping each other navigate the paranoia and isolation of peak deepfake chaos. Now they're something more: a chosen family bound by shared verification protocols and deeper understanding. They laugh about the early days when they'd spend half their time proving they were real. Now, verification is background music to genuine connection.

The afternoon brings a notification Maya chooses to engage with: a potential synthetic media attack on a local climate activist. Maya's part of a rapid response network that formed organically in the Bay Area. Within an hour, they've verified the fake, traced its origins, notified the platforms, and surrounded the activist with support. The deepfake still spreads, but it meets organized resistance at every turn.

Evening finds Maya at her nephew's birthday party. No phones allowed—not from paranoia but from presence. The children play with physical toys, their laughter unrecorded but deeply felt. The adults tell stories, their voices unverified but trusted. For these few hours, they live like humans always have: through direct connection, shared experience, embodied presence.

. . .

Before bed, Maya reflects on the strange beauty of their adapted world. Yes, synthetic media has made them more cautious, more intentional about trust. But it's also made them more appreciative of authentic connection, more skilled at building real community, more conscious about how they live.

Her daughter texts a goodnight message—through their verified channel, of course, but what matters is the words: "Thanks for your help today. Love you."

Maya smiles. They're living authentically in a synthetic world—not by rejecting the digital but by choosing how to engage with it, not by building perfect defenses but by building meaningful connections, not by eliminating all risk but by facing it together.

This is what adaptation looks like: not a return to some imaginary past, but a conscious navigation of an unprecedented present. They've learned to thrive not despite synthetic media but because of what resisting it has taught them about being human.

PERSONAL STRATEGIES FOR SYNTHETIC RESILIENCE

The fictional day in Maya's life illustrates something profound: living authentically in a synthetic world isn't about perfect security or constant vigilance. It's about developing sustainable practices that preserve your humanity while navigating digital complexity. The strategies that emerge from real experiences of those already adapting point toward a middle path—neither naive trust nor paranoid isolation.

. . .

Build Your Reality Anchors

Just as ships need anchors to keep from drifting, humans need connections to unmediated reality that synthetic media cannot corrupt:

Physical Practices: Maintain some analog habits that ground you in the physical world. This might be:

- A handwritten journal that captures your thoughts without digital intermediation
- Physical photo albums that preserve memories without algorithmic curation
- Regular time in nature where reality isn't filtered through screens
- Crafts or hobbies that engage your hands and create tangible results

Temporal Anchors: Create rhythms that synthetic media cannot disrupt:

- Morning routines completed before engaging with digital devices
- Weekly digital sabbaths where you disconnect entirely
- Seasonal rituals that mark time's passage independent of online cycles
- Regular in-person gatherings that maintain human connection

. . .

Sensory Grounding: Engage senses that screens cannot replicate:

- Cooking meals that fill your home with real aromas
- Playing musical instruments that create vibrations you feel
- Gardening to connect with growth cycles beyond algorithms
- Exercise that reminds you of your body's reality

Develop Verification Habits Without Paranoia

The key to sustainable verification is making it as natural and unobtrusive as other safety habits:

Graduated Verification: Not every interaction needs the same level of scrutiny:

- Casual conversations: basic behavioral consistency
- Financial requests: multiple channel confirmation
- Identity claims: cryptographic verification
- Emergency messages: established family protocols

Verification Rituals: Make authentication feel like connection, not suspicion:

- Family code words that double as inside jokes
- Friend verification that includes sharing positive memories
- Professional protocols that build team cohesion
- Community practices that strengthen bonds

Trust But Verify Culture: Normalize verification without stigma:

- "Let me verify that" becomes as routine as "let me Google that"
- Checking sources becomes a sign of care, not distrust
- Verification requests are met with appreciation, not offense
- Everyone understands it's about the system, not the person

Create Intentional Information Practices

Your information diet shapes your reality as much as your food diet shapes your health:

Conscious Consumption: Choose your inputs deliberately:

- Subscribe directly to trusted sources rather than relying on algorithms
- Set specific times for news consumption rather than continuous updates

- Balance negative awareness with positive possibilities
- Seek primary sources over interpretations

Active vs. Passive Engagement: Transform from consumer to participant:

- Comment thoughtfully rather than just scrolling
- Create content, don't just consume it
- Share verified information, not just viral content
- Build rather than just browse

Information Fasting: Regular breaks reset your perspective:

- Daily periods without any digital input
- Weekly longer disconnections
- Monthly deep dives into single topics rather than scattered attention
- Annual extended breaks for perspective

Build Your Concentric Circles of Trust

Organize your relationships in circles of increasing verification and decreasing friction:

Inner Circle (3-8 people): Family and closest friends

- Highest trust, lowest verification friction
- Share verification methods that are intimate and unique
- Create closed channels for authentic communication
- Maintain some fully private, undigital connections

Trust Circle (20-50 people): Close friends and key colleagues

- Regular verification but integrated into connection
- Shared protocols everyone understands
- Mutual support for verification and synthetic media defense
- Group activities that build collective resilience

Community Circle (100-500 people): Extended network

- Basic verification for significant interactions
- Participation in collective defense networks
- Shared resources and information
- Community standards for synthetic media response

Public Circle (everyone else): Default skepticism with openness

- Verify before trusting
- Share carefully
- Maintain boundaries
- Expect synthetic media

Practice Cognitive Sovereignty Daily

Reclaiming your mental autonomy requires daily practice:

Attention Ownership: Take control of where your focus goes:

- Start each day with intention-setting
- Notice when your attention is captured versus chosen
- Practice returning to the present when distracted
- End each day reviewing where your attention went

Emotional Regulation: Recognize and resist manipulation:

- Notice emotional triggers in media consumption
- Pause between feeling and reacting
- Question who benefits from your emotional response
- Choose responses aligned with your values

Critical Thinking Habits: Make skepticism productive:

- Ask "what if this is synthetic?" without paranoia
- Look for evidence, not just claims
- Consider multiple explanations
- Remain open to being wrong

Maintain Hope and Connection

Perhaps most importantly, don't let defensive necessities destroy what makes life meaningful:

Celebrate Small Victories: Acknowledge progress:

- Successfully verifying a suspicious message
- Helping someone else avoid synthetic deception
- Building stronger real relationships
- Creating something authentic

Focus on Growth: Frame challenges as opportunities:

- Each synthetic media encounter teaches discernment
- Verification practices deepen relationships
- Challenges build collective resilience
- Adaptation develops new capacities

Preserve Wonder: Don't let caution eliminate joy:

- Technology can still enable beautiful connections
- Verification can become a form of care
- Community defense builds deeper bonds
- Human creativity always finds new expression

THE NEW DIGITAL LITERACY

Traditional digital literacy focused on using tools—how to search, create documents, navigate interfaces. But synthetic media demands a fundamentally different literacy: the ability to navigate uncertainty, verify authenticity, and maintain humanity while using powerful technologies. This new literacy isn't just technical skill but wisdom for living.

Reality Testing as Core Competency

Just as traditional literacy starts with recognizing letters, synthetic age literacy starts with recognizing what's potentially fake:

Pattern Recognition: Developing intuition for synthetic content:

- Too-perfect scenarios that lack messy reality
- Emotional manipulation that feels crafted
- Timing that seems strategically suspicious
- Claims that conveniently can't be verified

Verification Skills: Moving beyond "this looks real" to proof:

- Reverse image searching as second nature
- Cross-referencing across multiple sources
- Understanding cryptographic verification
- Building networks for collective checking

Uncertainty Tolerance: Functioning without perfect knowledge:

- Acting on best available information
- Holding provisional beliefs
- Updating views with new evidence
- Accepting some things remain unknown

Relationship Literacy in Synthetic Context

Understanding how synthetic media changes human connection:

Authentic Communication: Recognizing real human connection:

- Imperfection as a sign of authenticity
- Emotional resonance beyond words
- Consistent patterns over time
- Vulnerability as trust signal

Synthetic Awareness: Identifying manufactured relationships:

- Love bombing and rapid intimacy
- Requests that escalate unusually
- Inconsistencies in life details
- Pressure tactics and urgency

Boundary Management: Protecting yourself while remaining open:

- Different verification for different relationships
- Information sharing on need-to-know basis
- Exit strategies for compromised connections
- Recovery protocols for breaches

Technical Literacy Without Expertise

Understanding enough to protect yourself without becoming a technologist:

Conceptual Understanding: Grasping how not what:

- How deepfakes work conceptually
- Why cryptographic signatures matter
- What makes verification possible
- Where vulnerabilities exist

Tool Competence: Using protection without understanding internals:

- Password managers without cryptography knowledge
- Verification apps without technical details
- Privacy tools without networking expertise
- Security practices without paranoia

Update Awareness: Staying current without obsession:

- Major shifts in synthetic capabilities
- New verification methods available
- Emerging threats to watch for
- Community resources for learning

Emotional and Psychological Literacy

Understanding synthetic media's psychological impact:

Stress Recognition: Identifying when you're overwhelmed:

- Verification fatigue symptoms
- Paranoia versus reasonable caution
- Social withdrawal patterns
- Reality dissociation signs

Coping Strategies: Managing synthetic media stress:

- Scheduled verification breaks
- Reality anchoring practices
- Support network activation
- Professional help when needed

Resilience Building: Growing stronger through challenge:

- Reframing threats as skill-building
- Finding meaning in collective defense
- Building confidence through practice
- Celebrating adaptation success

Cultural and Social Literacy

Understanding synthetic media's broader implications:

Power Dynamics: Recognizing who benefits and who suffers:

- Synthetic media as tool of oppression
- Digital divides in protection access
- Collective action possibilities
- Systemic versus individual solutions

Ethical Navigation: Making good choices in gray areas:

- When to verify versus trust
- How to call out synthetic media kindly
- Whether to use synthetic tools ethically
- Where to draw personal boundaries

Future Orientation: Preparing for what's next:

- Assuming capabilities will increase

- Building adaptable rather than fixed defenses
- Teaching others what you learn
- Contributing to collective wisdom

This new literacy isn't mastered through courses but developed through practice. Every day in the synthetic age offers opportunities to build these competencies, to help others develop them, and to collectively become wiser about navigating our strange new world.

COMMUNITIES OF TRUST IN A TRUSTLESS WORLD

[The following section explores how communities might organize in response to synthetic media threats, based on historical patterns of mutual aid and collective defense. While some early examples of collaborative verification exist (like fact-checking groups), the specific organizational forms described here remain largely speculative projections of how human communities typically adapt to new challenges.]

While the scenario of Maya's trust circle was fictional, it represents the kind of community responses we might expect to emerge: faced with synthetic media's assault on individual verification, people would likely build new forms of community based on mutual authentication and collective defense. These wouldn't be returns to pre-digital communities but entirely new social formations adapted to synthetic age challenges.

The Trust Circle Movement

. . .

Around the world, small groups could form with a specific purpose: mutual verification and support in navigating synthetic media:

Formation Patterns: How trust circles emerge:

- Often sparked by shared synthetic media experience
- Usually 5-12 people for manageability
- Mix of technical and non-technical members
- Diverse perspectives but shared values

Core Practices: What trust circles do:

- Regular in-person meetings to maintain human connection
- Shared verification protocols everyone understands
- Rapid response to member synthetic media threats
- Skill sharing and mutual education
- Emotional support for synthetic media stress

Evolution Stages: How trust circles mature:

- Initial formation around shared vulnerability
- Development of working verification methods
- Expansion to include families and close friends
- Connection with other circles for broader network
- Formalization of practices that work

Neighborhood Verification Networks

Geographic proximity creates unique opportunities for synthetic media defense:

Local Advantages: Why physical neighbors matter:

- Can verify physical presence quickly
- Share local context outsiders miss
- Build on existing social infrastructure
- Create rapid response capability

Community Practices: What neighborhoods are doing:

- Block parties that include digital literacy components
- Shared verification resources and tools
- Rapid alert systems for local synthetic media
- Support for vulnerable neighbors
- Children's education programs

Infrastructure Building: Creating lasting protection:

- Neighborhood verification registries
- Local business authentication networks
- Community-owned verification tools
- Shared defense funds
- Regular training and drills

Professional Verification Networks

Industries and professions create their own defensive structures:

Industry Initiatives: Sector-specific solutions:

- Journalists creating verification collaboratives
- Financial professionals sharing fraud patterns
- Educators building synthetic media curricula
- Healthcare workers protecting patient privacy
- Artists defending against style theft

Cross-Organization Cooperation: Breaking down silos:

- Competitors sharing synthetic media intelligence
- Industry-wide verification standards
- Collective response to sector attacks
- Shared training resources
- Joint advocacy efforts

Professional Development: New skills for synthetic age:

- Verification as core competency
- Synthetic media awareness training
- Client/customer protection protocols
- Ethical guidelines for synthetic tools

- Recovery and response procedures

Global Solidarity Networks

Distance doesn't prevent collective defense:

International Connections: Building global resilience:

- Language-specific verification communities
- Diaspora networks maintaining cultural identity
- Professional communities crossing borders
- Shared defense against state-level attacks
- Technology transfer between regions

Resource Sharing: Collective capacity building:

- Open-source verification tools
- Translated educational materials
- Shared threat intelligence
- Collaborative response teams
- Funding for under-resourced communities

Cultural Exchange: Learning from different approaches:

- How different cultures handle trust
- Varied verification methods

- Alternative community structures
- Diverse resilience strategies
- Cross-cultural synthetic media patterns

The Commons We're Building

These various community formations are creating something new: a commons of trust in an age of synthetic deception. This isn't centralized or controlled but emerges from countless small groups choosing connection over isolation, collective defense over individual paranoia.

Characteristics of the emerging trust commons:

Distributed but Connected: Independent groups share methods and learn from each other without central control

Resilient through Diversity: Different approaches for different contexts prevent single points of failure

Inclusive by Design: Communities actively work to include those most vulnerable to synthetic media

Evolving Constantly: Practices adapt as threats change, spreading successful innovations

. . .

Humanizing Technology: Tools serve human connection rather than replacing it

The trust commons proves something important: even in a world where anything can be faked, humans can create authentic community. The same social instincts that make us vulnerable to deception also enable our collective defense.

BUILDING THE MOVEMENT FOR DIGITAL AUTHENTICITY

[The following explores how a movement for digital authenticity might emerge, drawing from patterns observed in other technology-focused social movements like digital rights, open source software, and privacy advocacy. While elements of such a movement exist in current digital literacy and fact-checking initiatives, the comprehensive movement described here is a speculative projection of how civil society might organize around synthetic media challenges.]

Beyond individual practices and community formations, a broader movement for digital authenticity is emerging—not through central organization but through countless aligned actions by people choosing real over synthetic, connection over isolation, and collective wisdom over individual struggle.

Movement Principles Emerging

Though no manifesto exists, common principles appear across contexts:

. . .

Authenticity as Resistance: In a world of synthetic everything, choosing to be real becomes revolutionary:

- Sharing imperfect real content over polished fake
- Admitting uncertainty rather than false confidence
- Showing vulnerability as strength
- Celebrating human messiness

Verification as Care: Checking authenticity becomes act of love:

- Verifying to protect others, not just yourself
- Making verification feel like connection
- Building trust through transparency
- Creating safety for authentic expression

Collective Over Individual: Recognizing no one survives alone:

- Sharing verification labor
- Building tools for community use
- Teaching what you learn
- Supporting those struggling

Joy Despite Threat: Refusing to let defense destroy life:

- Finding humor in verification rituals
- Celebrating successful defenses
- Building beautiful tools
- Creating amid chaos

. . .

Practical Movement Building

The movement grows through concrete actions:

Education Initiatives: Teaching the next generation:

- School programs on synthetic media literacy
- Community workshops for elders
- Professional development courses
- Peer-to-peer learning networks
- Intergenerational knowledge transfer

Tool Development: Building what we need:

- Open-source verification software
- Community-owned platforms
- Privacy-respecting alternatives
- Accessible interfaces
- Local language support

Policy Advocacy: Demanding systemic change:

- Right to authentic identity laws
- Platform accountability measures
- Public funding for verification infrastructure
- Protection for synthetic media victims

- International cooperation frameworks

Cultural Production: Changing hearts and minds:

- Art that explores synthetic/authentic tension
- Stories celebrating human connection
- Music about digital age challenges
- Games teaching verification skills
- Memes spreading awareness

Signs of Success

Evidence the movement is working:

Normalized Verification: Checking sources becomes as routine as hand washing

Reduced Shame: Being fooled by synthetic media carries no stigma

Increased Connection: Verification rituals deepen rather than strain relationships

Technical Adoption: Verification tools achieve mass usage

. . .

Policy Progress: Governments implement protective frameworks

Cultural Shift: Authenticity valued over perfection

Challenges and Responses

Such a movement would likely face predictable obstacles based on patterns from other digital rights movements:

Sophistication Gap: Synthetic media would likely improve faster than defenses

- Response: Focus on collective intelligence over perfect technical solutions

Resource Inequality: Not everyone would have equal access to protection

- Response: Build commons-based solutions and mutual aid networks

Exhaustion Risk: Constant vigilance could burn people out

- Response: Rotate responsibilities and build sustainable practices

. . .

Co-optation Danger: Commercial interests might try to capture movement energy

- Response: Maintain focus on human agency over profit

Despair Temptation: The task could seem impossible

- Response: Celebrate small victories and build hope through action

Your Role in the Movement

Everyone has something to contribute:

If you're technical: Build tools that empower rather than exhaust

If you're social: Create communities of mutual verification

If you're creative: Make content that inspires authentic connection

If you're political: Advocate for policies protecting digital dignity

. . .

If you're educational: Teach the next generation synthetic media wisdom

If you're none of the above: Your authentic presence and willingness to connect matter most

The movement for digital authenticity isn't waiting for leaders or permission. It's happening every time someone chooses verification over viral sharing, every time communities practice collective defense, every time humans insist on staying human despite synthetic temptation.

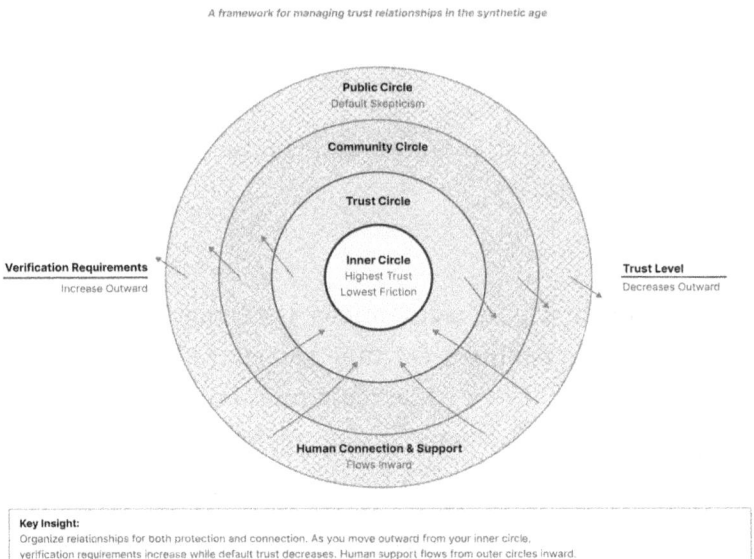

Figure 17.1: *The Concentric Circles of Trust*. A framework for organizing relationships in the synthetic age, balancing protection with human connection. The diagram illustrates how trust operates on a gradient—from the Inner Circle of highest trust requiring minimal verification, to the Public Circle where default skepticism and maximum verification prevail. While verification requirements increase and trust decreases moving outward (shown by directional arrows), human connection and support flow inward, creating a reciprocal system that maintains both security and meaningful relationships. This model helps individuals navigate the paradox of needing both stronger boundaries and deeper connections in an era of synthetic threats.

FINAL TAKEAWAY: YOU ARE NOT POWERLESS

As we reach the end of this journey through the synthetic age—from understanding the threats to building defenses, from individual practices to collective movements—one truth stands above all: you are not powerless.

Yes, the challenges are real:

- Synthetic media grows more sophisticated daily
- Perfect security is impossible
- Individual defenses alone cannot succeed
- The pace of change exhausts human adaptation

But so is your capacity to respond:

- Human intuition still catches what algorithms miss
- Communities provide strength individuals lack
- Every small action contributes to collective defense
- Adaptation is humanity's superpower

What You Can Do Today

Start where you are with what you have:

Personal Foundation:

- Choose one reality anchor practice to begin
- Set up basic verification with family
- Join or form a trust circle
- Practice conscious media consumption
- Document your authentic life

Community Building:

- Share what you learn with others
- Support someone facing synthetic attack
- Contribute to collective verification efforts
- Model healthy synthetic media practices
- Build bridges, not walls

Systemic Change:

- Support organizations advancing digital rights
- Advocate for protective policies
- Choose platforms respecting human agency
- Fund tools serving collective good
- Vote for leaders who understand

The Path Forward

Living authentically in a synthetic world isn't about perfect defense—it's about conscious choice. Every day you'll face decisions: trust or verify, share or pause, connect or protect. There's no universal right answer, only the ongoing practice of navigating with wisdom.

The synthetic age isn't just a threat—it's a mirror showing us what we value about being human. In fighting to preserve authentic connection, we discover what authenticity means. In building collective defenses, we create deeper community. In facing unprecedented challenges, we develop new capacities.

. . .

Hope in Action

Hope in the synthetic age isn't passive optimism—it's active construction of the world we want to inhabit. Every time you:

- Verify before sharing
- Build real connections despite digital risks
- Teach someone else protective practices
- Choose human wisdom over algorithmic ease
- Insist on staying human

You're not just surviving the synthetic age—you're helping create a future where human authenticity thrives despite technological capability for deception.

The tools of synthesis are powerful, but so are the tools of human connection, collective wisdom, and stubborn insistence on truth. We're not returning to a pre-synthetic world, but we're not surrendering to synthetic dominion either. We're building something new: a world where humans use powerful technologies while maintaining their humanity, where verification enables rather than replaces trust, where collective defense creates deeper community.

The Choice Is Ours

The synthetic age presents a choice that each generation faces in its own way: will we let our tools define us, or will we define how we use our tools? Will we surrender agency for convenience, or maintain humanity despite difficulty? Will we face challenges alone, or together?

History suggests humans choose connection, choose agency, choose hope—not because it's easy but because it's human. The synthetic age is our generation's test. How we respond will echo through generations.

You're not just living through unprecedented change—you're helping determine what human means in an age where humanity itself can be synthesized. That's not a burden—it's an opportunity. Not a crisis—but a chrysalis.

The future remains unwritten. Your choices help write it. In a world where everything can be faked, your authentic action matters more than ever.

Stay human. Stay connected. Stay hopeful.

The revolution for human authenticity in the synthetic age has begun. You're already part of it.

Welcome to the rest of your life.

∼

Appendix A: Zero Trust Implementation Checklist

"Never trust, always verify" isn't paranoia—it's prudence in the synthetic age.

This checklist translates the principles explored throughout this book into concrete actions you can take today. Start with the basics and gradually build more sophisticated defenses. Remember: perfect security is impossible, but meaningful protection is achievable.

PERSONAL SECURITY AUDIT

LEVEL 1: FOUNDATION (START HERE)

Complete these basics before moving to advanced measures.

Digital Inventory

- [ ] List all devices you own (phones, computers, tablets, smart home devices)
- [ ] Document which devices have biometric data (fingerprint, face, voice)
- [ ] Identify where your photos and videos are stored
- [ ] Note which apps have access to your camera and microphone
- [ ] Review what personal data you've shared on social media

Authentication Baseline

- [ ] Enable two-factor authentication on all critical accounts
- [ ] Use unique passwords for every service (password manager recommended)
- [ ] Document your security questions and ensure answers aren't publicly discoverable
- [ ] Set up account recovery options that don't rely on SMS
- [ ] Create a list of your most critical accounts requiring highest security

Communication Channels

- [ ] Install at least one end-to-end encrypted messaging app (Signal, Threema, Wire, Element)
- [ ] Identify which channels you use for sensitive communications
- [ ] Establish preferred channels for different types of contacts
- [ ] Review and clean up your contact lists
- [ ] Set up verified communication channels with immediate family

LEVEL 2: ENHANCED PROTECTION

Build on the foundation with these additional measures.

Synthetic Media Awareness

- [ ] Learn to use reverse image search tools
- [ ] Install browser extensions for fact-checking
- [ ] Practice identifying common deepfake artifacts
- [ ] Bookmark trusted verification resources
- [ ] Join at least one fact-checking community

Privacy Hardening

- [ ] Review and restrict app permissions on all devices
- [ ] Limit biometric data sharing to essential services only
- [ ] Use privacy-focused browsers and search engines
- [ ] Enable privacy settings on all social media accounts
- [ ] Consider using a VPN for sensitive browsing

Behavioral Security

- [ ] Develop habits of pausing before sharing content
- [ ] Practice verifying unusual requests through alternate channels
- [ ] Create regular backups of important data
- [ ] Document your normal communication patterns
- [ ] Establish "reality anchors" (analog practices that ground you)

LEVEL 3: ADVANCED MEASURES

For those facing higher risks or wanting maximum protection.

Cryptographic Identity

- [ ] Obtain hardware security keys (YubiKey or similar)
- [ ] Set up PGP keys for email encryption
- [ ] Learn basic cryptographic signature verification
- [ ] Create secure backups of all cryptographic keys
- [ ] Establish key exchange protocols with trusted contacts

Compartmentalization

- [ ] Separate devices or user accounts for different activities
- [ ] Use different email addresses for different purposes
- [ ] Maintain distinct online identities for various contexts
- [ ] Implement network segmentation at home
- [ ] Create isolated environments for sensitive work

Active Defense

- [ ] Monitor for unauthorized use of your likeness online
- [ ] Set up alerts for your name and variations
- [ ] Document all your legitimate online presence
- [ ] Create a response plan for identity theft
- [ ] Build relationships with legal and technical experts

FAMILY VERIFICATION PROTOCOLS

BASIC FAMILY SECURITY

Essential steps every family should take.

Establishing Trust Signals

- [ ] Create family code words that rotate monthly

- [ ] Establish verification questions only family members know
- [ ] Set up a family group on encrypted messaging
- [ ] Create rules for money requests and transfers
- [ ] Practice verification scenarios regularly

Communication Protocols

- [ ] Designate primary and backup communication channels
- [ ] Establish check-in schedules for family members
- [ ] Create protocols for emergency situations
- [ ] Set up location sharing among trusted family
- [ ] Define what information is never requested via digital channels

Children's Digital Safety

- [ ] Educate children about synthetic media age-appropriately
- [ ] Establish rules for sharing photos and videos
- [ ] Monitor children's digital footprint
- [ ] Teach verification before trust
- [ ] Create safe spaces for children to report concerns

EXTENDED FAMILY NETWORKS

Protecting broader family connections.

Elderly Family Members

- [ ] Provide simplified verification methods
- [ ] Regular education about evolving threats
- [ ] Set up trusted contact lists on their devices

- [ ] Create easy reporting mechanisms for suspicious contact
- [ ] Establish power of attorney for digital matters if needed

Geographic Distribution

- [ ] Account for time zones in verification protocols
- [ ] Establish regional family points of contact
- [ ] Create redundant communication channels
- [ ] Plan for international communication restrictions
- [ ] Document family network structure

ORGANIZATIONAL TRUST POLICIES

SMALL BUSINESS IMPLEMENTATION

For businesses with limited resources.

Basic Business Security

- [ ] Implement multi-person approval for financial transactions
- [ ] Create verification protocols for remote workers
- [ ] Establish secure channels for sensitive communications
- [ ] Train all employees on synthetic media threats
- [ ] Document normal business communication patterns

Customer Protection

- [ ] Implement customer identity verification procedures
- [ ] Create clear policies about what you'll never ask via email

- [ ] Establish secure channels for customer verification
- [ ] Train customer service on synthetic media awareness
- [ ] Create public awareness about your security practices

ENTERPRISE IMPLEMENTATION

For larger organizations with dedicated resources.

Governance Structure

- [ ] Establish a synthetic media response team
- [ ] Create clear escalation procedures
- [ ] Implement regular security awareness training
- [ ] Conduct synthetic media attack simulations
- [ ] Establish relationships with law enforcement

Technical Infrastructure

- [ ] Deploy enterprise-grade authentication systems
- [ ] Implement content authenticity verification tools
- [ ] Create secure communication platforms
- [ ] Establish cryptographic signing for official communications
- [ ] Build redundant verification systems

Supply Chain Security

- [ ] Verify all vendor communications through multiple channels
- [ ] Establish secure communication protocols with partners
- [ ] Create supplier verification databases
- [ ] Implement code signing for software suppliers
- [ ] Regular audits of third-party security practices

COMMUNITY RESPONSE PLANS

NEIGHBORHOOD NETWORKS

Building local resilience.

Community Organization

- [ ] Form local digital safety groups
- [ ] Organize regular education sessions
- [ ] Create neighborhood alert systems
- [ ] Establish physical meeting spaces
- [ ] Build relationships with local law enforcement

Resource Sharing

- [ ] Pool resources for security tools
- [ ] Share threat intelligence locally
- [ ] Create skill-sharing programs
- [ ] Establish tool lending libraries
- [ ] Coordinate bulk purchases of security devices

PROFESSIONAL COMMUNITIES

Industry-specific protections.

Sector Coordination

- [ ] Join industry-specific security groups
- [ ] Share threat intelligence within your sector
- [ ] Coordinate responses to sector-wide attacks
- [ ] Establish cross-organization verification
- [ ] Create industry standards for verification

Knowledge Networks

- [ ] Participate in professional security forums
- [ ] Contribute to open-source verification projects
- [ ] Share lessons learned from incidents
- [ ] Mentor others in your field
- [ ] Build international professional connections

IMPLEMENTATION TIMELINE

MONTH 1: FOUNDATION

- Complete Level 1 Personal Security Audit
- Establish basic family protocols
- Begin community connections

MONTH 2-3: ENHANCEMENT

- Implement Level 2 security measures
- Expand family protocols to extended network
- Formalize organizational policies

MONTH 4-6: ADVANCEMENT

- Deploy Level 3 measures as needed
- Conduct family and organizational drills
- Strengthen community networks

ONGOING: MAINTENANCE

- Monthly verification protocol reviews
- Quarterly security audits

- Annual comprehensive assessment
- Continuous education and updates

RED FLAGS: WHEN TO SEEK HELP

Immediately escalate if you encounter:

- Requests for money with unusual urgency
- Communications that don't match established patterns
- Threats or coercion of any kind
- Evidence of synthetic media using your likeness
- Systematic targeting of your organization
- Compromise of verification channels

RESOURCES FOR CONTINUED LEARNING

Verification Tools

- See *Appendix C: Resources and Tools*.

Educational Resources

- Online courses in digital verification
- Community workshops and training
- Professional certification programs
- Academic research centers

Support Networks

- Digital rights organizations
- Victim support services
- Legal aid resources
- Technical assistance programs

REMEMBER: PROGRESS, NOT PERFECTION

This checklist can feel overwhelming. Don't try to implement everything at once. Start with the basics, build gradually, and remember that any improvement in your security posture is valuable. The goal isn't to become a security expert overnight—it's to steadily build resilience against synthetic threats while maintaining the connections and activities that make life meaningful.

The most important step isn't the most sophisticated technical measure—it's the decision to take your digital security seriously and start somewhere. Every checkbox you complete makes you, your family, and your community slightly safer in the synthetic age.

∼

Begin today. Build consistently. Stay human.

∼

APPENDIX B: TECHNICAL DEEP DIVES

For those who want to understand not just what to do, but how it works.

This appendix provides deeper technical explanations of key concepts discussed throughout the book. While the main text keeps technical details accessible, here we explore the mathematics, algorithms, and engineering that make these systems work—or fail.

UNDERSTANDING PUBLIC KEY CRYPTOGRAPHY

THE MATHEMATICAL FOUNDATION

Public key cryptography seems like magic: how can you have a key that locks but can't unlock? The answer lies in mathematical operations that are easy in one direction but nearly impossible to reverse.

The Basic Principle

Imagine multiplying two large prime numbers:

- 1,019 × 1,013 = 1,032,247 (easy to calculate)
- Given 1,032,247, find its prime factors (much harder)

With small numbers, factoring is manageable. But with primes hundreds of digits long, even supercomputers would need centuries. This "one-way" mathematical property enables public key systems.

How RSA Works

RSA (Rivest-Shamir-Adleman) uses this principle:

1. **Key Generation:**
    - Choose two large primes (p and q)
    - Calculate n = p × q
    - Choose public exponent e (commonly 65,537)
    - Calculate private exponent d (using p, q, and e)
    - Public key: (n, e)
    - Private key: (n, d)

2. **Encryption:**
    - Message^e mod n = Ciphertext

3. **Decryption:**
    - Ciphertext^d mod n = Message

The security relies on the difficulty of factoring n back into p and q.

Real-World Implications

- Current standard: 2048-bit keys (617 decimal digits)
- Quantum computers threaten this model (see below)

- Post-quantum cryptography uses different hard problems

DIGITAL SIGNATURES EXPLAINED

Digital signatures prove authenticity and integrity using the reverse of encryption:

1. **Signing:** Hash the message, then encrypt hash with private key
2. **Verification:** Decrypt signature with public key, compare to message hash

If hashes match, the signature is valid and the message unchanged.

Why This Matters for Synthetic Media

- Every piece of verified content could carry a signature
- Tampering breaks the mathematical relationship
- But the signature only proves the signer—not truth

HOW DEEPFAKES WORK

GENERATIVE ADVERSARIAL NETWORKS (GANS)

Deepfakes primarily use GANs, where two neural networks compete:

The Generator creates fake content

- Starts with random noise
- Learns to transform noise into realistic images/video
- Goal: fool the discriminator

The Discriminator detects fakes

- Trained on real images/videos
- Learns to spot synthetic content
- Goal: correctly identify generator's fakes

They train together in an arms race:

1. Generator creates fake image
2. Discriminator judges real or fake
3. Both update based on results
4. Repeat millions of times

THE TECHNICAL PIPELINE

Data Collection

- Gather hours of target video/audio
- Multiple angles, lighting conditions, expressions
- More data = more convincing fakes

Face Extraction and Alignment

- Detect faces in each frame
- Normalize size, orientation, lighting
- Create standardized training dataset

Training Process

- Encoder learns to compress faces to essential features
- Decoder learns to reconstruct faces from features
- Swap decoders to put one person's expressions on another's face

Post-Processing

- Blend edges for seamless integration
- Match lighting and color
- Add realistic motion blur
- Sync audio if needed

WHY DETECTION IS DIFFICULT

Technical Challenges:

- GANs improve faster than detectors
- Compression artifacts hide tells
- Each generation gets more sophisticated
- Adversarial training defeats detectors

Practical Challenges:

- Need original for comparison
- Real-time detection computationally expensive
- False positives damage legitimate content
- Arms race favors attackers

BLOCKCHAIN AND DISTRIBUTED LEDGERS EXPLAINED

CORE CONCEPTS

What Is a Blockchain?

A blockchain is a chain of blocks, where each block contains:

- Transaction data
- Timestamp
- Hash of previous block
- Nonce (number used once)

This creates an immutable history—change any past block, and all subsequent hashes break.

Consensus Mechanisms

How do distributed systems agree on truth?

Proof of Work (Bitcoin):

- Miners compete to solve mathematical puzzles
- First to solve gets to add block
- Extremely energy-intensive
- Security through computational cost

Proof of Stake (Ethereum 2.0):

- Validators chosen based on stake held
- Less energy-intensive
- Security through economic incentives
- Risk of centralization

Byzantine Fault Tolerance:

- Nodes vote on valid transactions
- Can tolerate up to 1/3 malicious nodes
- Faster but requires known participants

APPLICATION TO CONTENT AUTHENTICITY

Storing Hashes, Not Content

- Content too large for blockchain
- Store cryptographic hash instead
- Anyone can verify content matches hash

- Timestamp proves when it existed

Challenges:

- Blockchain proves when, not what
- Garbage in, garbage out
- Scalability limitations
- Energy consumption
- Permanence can be a bug, not feature

ZERO-KNOWLEDGE PROOFS DEMYSTIFIED

THE INTUITION

How can you prove you know something without revealing what you know?

The Classic Example: Colorblind Friend

- Friend has two balls (red and green) but can't see colors
- Friend wants to know if they're the same or different colors
- Friend shows you the balls, then hides them behind their back
- Friend either switches them between hands or keeps them the same
- Friend shows you the balls again and asks: "Did I switch them?"
- If the balls are different colors, you can always tell correctly
- If they were the same color, you'd only guess right 50% of the time
- After many rounds of always being correct, friend is convinced they're different colors

- Friend never learns which ball is red or green—only that they differ

MATHEMATICAL FOUNDATION

The Three Properties:

In our colorblind friend example:

- *You* are the Prover (claiming the balls are different colors)
- *Friend* is the Verifier (testing your claim)

1. **Completeness:** If statement is true, honest prover convinces honest verifier
    - Since the balls really are different colors, you can always identify switches correctly

2. **Soundness:** If statement is false, no cheating prover can convince honest verifier (except with small probability)
    - If the balls were the same color, you couldn't consistently identify switches

3. **Zero-Knowledge:** Verifier learns nothing except statement validity
    - Friend learns the balls are different but never learns which is red or green

REAL-WORLD ZKP SYSTEMS

zk-SNARKs (Zero-Knowledge Succinct Non-Interactive Arguments of Knowledge):

- Prove complex statements with tiny proofs
- Non-interactive (no back-and-forth needed)
- Requires trusted setup

- Used in Zcash cryptocurrency

zk-STARKs (Zero-Knowledge Scalable Transparent Arguments of Knowledge):

- No trusted setup needed
- Quantum-resistant
- Larger proof sizes
- More recent development

PRACTICAL APPLICATIONS

Age Verification Without Revealing Birthdate:

1. Government signs statement: "This person born before 2005"
2. Person presents proof they own this statement
3. Verifier confirms without learning actual birthdate

Financial Solvency Without Revealing Balance:

1. Prove account balance > X
2. Without revealing actual amount
3. Useful for loans, rentals, etc.

HARDWARE SECURITY MODULES AND SECURE ENCLAVES

TRUSTED EXECUTION ENVIRONMENTS (TEES)

What Makes Hardware Secure?

Software can be modified, but hardware provides physical guarantees:

- **Isolated Execution:** Separate processor, memory, storage
- **Secure Boot:** Cryptographically verified startup
- **Hardware Random Numbers:** True randomness from physical processes
- **Tamper Resistance:** Physical attacks trigger key destruction

COMMON IMPLEMENTATIONS

Apple Secure Enclave:

- Dedicated chip in iPhones/Macs
- Stores biometric data
- Handles cryptographic operations
- Never exposes keys to main processor

ARM TrustZone:

- Creates secure and normal worlds in same processor
- Used in billions of Android/mobile devices
- Switches between secure/normal execution modes
- Enables features like Samsung Knox

Intel SGX (Software Guard Extensions):

- Creates secure enclaves in main processor
- Encrypts memory regions
- Remote attestation capabilities
- Application-level security isolation

Microsoft Pluton:

- Security processor integrated into CPU
- Designed with AMD, Intel, Qualcomm

- Updateable firmware through Windows Update
- Protects credentials, keys, and identity

TPM (Trusted Platform Module):

- Industry standard chip
- Stores keys and certificates
- Measures boot process
- Enables BitLocker, etc.

ATTACK VECTORS AND DEFENSES

Physical Attacks:

- Power analysis (measuring consumption patterns)
- Electromagnetic emanation
- Fault injection (voltage glitches)
- Decapping chips for microscopy

Defenses:

- Power consumption randomization
- EM shielding
- Fault detection circuits
- Self-destructing keys

THE LIMITS OF CURRENT TECHNOLOGY

QUANTUM COMPUTING THREATS

Impact on Cryptography:

- Shor's algorithm breaks RSA/ECC
- Grover's algorithm weakens symmetric crypto

- Timeline uncertain (10-30 years?)
- Post-quantum cryptography being developed

AI ADVANCEMENT TRAJECTORIES

Near-Term (1-3 years):

- Real-time voice conversion improvement
- Better emotional synthesis
- Reduced training data needs
- Mobile device generation

Medium-Term (3-10 years):

- Full body synthesis
- Behavioral pattern replication
- Cross-modal synthesis
- Reduced computational requirements

Long-Term Speculation:

- Brain-computer interfaces
- Thought pattern synthesis
- Memory implantation
- Reality indistinguishability

DEFENSIVE TECHNOLOGY GAPS

Current Limitations:

- Detection lags generation
- Computational asymmetry favors attackers
- Human factors remain weakest link
- Legal frameworks lag technology

- Global coordination challenges

Promising Research:

- Provenance from capture
- Behavioral anomaly detection
- Distributed verification
- Privacy-preserving authentication
- Quantum-resistant systems

PRACTICAL IMPLEMENTATION GUIDE

FOR DEVELOPERS

Best Practices:

1. Never roll your own crypto
2. Use established libraries
3. Keep keys in hardware when possible
4. Implement defense in depth
5. Plan for algorithm agility

Common Mistakes:

- Weak random number generation
- Improper key storage
- Side-channel vulnerabilities
- Ignoring user experience
- Over-engineering solutions

FOR ORGANIZATIONS

Technology Stack Considerations:

- Start with threat modeling
- Choose boring, proven technology
- Plan for migration/updates
- Consider total cost of ownership
- Don't forget the human element

FOR INDIVIDUALS

Understanding Your Tools:

- You don't need to understand elliptic curves
- Do understand what guarantees tools provide
- Know the failure modes
- Have backup plans
- Stay informed but not paranoid

FURTHER READING

Academic Papers:

- "The Science of Deepfakes" (2023)
- "Post-Quantum Cryptography Survey" (2024)
- "Zero-Knowledge Proofs: A Tutorial" (2023)

Technical Books:

- *Applied Cryptography* (Schneier)
- *The Hardware Security Handbook*
- *Deep Learning* (Goodfellow, Bengio, Courville)

Online Resources:

- Cryptography Course (Coursera)
- Blockchain Fundamentals (MIT)

- AI Safety Resources (Various)

∽

Remember: Technical knowledge empowers but shouldn't overwhelm. Use this appendix to deepen understanding where helpful, but don't feel you need to master every detail. The goal is informed action, not academic expertise.

∽

APPENDIX C: RESOURCES AND TOOLS

Your toolkit for navigating the synthetic age.

This appendix provides a curated collection of resources, tools, and services to help you implement the concepts discussed throughout this book. Resources are organized by category and include both free and paid options. Remember: tools are only as effective as your understanding of how to use them.

IMPORTANT DISCLAIMERS

Everything Changes: This information represents a snapshot at the time of writing. By the time you read this:

- Services may have shut down or changed ownership
- Free tools may now charge fees
- Paid services may have different pricing

- Trusted organizations may have changed leadership or mission
- Secure tools may have been compromised

Pricing Volatility:

- "Free" designations were accurate when researched but may change
- Prices listed are estimates only—always verify with the actual provider
- Many services use dynamic pricing based on usage, features, or user type
- "Enterprise pricing" means you'll need to contact them for a quote

Trust But Verify:

- A recommendation here is not perpetual endorsement
- Good actors can become bad actors through acquisition, leadership changes, or pivots
- Always research current ownership and recent news before trusting a service
- Check privacy policies and terms of service—they change frequently

Geographic Limitations:

- Some resources may not be available in all countries
- Legal protections vary by jurisdiction
- Services may work differently in different regions
- Local alternatives may be more appropriate for your area

No Guarantees:

- Inclusion here doesn't guarantee effectiveness for your specific needs
- Security tools require proper configuration and use
- No tool provides perfect protection
- Your threat model determines appropriate tools

Do Your Homework:

- Research current reviews and security audits
- Verify the tool is still actively maintained
- Check for known vulnerabilities or breaches
- Ensure compatibility with your devices and systems
- Read the fine print—especially for "free" services

The most important tool is your own judgment. Use this list as a starting point, not gospel.

VERIFICATION SERVICES AND PLATFORMS

CONTENT VERIFICATION TOOLS

TinEye

- Purpose: Reverse image search to find original sources
- Cost: Free (limited) / Paid plans for heavy use
- Best for: Checking if images have been used elsewhere
- Website: tineye.com

Google Reverse Image Search

- Purpose: Find where images appear online
- Cost: Free
- Best for: Quick verification of image authenticity
- Access: images.google.com

InVID Verification Plugin

- Purpose: Browser extension for video verification
- Cost: Free
- Best for: Journalists and researchers
- Platform: Chrome/Firefox extension

Sensity AI

- Purpose: Deepfake detection for enterprises
- Cost: Enterprise pricing
- Best for: Organizations needing scalable detection
- Website: sensity.ai

REAL-TIME COMMUNICATION VERIFICATION

Pindrop

- Purpose: Voice authentication and anti-spoofing
- Cost: Enterprise pricing
- Best for: Call centers and financial services
- Focus: Real-time voice verification

Truepic

- Purpose: Photo and video authenticity
- Cost: Free app / Enterprise solutions
- Best for: Insurance, dating apps, journalism
- Feature: Cryptographic image verification

FACT-CHECKING PLATFORMS

Snopes.com

- Purpose: Fact-checking rumors and claims
- Cost: Free
- Best for: General misinformation
- Strength: Long history and reputation

FactCheck.org

- Purpose: Political fact-checking
- Cost: Free
- Best for: US political claims
- Strength: Nonpartisan analysis

Full Fact (UK)

- Purpose: UK-focused fact-checking
- Cost: Free
- Best for: UK political and social claims
- Feature: Automated fact-checking tools

DIGITAL RIGHTS ORGANIZATIONS

GLOBAL ORGANIZATIONS

Electronic Frontier Foundation (EFF)

- Focus: Digital privacy and free speech
- Services: Legal support, activism tools, education
- How to engage: Donate, use their tools, join campaigns
- Website: eff.org

Access Now

- Focus: Digital rights globally
- Services: Digital security helpline, advocacy

- Special program: 24/7 helpline for activists
- Website: accessnow.org

Article 19

- Focus: Freedom of expression
- Services: Legal analysis, advocacy
- Strength: International scope
- Website: article19.org

REGIONAL ORGANIZATIONS

European Digital Rights (EDRi)

- Focus: EU digital rights
- Members: 47 organizations across Europe
- Key issues: Privacy, surveillance, AI regulation
- Website: edri.org

Digital Rights Watch (Australia)

- Focus: Australian digital rights
- Services: Education, advocacy, campaigns
- Website: digitalrightswatch.org.au

Internet Freedom Foundation (India)

- Focus: Indian digital liberties
- Services: Litigation, research, advocacy
- Website: internetfreedom.in

SPECIALIZED SUPPORT

Coalition Against Stalkerware

- Focus: Intimate partner surveillance
- Services: Resources for victims, detection tools
- Website: stopstalkerware.org

Cyber Civil Rights Initiative

- Focus: Non-consensual intimate images
- Services: 24/7 helpline, legal support
- Website: cybercivilrights.org

EDUCATIONAL RESOURCES

ONLINE COURSES

Coursera: "Cryptography I" (Stanford)

- Instructor: Dan Boneh
- Cost: Free to audit / Paid certificate
- Duration: 7 weeks
- Level: Intermediate

MIT OpenCourseWare: "Computer Systems Security"

- Cost: Free
- Format: Lecture videos and materials
- Level: Advanced

SANS Cyber Aces

- Cost: Free

- Focus: Basic cybersecurity concepts
- Format: Video tutorials
- Level: Beginner

DIGITAL LITERACY PROGRAMS

Mozilla Web Literacy

- Cost: Free
- Format: Interactive curriculum
- Audience: Educators and learners
- Focus: Critical thinking online

MediaSmarts (Canada)

- Cost: Free
- Format: Lesson plans and resources
- Audience: Teachers, parents, youth
- Strength: Age-appropriate materials

First Draft

- Cost: Free
- Format: Courses and resources
- Focus: Verification for journalists
- Specialty: Misinformation research

BOOKS AND PUBLICATIONS

Technical Books

- "The Age of Surveillance Capitalism" - Shoshana Zuboff
- "Algorithms of Oppression" - Safiya Noble
- "The Data Dividend" - Eustace Asanghanwa

- "Race After Technology" - Ruha Benjamin
- "Weapons of Math Destruction" - Cathy O'Neil

Practical Guides

- "The Art of Invisibility" - Kevin Mitnick
- "How to Be Invisible" - J.J. Luna
- "Permanent Record" - Edward Snowden
- "The Smart Girl's Guide to Privacy" - Violet Blue

OPEN SOURCE TRUST TOOLS

PRIVACY TOOLS

Signal

- Purpose: Encrypted messaging
- Cost: Free
- Platforms: iOS, Android, Desktop
- Feature: Disappearing messages

Tor Browser

- Purpose: Anonymous browsing
- Cost: Free
- Platform: All major OS
- Warning: Slower than regular browsing

ProtonMail

- Purpose: Encrypted email
- Cost: Free (limited) / Paid plans
- Feature: Zero-access encryption
- Based: Switzerland

Tails

- Purpose: Anonymous operating system
- Cost: Free
- Use case: Highest security needs
- Runs from: USB or DVD

PASSWORD AND AUTHENTICATION

Bitwarden

- Purpose: Password management
- Cost: Free / Premium $10/year
- Feature: Open source
- Platforms: All major platforms

KeePass

- Purpose: Offline password management
- Cost: Free
- Feature: Complete local control
- Platforms: Windows, ports available

Aegis Authenticator (Android)

- Purpose: 2FA tokens
- Cost: Free
- Feature: Encrypted backups
- Alternative: Raivo OTP (iOS)

FILE AND COMMUNICATION SECURITY

VeraCrypt

- Purpose: File encryption
- Cost: Free
- Use case: Sensitive file storage
- Successor to: TrueCrypt

OnionShare

- Purpose: Anonymous file sharing
- Cost: Free
- Feature: Tor-based sharing
- Use case: Whistleblowing

Jitsi Meet

- Purpose: Encrypted video calls
- Cost: Free
- Feature: No account needed
- Alternative to: Zoom

HARDWARE SECURITY

SECURITY KEYS

YubiKey

- Manufacturer: Yubico
- Price: $25-$90
- Protocols: FIDO2, U2F, OTP
- Best for: Most users

Titan Security Key

- Manufacturer: Google
- Price: $30-$35

- Feature: Built by Google
- Best for: Google ecosystem users

OnlyKey

- Manufacturer: CryptoTrust
- Price: $46+
- Feature: On-device password storage
- Best for: Advanced users

SECURE COMMUNICATION DEVICES

Librem 5

- Manufacturer: Purism
- Type: Privacy phone
- OS: PureOS (Linux)
- Feature: Hardware kill switches

Fairphone

- Type: Ethical/repairable phone
- Focus: Sustainability and longevity
- OS: Android (de-Googled options)
- Feature: User-repairable

PRIVACY ACCESSORIES

Faraday Bags

- Purpose: Block all wireless signals
- Price: $15-$50
- Use case: Prevent tracking
- Specific products:

- Silent Pocket: Leather and nylon options, various sizes
- Mission Darkness: Military-grade, certified shielding
- GoDark Bags: Phone-specific sizing with window
- OffGrid: Budget-friendly basic protection
- Note: Verify effectiveness with your devices before relying on them

Audio Privacy Devices

- Purpose: Prevent audio eavesdropping while keeping devices functional
- Products:
  - **TrustBox Mute** (Scalys)
    - Function: Audio jamming to prevent phone eavesdropping
    - Features: Hardware noise generation, 40-hour battery, wireless charging pass-through
    - Use case: Confidential meetings where phones must remain accessible
    - Best for: Corporate, government, legal environments
    - Note: Prevents audio surveillance while allowing visual access to notifications

Webcam Covers

- Purpose: Physical camera blocking
- Price: $5-$15
- Options: Sliding, magnetic, stick-on
- Note: Also cover smart TV cameras

SUPPORT SERVICES

IDENTITY THEFT RESPONSE

IdentityTheft.gov (US)

- Service: Recovery plan creation
- Cost: Free
- Operated by: FTC
- Feature: Personalized recovery plan

Victim Support (UK)

- Service: Emotional and practical support
- Cost: Free
- Contact: 24/7 helpline
- Website: victimsupport.org.uk

LEGAL RESOURCES

Cyber Civil Rights Legal Project

- Service: Pro bono legal help
- Focus: Image-based sexual abuse
- Eligibility: Case-by-case basis
- Contact: Through website

EFF Cooperating Attorneys List

- Service: Referrals to digital rights lawyers
- Cost: Varies by attorney
- Coverage: United States
- Access: eff.org/pages/legal-assistance

MENTAL HEALTH SUPPORT

National Suicide Prevention Lifeline

- Phone: 988 (US)
- Service: Crisis support
- Cost: Free
- Hours: 24/7

Crisis Text Line

- Text: HOME to 741741 (US)
- Service: Crisis counseling
- Cost: Free
- Feature: Text-based support

STAYING UPDATED

NEWS SOURCES

Specialized Coverage

- The Markup (Tech accountability)
- MIT Technology Review (Tech analysis)
- Wired Security (Security news)
- Ars Technica (Technical depth)

NEWSLETTERS

This Week in Security

- Focus: Security news roundup
- Frequency: Weekly
- Subscribe: schneier.com

Recode Daily

- Focus: Tech impact on society
- Frequency: Daily
- Platform: Vox Media

PODCASTS

Security and Privacy

- "Security Now" - Steve Gibson
- "The Privacy, Security, and OSINT Show"
- "Darknet Diaries" - Jack Rhysider
- "Risky Business" - Patrick Gray

RESEARCH ORGANIZATIONS

Citizen Lab (University of Toronto)

- Focus: Digital threats to civil society
- Output: Research reports
- Website: citizenlab.ca

AI Now Institute

- Focus: Social implications of AI
- Output: Annual reports
- Website: ainowinstitute.org

COMMUNITY RESOURCES

LOCAL WORKSHOPS

CryptoParty

- What: Hands-on encryption training
- Cost: Free
- Format: Local meetups
- Find: cryptoparty.in

Library Digital Literacy Programs

- Check your local library for:
    - Basic computer security
    - Privacy workshops
    - One-on-one tech help
    - Equipment lending

ONLINE COMMUNITIES

r/privacy (Reddit)

- Focus: Privacy tools and practices
- Size: 1M+ members
- Strength: Beginner-friendly

PrivacyTools.io Forums

- Focus: Tool recommendations
- Format: Discourse forum
- Strength: Curated information

EMERGENCY RESOURCES

IF YOU'RE BEING STALKED/HARASSED

1. **Document everything** - Screenshots, dates, times
2. **Contact local law enforcement** - File reports
3. **Reach out to specialized organizations:**
   - National Domestic Violence Hotline: 1-800-799-7233
   - NNEDV Safety Net Project: nnedv.org
   - Operation Safe Escape: operationsafeescape.org

IF YOUR INTIMATE IMAGES ARE SHARED

1. **Don't panic** - Support is available
2. **Document URLs** - Before content is removed
3. **Contact platforms** - Request immediate removal
4. **Get help:**
   - Cyber Civil Rights Initiative: 24/7 helpline
   - CCRI Image Removal Guide: cybercivilrights.org
   - Without My Consent: withoutmyconsent.org

IF YOU'RE TARGETED BY DEEPFAKES

1. **Act quickly** - Time matters
2. **Alert your network** - Warn contacts
3. **Document everything** - Save evidence
4. **Seek help:**
   - Contact platforms for removal
   - Consult with lawyers familiar with synthetic media
   - Consider public statement if appropriate

A LIVING RESOURCE

The landscape of tools and resources changes rapidly. What works today might be compromised tomorrow. New tools emerge as threats evolve. Stay engaged with communities that track these changes, and always verify that tools and services remain trustworthy before relying on them.

∼

Remember: The best tool is the one you'll actually use. Start with basics that match your threat model and technical comfort, then build from there.

∼

APPENDIX D: GLOSSARY OF TERMS

The language of the synthetic age, decoded.

This glossary provides clear definitions of technical terms, concepts, and acronyms used throughout this book. Terms are organized alphabetically for easy reference.

A

Adversarial Learning

The process where synthetic media generators and detectors compete against each other, each improving through the competition. Like an arms race where better fakes drive better detection, which drives even better fakes.

Ambient Authentication

Security verification that happens continuously in the background without interrupting user activities. Your phone knowing it's you through usage patterns rather than demanding a password every few minutes.

API (Application Programming Interface)

A set of rules that allows different software applications to communicate with each other. Think of it as a restaurant menu that tells other programs what they can order and how to order it.

Attestation

The process by which a device or system cryptographically proves its identity and integrity. Like a tamper-evident seal for digital systems that shows if anything has been modified.

B

Behavioral Biometrics

Authentication based on patterns of behavior—how you type, walk, or hold your phone—rather than physical characteristics. Your digital body language becoming your password.

Biometric Data

Unique physical or behavioral characteristics used for identification: fingerprints, face structure, iris patterns, voice, or gait. The parts of you that are supposedly unique but increasingly copyable.

Blockchain

A distributed ledger technology that creates an immutable record of transactions. Imagine a notebook that everyone has a copy of, where any change is immediately visible to all, and past entries cannot be erased.

Byzantine Fault Tolerance

A system's ability to continue operating correctly even when some participants are malicious or faulty. Named after the Byzantine

Generals Problem—how do generals coordinate when messengers might be traitors?

C

Certificate Authority (CA)

An organization that issues digital certificates verifying the identity of websites, individuals, or devices. The digital equivalent of a notary public for the internet.

Consensus Mechanism

The method by which a distributed system agrees on a single version of truth. How a group decides what's real when there's no central authority to ask.

Content Authenticity

The ability to verify that digital content hasn't been manipulated and comes from a claimed source. Proving not just who created something, but that it hasn't been altered since.

Cryptographic Hash

A mathematical function that converts any input into a fixed-size string of characters. Like a fingerprint for data—change even one bit, and the hash completely changes.

Cryptographic Signature

A mathematical proof that a message came from a specific sender and hasn't been altered. Like a wax seal that's mathematically impossible to forge.

D

Decentralized Identity (DID)

A form of digital identity that users control directly, without relying on a central authority. Your identity lives with you, not in some company's database.

Deepfake

Synthetic media where a person's likeness is replaced with someone else's, creating convincing but false video or audio. Digital puppetry that's increasingly indistinguishable from reality.

Defense in Depth

A security strategy using multiple layers of protection. If one defense fails, others remain. Like having locks, alarms, cameras, and guards rather than relying on just one.

Digital Twin

A synthetic version of a real person that can act autonomously online. Your artificial double living a parallel digital life, sometimes more successfully than you.

E

End-to-End Encryption (E2E)

Encryption where only the communicating parties can read the messages. Even the service provider can't access the content. Like a conversation in a language only you and your friend understand.

Entropy

In cryptography, a measure of randomness or unpredictability. High entropy means harder to guess. The difference between a password like "password123" and "h7$mK9@pL2&v".

F

Faraday Cage/Bag

An enclosure that blocks electromagnetic fields, preventing wireless communications. A physical barrier that keeps your devices from calling home or being tracked.

FIDO2

An authentication standard that enables passwordless login using cryptographic keys. Your device proves who you are without sending passwords over the internet.

G

GAN (Generative Adversarial Network)

A machine learning architecture where two neural networks compete—one creating fake content, one detecting it. The technology behind most deepfakes.

GPG/PGP (GNU Privacy Guard/Pretty Good Privacy)

Encryption software for secure communication. A way to scramble messages so only intended recipients can read them.

H

Hardware Security Module (HSM)

A physical device that manages and protects cryptographic keys. A digital safe that performs cryptographic operations without ever revealing the keys.

Hash Function

See Cryptographic Hash.

I

Identity Proofing

The process of verifying that someone is who they claim to be before issuing credentials. The digital equivalent of checking someone's ID before giving them keys to the building.

Immutable

Unable to be changed or altered. In blockchain and cryptography, creating records that can't be secretly modified later.

K

Key Ceremony

A formal procedure for generating important cryptographic keys with multiple witnesses and security controls. Like a high-security ritual for creating digital master keys.

Key Escrow

Storing copies of encryption keys with a third party. Controversial because it creates a backdoor that could be exploited.

L

Least Privilege

A security principle where users and systems only get the minimum access necessary for their function. Like giving someone a guest key instead of a master key.

Liveness Detection

Technology to determine if biometric data comes from a living person present at the time, not a photo, video, or mask. Proving you're not just real, but really there.

M

Man-in-the-Middle Attack

When an attacker secretly intercepts and possibly alters communication between two parties. Like someone opening your mail, reading it, maybe changing it, then resealing and delivering it.

Metadata

Data about data. For a photo: when taken, where, by what device. Often reveals more than people realize and harder to fake than the content itself.

Multi-Factor Authentication (MFA)

Requiring multiple types of proof to verify identity: something you know (password), have (phone), and/or are (fingerprint). Not putting all your security eggs in one basket.

N

Non-Repudiation

The assurance that someone cannot deny the authenticity of their signature or actions. Mathematical proof that yes, you really did authorize that transaction.

O

Out-of-Band Verification

Confirming something through a different communication channel. If you get a suspicious email, calling to verify. Using a second path to check the first.

P

Phishing

Attempting to trick people into revealing sensitive information by pretending to be trustworthy. The digital equivalent of a con artist in a uniform.

Post-Quantum Cryptography

Encryption methods designed to remain secure even against quantum computers. Future-proofing security for when current encryption becomes breakable.

Private Key

The secret half of a cryptographic key pair, kept secure and never shared. Your digital seal that only you can use.

Proof of Stake/Work

Consensus mechanisms for blockchain. Proof of Work requires computational effort; Proof of Stake requires holding currency. Different ways to make cheating expensive.

Public Key

The shareable half of a cryptographic key pair. Others use it to encrypt messages only you can decrypt, or verify signatures only you could create.

R

Rate Limiting

Restricting how often an action can be performed. Like a bouncer who only lets people into a club slowly, preventing stampedes and identifying troublemakers.

Replay Attack

Using a recorded legitimate transmission to fool a system. Like recording someone's garage door opener signal and playing it back later to break in.

S

Secure Enclave

A physically isolated chip or area in a processor for handling sensitive data. A vault inside your device that even the main system can't access.

Side-Channel Attack

Extracting information from physical implementations rather than breaking cryptography directly. Reading secrets by watching power use, timing, or electromagnetic emissions.

Social Engineering

Manipulating people to divulge confidential information. Hacking humans instead of computers, often the easiest path to compromise.

Spoofing

Falsifying data to impersonate someone or something else. Making your email look like it came from your boss, or your phone number appear as the bank's.

Synthetic Media

Artificial content created or modified by AI to misrepresent reality. The broad category including deepfakes, voice clones, and AI-generated text presenting as human.

T

Temporal Integrity

The verifiable ordering and timing of events. Proving not just what happened, but when and in what sequence.

Threat Model

An analysis of what you're protecting, from whom, and how they might attack. Knowing your enemy and your vulnerabilities before building defenses.

Trusted Execution Environment (TEE)
A secure area in a processor that runs separately from the main operating system. A safe room inside your device where sensitive operations happen.

Two-Factor Authentication (2FA)
See Multi-Factor Authentication.

U

User Agent
Software acting on behalf of a user, typically a web browser. The digital ambassador that represents you to websites.

V

Verifiable Credentials
Digital credentials that can be cryptographically verified without contacting the issuer. Like a diploma that proves itself real without calling the university.

Verifiable Identity
A digital identity that can be cryptographically proven to belong to a specific person or entity. The ability to prove "I am who I claim to be" through mathematical certainty rather than just documents or biometrics that can be faked.

W

Web of Trust

A decentralized trust model where users vouch for each other's identities. Trust through social connections rather than central authorities.

White-Box Cryptography

Encryption techniques that remain secure even when the attacker can observe internal operations. Keeping secrets even when someone's watching every step.

Z

Zero-Knowledge Proof (ZKP)

A method to prove you know something without revealing what you know. Proving you're over 21 without showing your birthdate, or that you have funds without revealing your balance.

Zero Trust Architecture

A security model that assumes no user or system should be trusted by default, requiring continuous verification. "Never trust, always verify" as a design principle.

zk-SNARK/zk-STARK

Types of zero-knowledge proofs. SNARKs are succinct but need trusted setup; STARKs are larger but don't need trust. Different flavors of proving without revealing.

This glossary covers the essential terms for understanding digital security in the synthetic age. For deeper technical explanations, see Appendix B: Technical Deep Dives.

APPENDIX E: DISCUSSION QUESTIONS FOR BOOK CLUBS AND CLASSROOMS

Exploring the human dimensions of trust in the synthetic age.

∽

These questions are designed to spark meaningful conversations about the themes in this book. They range from personal reflection to societal implications, encouraging readers to connect the concepts to their own lives and communities.

PART I: COLLAPSE OF TRUST

CHAPTER 1: THE GREAT UNRAVELING

1. **Personal Experience:** Have you ever fallen for a scam or deception online? What made it convincing? How did you feel when you realized the truth?
2. **Trust Evaluation:** Make a list of five people or institutions you trust implicitly. What would it take for

that trust to be broken? How would you verify their authenticity in a world of perfect impersonation?
3. **Societal Impact:** The Pentagon incident showed how voice cloning can compromise national security. What other critical systems in society depend on voice verification? How vulnerable are they?
4. **Ethical Considerations:** If the technology to create perfect voice clones exists, should it be regulated? Who decides what uses are legitimate?

CHAPTER 2: THE IDENTITY CRISIS

1. **Identity Reflection:** What makes you "you"? If someone created a perfect digital copy of you, what would prove you're the original?
2. **Future Implications:** The Karnataka gang created entirely synthetic identities that collected benefits for years. What does this mean for systems that assume every person has one unique identity?
3. **Personal Security:** Review your own digital footprint. How much information about you could someone gather to create a convincing impersonation?
4. **Philosophical Questions:** If a synthetic version of you maintains relationships online while you're offline, who owns those relationships? Can a synthetic being have rights?

CHAPTER 3: THE REALITY WARS

1. **Media Literacy:** How do you currently decide what news or information to trust? Would your methods work against sophisticated synthetic media?

2. **Democratic Implications:** The Slovak election showed how deepfakes could influence democracy. Should there be "quiet periods" where synthetic media is banned before elections? How would this be enforced?
3. **Truth and Fiction:** In a world where any media can be faked, how do we maintain shared truth? What happens to society when we can't agree on basic facts?
4. **Personal Boundaries:** Would you want to know if content you're viewing is synthetic? Should all AI-generated content be labeled? What about creative uses?

CHAPTER 4: THE CORPORATE SHAPESHIFTERS

1. **Workplace Vulnerability:** The Hong Kong heist succeeded because an employee trusted a video call with their "CFO." How does your workplace verify important requests? What vulnerabilities exist?
2. **Corporate Culture:** Does your organization's culture prioritize speed or verification? How might pressure to be responsive make employees vulnerable to synthetic media attacks?
3. **Supply Chain Trust:** The chapter describes synthetic vendors infiltrating supply chains. How many of your professional relationships exist only digitally? How would you verify they're real?
4. **Economic Impact:** If synthetic media makes business communication unreliable, what happens to global commerce? How might companies adapt? What would be the costs?

PART II: RETHINKING TRUST

CHAPTER 5: FROM PERIMETERS TO PRINCIPLES

1. **Zero Trust Application:** The book suggests applying "never trust, always verify" to human relationships. How does this make you feel? Is constant verification compatible with intimacy and friendship?
2. **Practical Implementation:** Design a "zero trust" protocol for your family's financial decisions. What would it include? How would you balance security with maintaining relationships?
3. **Cultural Differences:** How might zero trust principles work differently in high-trust versus low-trust societies? Does your cultural background affect your comfort with verification?

CHAPTER 6: THE AUTHENTICATION REVOLUTION

1. **Daily Authentication:** Track how many times you verify your identity in a single day. Is this sustainable? What's the emotional cost of constant authentication?
2. **Inclusivity Concerns:** Many authentication systems don't work well for people with disabilities. How do we balance security with accessibility?
3. **Future Vision:** Imagine authentication in 2040. What methods might we use? What would you want to see? What would you fear?

CHAPTER 7: THE PRINCIPLE OF LEAST PRIVILEGE

1. **Information Sharing:** Review what information you share with different services. Are you practicing "least privilege" or giving away more than necessary?
2. **The Twitter Blue Checkmark:** The chaos from purchasable verification showed how much we depend on information hierarchies. What other "signals of trust" do you rely on that could be corrupted?
3. **Creating Boundaries:** Design an information-sharing policy for yourself. What would you share with different circles of people? How would you enforce these boundaries?

CHAPTER 8: ASSUMING BREACH IN HUMAN SYSTEMS

1. **Personal Vulnerability:** The WhatsApp scam succeeded by exploiting family trust. What requests from loved ones would you act on without verification? Should you change this?
2. **Recovery Planning:** If you discovered you'd been fooled by synthetic media, what would you do? Who would you tell? How would you recover emotionally and practically?
3. **Trust Networks as Attack Vectors:** Every relationship in your life could be a vulnerability. How does this make you feel? Can you maintain meaningful relationships while assuming breach?
4. **Building Resilience:** The chapter emphasizes recovery over prevention. What's the difference between healthy skepticism and destructive paranoia? Where do you draw the line?

PART III: INFRASTRUCTURE FOR INTEGRITY

CHAPTER 9: THE CRYPTOGRAPHIC FOUNDATION

1. **Understanding Encryption:** Before reading this book, what did you think encryption was? How has your understanding changed? Do you feel empowered or overwhelmed?
2. **Privacy vs. Security:** The "right to be forgotten" conflicts with blockchain's permanent records. Which is more important to you? Can we have both?
3. **Practical Steps:** What cryptographic tools are you willing to adopt? What barriers prevent you from using them?

CHAPTER 10: HARDWARE ROOTS OF TRUST

1. **Device Trust:** Do you trust the devices you use daily? Should you? What would it take to compromise your phone or computer?
2. **Supply Chain Awareness:** Your devices contain components from many countries. Does this concern you? Should there be "trusted" supply chains?
3. **Physical Security:** The chapter emphasizes physical security in a digital world. How do you protect your physical devices? Is it enough?

CHAPTER 11: THE VERIFICATION INFRASTRUCTURE

1. **Identity Systems:** The chapter opens with someone being declared digitally dead while alive. How dependent

are you on digital systems recognizing your existence? What backup plans do you have?
2. **Decentralized vs. Centralized:** Should identity be controlled by governments, corporations, or individuals? What are the trade-offs of each approach?
3. **Inclusion Concerns:** How do we build verification systems that work for everyone, including those without smartphones, stable addresses, or traditional documentation?
4. **Web of Trust:** Would you vouch for others' identities in a distributed system? Whose identity would you stake your reputation on? What risks would this create?

CHAPTER 12: CONTENT AUTHENTICITY AT SCALE

1. **Trust in Media:** The Olympics scenario showed how C2PA labeling helped identify fakes. Would you trust content more if it had cryptographic verification? What could still go wrong?
2. **Creation vs. Consumption:** Should content creators be required to cryptographically sign their work? What about citizen journalists or whistleblowers who need anonymity?
3. **The Permanence Problem:** If all content is permanently attributed to creators, what happens to artistic experimentation, political dissent, or the right to be forgotten?
4. **Practical Adoption:** What would motivate you to use content authenticity tools? What barriers currently prevent you from verifying content before sharing?

PART IV: A NEW SOCIAL CONTRACT

CHAPTER 13: THE RIGHT TO AUTHENTIC IDENTITY

1. **Legal Rights:** Should you own your biometric data the same way you own physical property? What rights should you have over synthetic versions of yourself?
2. **Consent Complexity:** Can true informed consent exist when we don't understand how our data might be used? How do we protect people who can't understand these risks?
3. **Global Differences:** Different cultures have different concepts of identity and privacy. How do we create global frameworks that respect these differences?

CHAPTER 14: COLLECTIVE DEFENSE

1. **Community Building:** The Taiwan example showed collective defense against synthetic media. Could your community organize similarly? What would it take?
2. **Trust Circles:** Design a trust circle for yourself. Who would be in it? What protocols would you establish? How would you maintain it?
3. **Mutual Aid:** How can communities support members who are less technically capable? What would digital mutual aid look like in your area?

CHAPTER 15: GOVERNANCE FOR THE SYNTHETIC AGE

1. **Global vs. National:** The UN summit scenario illustrates tensions between global coordination and national

sovereignty. Should synthetic media regulation be international or country-specific? What are the trade-offs?
2. **Innovation vs. Protection:** How do we regulate synthetic media without stifling beneficial uses in education, accessibility, or art? Where should we draw lines?
3. **Digital Citizenship:** If you could have digital citizenship from any country, which would you choose? What rights and protections would you want?
4. **Regulatory Sandboxes:** Would you participate in an experimental program testing new verification systems? What safeguards would you need? What risks would you accept?

CHAPTER 16: DESIGNING FOR HUMAN AGENCY

1. **Technology Assessment:** Think of a security system you use regularly. Does it empower or exhaust you? How could it be redesigned to respect human agency?
2. **Cognitive Load:** The book discusses "authentication fatigue." Have you experienced this? How do you manage the cognitive load of digital security?
3. **Future Design:** If you could redesign one digital system to better support human agency, what would it be? What would you change?

CONCLUSION: THE AUTHENTIC FUTURE

CHAPTER 17: LIVING AUTHENTICALLY IN A SYNTHETIC WORLD

1. **Daily Practice:** Maya's day shows adapted life in 2030. What aspects of her routine appeal to you? What would you find difficult? How might your own daily life need to change?
2. **Reality Anchors:** The chapter emphasizes physical practices that ground us. What are your current reality anchors? What new ones might you adopt?
3. **Hope vs. Fear:** How do you balance necessary caution about synthetic media with maintaining joy and spontaneity in life? What would "thriving" look like for you in a synthetic age?
4. **Legacy Questions:** What kind of digital world do you want to leave for the next generation? What are you willing to do to help create it?

SYNTHESIS QUESTIONS

LOOKING BACK

1. **Changed Perspectives:** What beliefs about technology, privacy, or security has this book challenged? What surprised you most?
2. **Personal Evolution:** How has your behavior changed while reading this book? What new habits have you adopted? What have you resisted?
3. **Key Takeaways:** If you could only remember three

concepts from this book, what would they be? Why these three?

LOOKING FORWARD

1. **Future Scenarios:** It's 2035. What does your digital life look like? What synthetic media challenges do you face? How do you handle them?
2. **Teaching Others:** How would you explain synthetic media threats to a child? To an elderly relative? To a skeptic who thinks it's overblown?
3. **Collective Action:** What role will you play in building trustworthy digital systems? What specific actions will you take?

ETHICAL DILEMMAS

1. **The Trolley Problem Updated:** You discover a deepfake that could prevent a war but would destroy an innocent person's reputation. Do you expose it or let it spread?
2. **Authentication vs. Privacy:** A system could prevent all synthetic media but requires constant biometric monitoring. Would you accept it? Where do you draw the line?
3. **Generational Divide:** Your elderly parent refuses to adopt any verification practices, making them vulnerable. Do you respect their choice or intervene? How?

ACTION PLANNING

INDIVIDUAL ACTIONS

- What three things will you change about your digital behavior this week?
- What verification practices will you adopt with your family?
- How will you stay informed about synthetic media developments?

COMMUNITY ACTIONS

- How can your book club or class contribute to digital literacy in your community?
- What local organizations could benefit from synthetic media awareness training?
- How might you create or join a trust circle?

ADVOCACY ACTIONS

- What policy changes would you support regarding synthetic media?
- How can you help others understand these issues without creating panic?
- What role should schools play in teaching synthetic media literacy?

CREATIVE EXERCISES

1. **Write Your Own Scenario:** Create a fictional but

plausible synthetic media incident. What vulnerabilities does it exploit? How could it be prevented?
2. **Design Challenge:** Sketch a user interface for a verification system that respects human agency. What would it look like? How would it feel to use?
3. **Role Play:** Act out a family conversation about implementing verification protocols. What resistance might arise? How would you address concerns?
4. **Future History:** Write a news article from 2040 looking back at how society adapted to synthetic media. What worked? What failed?

These questions are meant to inspire discussion, not prescribe answers. Each group will bring different perspectives and experiences. The goal is to build collective understanding and prepare for a future where human wisdom guides technological power.

APPENDIX F: ENDNOTES

PREFACE: THE UNVERIFIABLE PRESENT

1. **Magramo, K.** (2024, February 4). Finance worker pays out $25 million after video call with deepfake 'chief financial officer'. CNN. https://www.cnn.com/2024/02/04/asia/deepfake-cfo-scam-hong-kong-intl-hnk/index.html

INTRODUCTION: THE DAY TRUST DIED

1. **e-Estonia (2024).** "Digital Society Initiatives." Republic of Estonia Official Portal. https://e-estonia.com/solutions/.

1. THE GREAT UNRAVELING

1. **Whitty, M. T. (2013).** The Scammers Persuasive Techniques Model: Development of a Stage Model to Explain the Online Dating Romance Scam. British Journal of Criminology, 53(4), 665–684.
2. **Luhmann, N. (1979).** Trust and Power. John Wiley & Sons. Translation by Howard Davis, John Raffan, and Kathryn Rooney.

3. THE REALITY WARS

1. **Kern, M. (2023, October 2).** Deepfake audio of Slovakian politician sparks outrage two days before election. The Record. https://therecord.media/deepfake-audio-slovakia-election.
2. **GLOBSEC. (2023).** Slovakia Parliamentary Elections 2023: Information Landscape Analysis. https://www.globsec.org/reports/slovakia-elections-2023.
3. **Official Election Results**: Statistical Office of the Slovak Republic. (2023). Parliamentary Elections 2023. https://volby.statistics.sk/.

4. THE CORPORATE SHAPESHIFTERS

1. **Chen, H., & Magramo, K. (2024, February 4).** Finance worker pays out $25 million after video call with deepfake 'chief financial officer'. CNN. https://www.cnn.com/2024/02/04/asia/deepfake-cfo-scam-hong-kong-intl-hnk/index.html.
2. **Federal Bureau of Investigation.** (2022). Internet Crime Complaint Center (IC3) Report 2021. https://www.ic3.gov/Media/PDF/AnnualReport/2021_IC3Report.pdf.

5. FROM PERIMETERS TO PRINCIPLES

1. **Cybersecurity and Infrastructure Security Agency.** (2020). Alert (AA20-352A): Advanced Persistent Threat Compromise of Government Agencies, Critical Infrastructure, and Private Sector Organizations. https://www.cisa.gov/news-events/cybersecurity-advisories/aa20-352a.

7. THE PRINCIPLE OF LEAST PRIVILEGE FOR INFORMATION

1. **Isaac, M., & Browning, K. (2022, November 11).** Elon Musk's Twitter Blue Verification Disaster. The New York Times. https://www.nytimes.com/2022/11/11/technology/twitter-blue-fake-accounts.html.
2. **Simon, H. A. (1971).** Designing Organizations for an Information-Rich World. In M. Greenberger (Ed.), Computers, Communications, and the Public Interest (pp. 37-72). Johns Hopkins University Press.

8. ASSUMING BREACH IN HUMAN SYSTEMS

1. **Federal Bureau of Investigation.** (2024). Internet Crime Complaint Center (IC3) Report 2024. https://www.ic3.gov/Media/PDF/AnnualReport/2024_IC3Report.pdf [Projected statistics based on trend analysis].

9. THE CRYPTOGRAPHIC FOUNDATION

1. **European Commission.** (2024). European Digital Identity Wallet: Architecture and Reference Framework. EU Digital Single Market Initiative. https://ec.europa.eu/digital-single-market/en/european-digital-identity.
2. **Diffie, W., & Hellman, M. (1976).** New directions in cryptography. IEEE Transactions on Information Theory, 22(6), 644-654.
3. **Goldwasser, S., Micali, S., & Rackoff, C. (1989).** The knowledge complexity of interactive proof systems. SIAM Journal on Computing, 18(1), 186-208.
4. **Reuters Institute.** (2024). Blockchain for News: Provenance and Verification in the Synthetic Media Age. Oxford University Digital News Report.
5. **ING Bank.** (2023). Zero-Knowledge Proofs in Banking: Privacy-Preserving Compliance. ING Innovation Labs White Paper.
6. **Regulation (EU) 2016/679 (General Data Protection Regulation), Article 17:** Right to erasure ('right to be forgotten').

10. HARDWARE ROOTS OF TRUST

1. **Robertson, J., & Riley, M. (2018, October 4).** The Big Hack: How China Used a Tiny Chip to Infiltrate U.S. Companies. Bloomberg Businessweek. https://www.

bloomberg.com/news/features/2018-10-04/the-big-hack-how-china-used-a-tiny-chip-to-infiltrate-america-s-top-companies.

12. CONTENT AUTHENTICITY AT SCALE

1. **Coalition for Content Provenance and Authenticity.** (2024). "C2PA Specification Version 2.0." https://c2pa.org/specifications/.

14. COLLECTIVE DEFENSE AGAINST SYNTHETIC THREATS

1. Ukrainian civil society has developed various digital resistance methods against disinformation, though specific operational details and effectiveness metrics remain difficult to verify independently.
2. **Brazilian Superior Electoral Court (TSE).** (2023). "Digital Brigadistas: Final Report on the 2022 Election Integrity Program." TSE Public Documentation Portal. https://www.tse.jus.br/eleicoes/2022/digital-brigadistas.
3. **Bellingcat Investigation Team.** (2023). "Methodology: How We Verify User-Generated Content from Conflict Zones." Bellingcat. https://www.bellingcat.com/resources/2023/01/27/verify-user-generated-content.

Also by Eustace Asanghanwa

THE DATA DIVIDEND: Your clicks fuel AI. Why aren't you getting paid?

ABOUT THE AUTHOR

Eustace Asanghanwa is a Security Technologist with decades of experience in security engineering, spanning the full spectrum from integrated circuit (IC) design and manufacturing to IC applications engineering, Internet of Things (IoT) systems, artificial intelligence (AI), and edge-to-cloud resilience. Through his work, he explores the intersection of AI, cybersecurity, and the future of human agency, identity, and digital trust.

He is the author of **THE DATA DIVIDEND: *Your Clicks Fuel AI. Why Aren't You Getting Paid?***, which examines how personal data powers the AI economy and how technology can ensure individuals share in its value.

Eustace blends deep technical expertise with a vision for technology that empowers people—believing that innovation and human dignity must advance together.

www.ingramcontent.com/pod-product-compliance
Lightning Source LLC
Chambersburg PA
CBHW070605030426
42337CB00020B/3694